How to Make the Best Use of Salvage

How to Make the
Best Use of Salvage

Barty Phillips

First published in Great Britain in 2010 by
Remember When
An imprint of
Pen & Sword Books Ltd
47 Church Street
Barnsley
South Yorkshire
S70 2AS

ISBN 978 1 84468 085 6

Typeset in 11pt Minion by Mac Style, Beverley, East Yorkshire
Printed in China through Printworks Int. Ltd

Pen & Sword Books Ltd incorporates the imprints of Pen & Sword Aviation, Pen & Sword Maritime, Pen & Sword Military, Wharncliffe Local History, Pen & Sword Select, Pen & Sword Military Classics, Leo Cooper, Seaforth Publishing and Frontline Publishing.

For a complete list of Pen & Sword titles please contact
PEN & SWORD BOOKS LIMITED
47 Church Street, Barnsley, South Yorkshire, S70 2AS, England
E-mail: enquiries@pen-and-sword.co.uk
Website: www.pen-and-sword.co.uk

Contents

Acknowledgements

My thanks to all the people who helped with ideas, information, enthusiasm, encouragement and pictures. Particular thanks to Edward Haes who spent time and energy looking out photographs, Paul Archer, Rabih Hage, Thornton and Ruby Kay of Salvo, Adam and Maria Hills of Retrouvius, Nadine at Architectural Forum, Carole Lucas of The Cobbled Yard, Arc Reclamation, Nor'East Architectural Salvage, Bob Lovell of Antique Oak Flooring, Paul of Paul's Emporium, Sarah Collins, Sarah Tisdall, Richard Westwood, John and Jenny Houston, Phil and Jane Glynn, Rosamund and Eion Downs, Gerry and Deborah Clark, John Phillips, Charlie and Penny Phillips, Pearson Phillips, Philippa Watkins, Pat Scheverin, Zena Flax, Michael Ann Mullen, Patrick Minns, Oliver Vicars-Harris, Mary Cruickshank, Nick Colwill, Diana Broad, Dorothy and John Knight, Brooke and Joanna Calverley, Pat Thomas, Marga Gervis and Christine Mannington.

Chapter One

The Basics

Your home reflects your character and if it is a traditional home from an earlier century, it also reflects the period in which it was built and some of the history of that time. There is something particularly attractive about an object that has a history and to retain the character of a period home is to capture a sense of the past. If the home has retained many of its original features, you are lucky. However, it may have lost many period items when they were thrown out during the 1960s and 70s as the passion for 'modernisation' took over from too much austerity following World War Two.

In recent years, people have begun to recognise the value of period features and original artefacts and many homes that were stripped of their 'old-fashioned' features are now having them lovingly put back. After all, period items were often made by skilled craftsmen who took pride in their work, understood the materials and techniques, and produced items that had a character all their own. And that's where architectural salvage comes into its own. Any salvaged item you buy has a story and you can spend happy hours looking for appropriate items to replace those that have worn out, become damaged or have been torn out.

Hunting for salvage has all the excitement of the chase. It's the never-ending detective story. You can learn to recognise the signs and the clues, to read the hidden meanings, to recognise the links and to uncover what's important to your own particular search among the wealth of false clues and strange objects you come across in your forage. Whether you are looking for authentic hand-made eighteenth-century tiles to match those used originally in your home, a cast-iron Victorian fireplace or a Utility extendable dining table, there are places where you can find practically anything you want, though you may have to winkle it out from somewhere hidden away behind other goods, tucked away in a tiny corner shop or lurking behind more popular items in a large architectural salvage depot.

Products that are not perfect can very much appeal to our sense of beauty and functionality and the rise in numbers of architectural salvage companies is symptomatic of a reaction against the prevalent fashion for flawlessness. Although the universally affordable answer to furnishing problems seems to be IKEA with its endlessly appropriate, adaptable and simple designs, most people would like to add something that makes their home 'different'. IKEA's enormously successful blockbuster storage range 'Billy' is undeniably a brilliant solution, but it definitely needs the addition of something warm, surprising or curious to stop it being exceedingly bland.

Anything from building materials such as wooden beams, stone, tiles or slates to antique or ethnic furniture, hand-woven rugs and ancient drinking troughs can be found and with imagination and a bit of creativity, used to add warmth, interest and even a touch of humour to your home.

These dusty old relics from a Lancashire shop would once have been burned or thrown into landfill, but will now be renovated for someone new to enjoy.

Old troughs and balustrading give any garden, large or small, a sense of timelessness and a very good framework against the changing pattern of the plants.

What is architectural salvage?

Architectural salvage can be described as anything that was once part of the fabric of a building or anything that was once used to decorate or furnish a building. It therefore includes materials such as bricks, stone, roof tiles, slates and chimney pots that have been reclaimed from a demolition site in a good enough condition to be used again. It is surprising how many bricks can be reclaimed in this way, making it possible to match up brickwork when adding an extension or repairing a wall. Other reclaimed materials include paving

This enormous solid wood door from Germany, with its painted trompe l'œil graining effect, will need to find a correspondingly imposing building to do it justice.

stones, Victorian garden edging, staddle stones and engineering bricks (which won't suffer from frost when used in the garden).

In fact, architectural salvage is more or less anything reclaimed from demolished buildings or house clearances that can be used again in the refurbishment, maintenance or decoration of existing homes. So it can sometimes include even whole buildings such as barns, as well as sinks and radiators, joinery, mouldings, flooring, stained glass, windows and doors and their frames, not to mention furniture and smaller items such as kitchen equipment and mirrors, glass and china. And it can importantly include garden and other outdoor items from metal railings and arbours to sculptures, edgings, fountains, ponds and plinths – in fact, there's not much it can't include.

Indoors there's a wealth of reclaimable things from windows to doors and frames, ancient oak floorboards, circular iron staircases, grand wooden staircases, Georgian and Victorian fireplaces (grand or bedroom) and French farmhouse fireplaces. There are interior fittings of all kinds, including sanitary ware such as baths, toilets, basins and sinks; kitchen units, even ancient refrigerators; furniture such as tables, chairs, benches, stools, beds, chests of drawers and wardrobes, glass-fronted cabinets and children's furniture. There are furniture and fittings from redundant churches: whole pews, to pulpits, lecterns and candlesticks. Offices, schools, pubs, hospitals, hotels and other public buildings, whether being refurbished or demolished, can all supply the reclaim business with solid, interesting, grand or practical items for the home. Reclaimed smaller items include housewares of all kinds such as decorative tins, and early radios. Then there are miscellaneous items such as post-boxes, telephone boxes, sentry boxes or enormous enamelled old London Underground maps and advertisements. It's hard to imagine anything more like Aladdin's cave than the reclamation world.

In the past, furniture and materials from houses being demolished or cleared were thrown away, smashed up or burned. Recently there has been a serious effort to salvage and reclaim such things so that they can be used again. There are so many good reasons for using second-hand and original items in your home that it's hard to know where to begin. Salvaging is virtuous as well as entertaining, enjoyable, satisfying and educational. There are many, many ways in which to find salvage from second-hand shops to flea markets to special architectural salvage centres. What you are doing is spending time in a vast countrywide museum and if you want to find out more about the items you are looking at, you may be lucky and find knowledgeable help is at hand.

Architectural features from pubs and churches offer tremendous potential for interesting and unusual interiors. You can obtain flooring or wainscoting, not to mention antique baths, sinks, taps, toilets, fireboxes, joinery, windows and doors. Features are still being salvaged from Victorian homes and one of the appeals of many of the items that find their way into salvage yards is the quality of the materials, however humble their origins may have been; another is their recent past history. There is something satisfying about knowing that your newly-acquired dining table came from the original British Library, when it was still housed in the British Museum. It's always worth asking about the provenance of an item if that side of things intrigues you. Most salvage yards have a very good idea of where their goods have come from and many items have an interesting background.

Where you'll find it

There is a range of sources and suppliers for reclaimed materials and once you start looking you will find yourself recognising salvage wherever you go, even sometimes before it has become salvage and is still attached to its original home.

Sale outlets vary from one-day flea markets or car boot sales and chaotic yards where everything is piled up together and it is difficult to see the treasures that might be hidden underneath, to beautifully organised spaces where everything is ordered, restored and displayed to best advantage.

Demolition evokes images of ball and chain, noise and waste. And you don't just need to look at traditional houses. Every building, however modern, generates reclaimable material. A steel frame building can provide a suitable structure for someone else's studio; reclaimed cladding sheets and steel can be used for new construction; crushed concrete can become aggregate for new roads and drives. A collapsed barn or ruin can be dismantled, labelled and put together again elsewhere. If pieces of the major fabric have deteriorated or been destroyed, these can be recreated to give the building new life.

You may glance across a huge reclamation yard and immediately be drawn by the vast choice of fireplaces with their pretty Victorian tiles, or to the corner where you can spy a gazebo and several old-fashioned red phone booths, or in another direction where there's a bevy of square white Belfast sinks waiting for a home in your kitchen or garden. Some have cleaned, painted iron radiators, all ready to be integrated into modern heating systems, polished and shining black fireplaces or pristine marble surrounds, everything in its place, easy to view and examine. The best-organised are always ready to give guidance and advice on the objects they are selling, their provenance and the history of their styles. Even 'Victorian' objects take in a number of periods and styles, so there is a great deal to learn if you are just beginning.

There are reclamation yards full of objects 'as found', leaning against each other, full of rust and nail holes and so closely jammed together you can hardly find a trail through. Prices in architectural salvage outlets are often reflected in how much work has gone into preparing items for the visitor.

Don't forget, you may find hidden salvageable secrets already concealed in your home. If you carefully strip layers of wallpaper, you may find a Victorian paper sheltering underneath. You might choose to keep this on at least one wall as a fascinating and unique background to your home.

There may be old floorboards or even parquet under a fitted carpet, just waiting to be discovered, polished up and enjoyed. And before you consider casting out your pink three-piece bathroom suite, installed in the 1970s, imagine what satisfaction you could get from basing your bathroom design around it. You may have solid panelled doors hidden under hardboard panels, from the 1950s: housewives were told the latter wouldn't need so much dusting. There may still be the odd Victorian cast-iron fireplace buried under modern plasterboard walls and even if you don't intend to burn a fire in it, there's nothing like a fireplace to provide good proportions and an interesting focal point in a traditional room. It is the tearing out of these original features around the 1950s that so many people are now trying to put right. And this is one of the most obvious ways of using architectural salvage yards.

Some auction houses, like this one in north London, are open during the week to sell certain items separately from the auction, acting as second-hand shops.

A modern hotel designed by Rabih Hage layers the old with the new. Here the wallpaper was found under layers of paint and the existing fitted cupboard has been retained.

During the 1960s and 70s, shocked by the wholesale vandalism of so many traditional features and artefacts, a few people began to recognise the folly and waste of throwing away all this fine stuff and the first architectural salvage companies were set up. Demolition companies soon began to cotton on and there are now architectural salvage and reclamation companies all over the country, saving items from buildings being refurbished or demolished, grand or humble.

On a somewhat humbler scale, there are house-clearance companies who empty the homes of people who have moved or died, whose relations have no room for the contents. There are regular reclamation and second-hand fairs where you can find an extraordinary selection of domestic items, large and small, and on a smaller scale, there are local markets, car boot sales and school or community sales, selling small items of furniture and domestic items where you can sometimes find a bargain.

It is also surprising what you might find put out into the street for anyone to take, or loaded into skips, to be carted away to landfill, so it's worth keeping an eye open as you go about your daily business. There is also the Internet where several web-based market places exist; notably eBay, but there are other dealers who sell solely through their own websites.

Items sometimes find their way to their final destination by roundabout routes. Demolition companies in many countries are now well aware of the value of the things they

Unusual agricultural items like these wooden buckets from Belgium can often be found in architectural salvage fairs. They can make interesting planters or, in a large room, waste paper baskets or other forms of storage.

find in historic buildings. Such companies are often tied in with architectural salvage companies and will deliver reclaimed building materials, built-in furniture and units, flooring and panelling directly to the salvage company. What the salvage company doesn't find interesting will then go to the smaller second-hand shops where it may be sold for a very reasonable price indeed. Some demolition companies have their own reclamation outlets, especially of building materials. Salvage fairs can be educative and entertaining and excellent sources for a huge number of features. They take place throughout the year and are well worth visiting.

Where to look:
- Reclamation yards
- Second-hand furniture shops
- Street markets
- Car boot sales
- School or community sales
- Specialist fairs
- The Internet
- Check local directories: Yellow Pages are worth consulting under *Building Materials – used*; and *Salvage and Surplus*. Local newspapers are a fund of information on what's going on from week to week locally including jumble sales, car boot sales, markets and fairs. Local shops may also advertise in the local paper.

Source locally when possible

When it comes to looking for materials to extend, maintain or repair a traditional home, look for local materials to try to get a match. London stock bricks are a yellowy colour, Home Counties bricks a rosy red, Midland bricks a solid brick-red. These materials are heavy and expensive to transport so were made and used locally and can often be found locally in salvage centres. Even thatchers use the local varieties of reeds or grass for thatched roofs – not hay carted from hundreds of miles away – which is why thatched roofs in different areas have different characteristics. If you want to be authentic (and, incidentally, if you want to save on transport), source locally.

Sourcing from abroad

Although it makes sense to source locally, a certain amount of salvage finds its way from Europe and from parts of Asia. French farmhouse fireplaces have a distinctive character and vary from locality to locality; French farmhouse beams and railway sleepers are also available. But if you are on holiday in places where second-hand items are available, you can bring them home with you. In some countries it is illegal to export antiques, so beware.

The eighteenth-century Grand Tour can be compared with today's opportunities to travel far and wide and to bring back elements of the countries visited. In a modern building these can all help to give the interior an interest it might otherwise not achieve. Flats and apartments are likely to be built with a uniform, rather bland exterior with often rather boxy interiors that lend themselves to invention and individuality, and can be given interest and personality with antiques or exotic colours or 'hi-tech' solutions. Beware anything labelled 'authentic style': authentic to what?

It makes sense to respect the proportions of your home. A large converted barn would house an enormous French armoire with ease, but a small apartment in a modern block of flats would be dwarfed if you tried to squeeze a large refectory table into it. A high ceiling can accommodate a dado rail and picture rail, but only one would probably fit comfortably into a small room with a low ceiling.

Who can use salvage?

Absolutely anybody can enjoy using traditional materials and objects in their home. Apart from the obvious pleasure in returning the things that belong to a traditional building, many architectural salvage items are used in modern designs as a way of introducing interest, quality craftsmanship, a sense of history and even humour.

Whether you want to match up bricks to repair a wall or find a piece of narrow furniture that will fit into a narrow hallway, or are looking for enormous items to fit in with the proportions of a barn or warehouse conversion, you may find just what you need among the wonders of the salvage yard.

Materials often used in modern design – glass, plastic and concrete, for example – can benefit greatly from rubbing shoulders with items that have the patina of age. So a modern bathroom or kitchen can benefit from a floor of old wooden floorboards and a mezzanine-level bed will be made friendlier by the use of a ladder made of reclaimed wooden beams.

Stainless steel kitchen equipment and wood always seem to go remarkably well together in a modern kitchen, and chunky furniture made out of reclaimed wood can take on a stately quality when paired with curtains in a modern print. Designers working on the refurbishment of a pub, restaurant or the interior of a new hotel, owners of fashionable or traditional shops, or someone setting up an office in town can all use reclaimed items that can be better designed and much cheaper than anything they could afford new. Theatre and set designers can often find exactly what they need including columns, life-size knight's armour and a particular period of chair; some salvage yards may be prepared to rent items for the period of the shoot or the production.

Who can benefit?
- Owners of traditional homes who want to replace or match up original features.
- Owners of modern homes who would like to add something with character and a bit of history.
- Converted loft, barn or factory dwellers who have large spaces to fill and would like something solid and grand and with personality with which to fill them.
- Architects, designers and decorators, whether for hotels, restaurants, clubs, bars, offices or private homes.
- Collectors: of bric-a-brac, rugs, specific types of furniture or other traditional items.
- Anybody who hates to see waste will be happy to consider buying the increasing number of items for the home being made out of reclaimed materials, from farmhouse beams to cast-iron radiators.

Reclaimed double doors from France, being installed in a modern conversion of a terraced town house, add light and elegance to the room. Design: Paul Archer architects.

A large purposeful cast-iron radiator like this one, reclaimed from an old hospital, has been restored by Edward Haes and can complement and efficiently heat a large space in a warehouse or loft conversion.

This kitchen by Retrouvius with its clean modern lines and marble work surface (from the refurbished local fishmonger) is enhanced by the use of reclaimed wooden floorboards.

The dining table here is made from thick teak from a demolished hospital, offset by slabs of Norwegian slate reclaimed from the Department of the Environment, softened by a modern print by Timorous Beasties. Design: Retrouvius with Helm architects.

Why buy salvage?

Replacing original features

One main reason for buying architectural salvage has always been to replace items that have worn out or were torn out in the destructive 1970s, when, following release from the restrictions of the war and post-war years, modernism became the goal.

Livening up a modern home

However, you don't even need to be replacing old items. If you live in a modern home, reclaimed objects can add interest and personality to the most box-like interior, where there is no chimney breast to leave alcoves for shelving. If you like the clean, uncluttered lines of modern design, reclaimed items such as slate or wood can add a rich and attractive quality to your home.

Avoiding unnecessary waste

Recycling has been the driving force behind the reclamation industry. The reuse of serviceable materials is good reason for people to buy environmentally-friendly products for their homes. Reclaimed building materials and furniture are a great way of including recycled materials into your home.

The construction industry is the single largest source of waste in England, using over £30bn of building materials each year. Transport costs alone make up a third of all road freight traffic in the country. Reuse of building products reduces waste and maximises carbon savings. Yet an estimated 13 per cent of all building products (14 million tonnes a year) never get used and end up in landfill. BMRCs (building material re-use centres) would help the industry meet the Site Waste Management Plan legislation, while reducing the overall carbon footprint of a construction project.

The case for use of reclaimed exterior materials is compelling, both from a cost and an environmental point of view. Reclaimed timbers are now often used to create excellent floorboards and can be turned into tables and other furniture. The direct substitution of reclaimed materials for new can radically reduce the environmental impact of any particular item. It removes the need to extract raw materials and largely removes the need for processing and manufacture.

If you are interested in retaining or reinstating the original character of your home, there are several ways of getting information into its background. You can find out about its history through your local public library, for example, which may have a historic section with building records where you can find the date of construction and the name of the architect and builder. For a traditional house, the value of the property will be significantly enhanced by the use of relevant period materials including external brick and tiles. Harmonious and thoughtful use of period doors, floors and architectural features which are correctly weighted and matched to the size and period of a property is at the heart of the salvage industry.

The planning department or building regulations department of your local council may be helpful, too. If the house was built recently, there should be copies of the plans and drawings.

Reuse of construction materials helps reduce pollution and wasteful applications of fossil fuel and heavy new clay ware, not to mention the regrettably small reduction in deforestation and unnecessary timber production achieved by reclaiming railway sleepers.

Much modern refurbishment seems to be not just about updating a home, but about spending as much money as possible, tearing out everything that went before and introducing new features, equipment and finishes, whether necessary or not, at truly enormous expense. Councils are particularly bad at this and their recycling departments seem to be completely separate from their planning and maintenance departments, so that bottles and paper are carefully collected and categorised while perfectly good sinks, basins, baths and cookers, chairs, tables and beautiful second-hand tiles and fireplaces are simply thrown away. They are not even passed on to neighbours who would be glad to have them. Literally millions can be spent on refurbishment which could be done at half the price if some thought was given to what the actual tenants would prefer.

It's not just a question of avoiding landfill but also of avoiding landfill tax. In the 1960s and 70s such things would have been ruthlessly got rid of, thrown into skips and ended up in landfill sites. However, in recent years we have come to recognise the value of such objects in terms of design, workmanship and materials. We have even come to realise that the signs of their past life give them an added interest. If an old oak school desk has ink stains or a polished mahogany table has the odd dent from being moved around or even the pale ring from a vase of flowers, they all indicate an interesting and productive life in a well-appreciated past. Some things will take on a new life simply by being brightened up with a fresh coat of paint.

BMRCs

In the USA and Canada there are hundreds of building material re-use centres or BMRCs; one in almost every large community. These are financially sustainable retail outlets selling reclaimed, reusable building materials to the trade and the general public. The goods may be cut to size, adapted, cleaned up or refinished, but they fundamentally retain their original form.

The UK has not yet established a BMRC network, although there are good social enterprises throughout the country successfully retailing furniture from reclaimed wood and many successful private architectural salvage companies selling historic and traditional materials, features and furniture.

The not-for-profit company Bio-regional is working with wasteWISE and MASCo to develop up to five major BMRCs in the UK, run as social enterprises, which will complement existing salvage and recycling companies. MASCo has one of Britain's largest reclamation yards selling building materials and furniture.

One company, Tiger Enterprise, based in the South East of England, has set up a surplus building materials yard and collects surplus building materials, both new and old from big building contractors working on new buildings as well as from demolition contractors (including bricks, doors, paving slabs, roof and floor tiles, loft insulation, sanitary ware and concrete blocks) which it sells from its own yard.

Anti-pollution

Brickworks, and indeed, many types of manufacture, are major polluters of the environment, so reusing bricks and tiles and other items in your home means less production of harmful gasses.

Reclaimed terracotta roof tiles at Herts Architectural Reclamation and Salvage have been cleaned up and boxed ready to transport to their new destination.

Two old-fashioned galvanised watering-cans found in an architectural salvage fair in the west of England have been given a new lease of life with a coat of daffodil yellow paint.

A reclaimed oak pew can be sawn into separate seats and used as individual garden seating if you don't have room for a complete length. This would also be suitable for a library or converted warehouse.

As an investment

Here, we are looking at items that will enhance your home in various ways from the moment you buy them, because you like them, not specifically as a financial investment for the future. And we will look at how different pieces can be used, altered, given different functions and generally adjusted to your own lifestyle. However, objects that are less old can become collectors' items which can put their price up as though they were antiques. It is not always easy to know where to draw the line between antiques and salvage. It is to do with age, of course. An antique is something valued for its age, workmanship, beauty and/or rarity and generally applies to objects over 100 years old. However, it also has to do with the quality of the object and the amount of care it has received during its lifetime, and with how many people want it, which will determine how much it is seen as 'collectible'.

Pleasure rather than investment:
- Some people buy in the hope that the item will increase in value and become an investment. But for many people, the attraction is in the hunt.
- It's good to find a bargain; it's better to find a perfectly-fitting piece of the jigsaw that is your home.
- You will be more likely to find a good bargain if you look in places that will not be of interest to professional dealers. For example, a second-hand shop selling mostly wooden furniture and books will be quite happy to sell the odd china cup or plate, whereas if it specialises in china, the best pieces will quickly go at much higher prices.
- Avoid chipped or cracked objects unless they are extremely rare, but you would do that anyway if you want simply to enjoy the object for its own intrinsic value to you.
- Choose items that will enhance your home in various ways from the moment you buy them, because you like them.
- Respect what you find but don't be overawed: use, alter, or give an object a different function to its original one and generally adjust things to your own lifestyle.

Ways of approaching salvage:
- Look for something specific.
- Keep your eyes open permanently for you-don't-necessarily-know-what.
- Look for things that will be relevant to the style of your home.
- Look for things you can adapt.
- Look for anything that will make your home more interesting – the eclectic approach.

One of the pleasures of salvage-hunting is that you can rummage for small items to put up on shelves or use in the kitchen, or you can buy enormous furniture for your converted barn or, if you're lucky, or rich, you can buy a complete barn or even, as someone recently found out, the splendid old Baltic Exchange that used to sit on the site of what is now Norman Foster's iconic 'gherkin' in the City of London. Most of us would be happy with something rather smaller.

The Baltic Exchange

This is the splendid pediment of the Baltic Exchange in the City of London whose foundations were damaged by an IRA bomb in 1992. The pediment was photographed when it was on show at the Salvo fair.

The Baltic Exchange, a twentieth-century trading hall, was built in 1903 by Smith and Wimble and demonstrated, with grandeur and style, in red granite, coloured marble and Portland stone, the wealth and solidity of London's maritime trade. In 1992 its foundations were damaged by an IRA bomb that badly damaged the City and in 1998 this Grade II* listed building had to be dismantled. It spent some years in pieces in wooden crates in a barn near Canterbury. The plaster interiors remained intact, including a pediment complete with sea monsters and mermaids riding dolphins among the classical mouldings. Some parts of the plasterwork were sold separately and a buyer was eventually found for the building, so this exotic piece of architectural salvage will now begin a new life in Eastern Europe.

Furniture worth looking for

Many types of furniture can be found including seating, tables and storage from the down-to-earth to the highly exotic. Up until the post World War Two period, furniture was mostly made of solid wood, sometimes oak, often pine (often called deal at the time.) These may be no-nonsense, no-frills pieces of furniture, made to last a very long time and to put up with lots of abuse. They include nursery chairs, children's chairs, individual and dining chairs and also the Utility furniture that was the only furniture available during the war and for a

A narrow painted wooden table and chair with a plywood seat make a good writing or homework desk. (The carrier bag is made out of reclaimed fruit juice cartons.)

Here is a plethora of unexpected treasures from cigarette machines to dining tables. It's up to you, the salvage-hunter, to make of them what you will.

short time afterwards. All these 'plain Jane' pieces have a certain sturdy charm today and, of course, can be painted in bright colours which can transform them into very desirable pieces for different parts of the home. They can also be cannibalised and used in different ways. For example, the doors of a cupboard that would be too bulky to use as it is, could be taken off and used as doors to a cupboard under the stairs; the top could be taken off a dresser-like piece and the top and bottom pieces used quite separately, one in the kitchen and one in a child's room, say, or perhaps as storage in the garage. A small school desk can make a good all-purpose table in a child's room and miniature kindergarten chairs can sometimes be found that children love to sit in.

Assessing what you find

Don't be afraid to negotiate on price. There are no manufacturer's recommended prices in the salvage world – nothing cut and dried. You may be able to get a good deal by buying in bulk, if you are interested in floorboards, roof tiles or a number of industrial pendant lamps, and the price of furniture is often negotiable.

There is no guarantee of the quality of what you may find in a second-hand shop or salvage yard. Some outlets simply stack their items fairly chaotically under dubious shelters. Here

Telegraph poles are uncompromisingly large and solid but can make attractive fences, in this case dividing a wildlife centre from a main road.

you may find unexpected treasures, but you may also find rusty, broken or useless objects. Others are impeccably organised, so you can see exactly what you are looking at and much of it is in good order. Others again will only offer items that have already been refurbished, repaired and made ready for use (as in radiators or fireplaces, for example).

As a salvage-hunter it is up to you to make sure that the item you fall in love with is actually what you want. A beautiful Georgian door may be your idea of perfection, but doors come in many different sizes, so it may cost you a lot of money if your reclaimed one doesn't fit the existing opening in the wall. It's best to pick the door before you build the wall, if you don't want expensive extra building work. A nineteenth-century Heath Robinson-like garden sprinkler may be beautifully engineered but if there's a bit missing, you'll probably have to invent or manufacture the missing piece yourself if you want to use it on the lawn.

Researching

Do your research beforehand. If you live in a period house, take time to find out about relevant materials for the restoration of your house or refurbishment of a room. If you live in a modern house and simply want to add interest or entertainment, then you have a wider outlook and can choose to suit yourself. However, the understanding of a traditional house and the search for building materials and furnishings in keeping with it has an attraction and fascination all its own.

The whole thing can be very seductive, so it's important to make initial rules. Buy only things that will fit in with your chosen style, only things that will fit in with the proportions of your home – and importantly, only things that will actually physically fit into the space you have for them. (Always carry a tape measure!) You might find a really desirable metal arbour/pergola with seats running along both sides; it may be several minutes before you realise it would cover the whole of your garden, not just embellish a small corner.

Using what you find

Matching up

You may have a Victorian or Edwardian terraced house that has had everything of character torn out. That is quite common. So to put back all those items that would have been designed for such a house can lead to an exciting and exhilarating treasure hunt. Luckily, the interest in saving, salvaging, reusing and caring for traditional materials and furniture means that those things are certainly around. It's just a question of finding them. Remember that local salvage-hunting will most likely find local artefacts – especially bricks and local materials. If you live in an area where particular items were made, it will be a good place to start looking for them.

Don't hesitate to mix up your styles and periods. Some junk shops and salvage yards sell props from old theatre and film productions where you may find a set of Greek columns and two of these leading into the main room of your home may give it a presence which will enhance its interest value and amuse at the same time.

Apart from the obvious uses of reclaimed materials and artefacts, there are all sorts of different ways you can make the most of things that might seem bizarre. For example, slate mantelpieces can make solid garden seats, discarded roof tiles can be given new life as path or border edges, and old kitchen doors fixed between a fence or wall can appear to lead into a further part of a small garden, psychologically making the space seem larger. A popular use of old beams is to turn them into floorboards; there are numerous uses for old railway sleepers and redundant telegraph poles, and there are a number of companies creating furniture from old wood.

On the more bizarre side, you can sometimes find old riding boots acting as bases for table lamps, or old tennis rackets turned into washroom mirrors complete with a hook on which to hang a face towel. Once you let your imagination take over, there are innumerable uses for beautiful old objects.

In the garden, reclaimed bricks and stone can add character and make it look established very quickly. Reclaimed York stone and cast-iron fencing immediately add interest, old staddle stones, fountains, sundials, birdbaths and wire arbours make fascinating features to draw the eye; old watering-cans can be painted to cheer up a shady garden.

What style?

A specific style

Are you looking for a specific style to fit in with the period of your home or are you interested in any style that will fit in with your own particular taste or just brightening up a rather bland modern interior space? People often start randomly, being fascinated by everything and attracted to many, then find they are drawn to a particular period or taste. As you know more, your choices become more specific. For some it may be the craftsmanship, for some the nostalgia, for some the simplicity or perhaps a highly decorative quality. The more you know, the better you can search for what you want. Always ask questions. Many sellers of second-hand objects are very well informed about what they are selling. If you can shop at unpopular times you will have more opportunity to talk to the dealer and the more time he will be able to give to your queries and desires. Once you find yourself drawn to a particular era, craftsperson or designer, visit museums, exhibitions, question, read books and magazines, join societies and search the Internet for information.

Eclectic style

Victorian homes invite collections as they would have done when first built. However, if you live in a modern block of flats made up of square simply-shaped rooms with rather low ceilings and few of the eccentricities or design features created by chimney breasts, sloping attic ceilings or space under the stairs, you can very well afford to be more eclectic and collect all sorts of interesting and colourful objects of your own choice to add personality and interest.

Handmade and crafted objects in interesting woods or with carved finishes can add a quality of interest and individuality and make all the difference to your home. Have faith in your own choices. If you buy things you like they are likely to go together so you don't have to worry about matching colours or styles. The colours you like will almost certainly belong together, whereas if you try to fit in with 'fashion' your design will be bland and will soon seem out of date. Remember that some of the most interesting items and some of the most satisfying materials can come from what seem to be humble homes. For example, twentieth-century hospitals, schools and offices can provide excellent ideas for the modern home or other interior. Taps and sinks, space-saving cupboards, industrial lighting and laboratory workbenches can all be incorporated into other schemes in interesting and inventive ways.

This eclectic interior belonging to a modern fabric designer is almost Victorian in its variety, combining a set of wooden lockers from a lawyer's office with a reclaimed standard lamp, old kilims and a kilim-covered chair.

Being sensitive to a room's proportions may be more important than understanding its style. Whether you live in a tiny box-like studio apartment or a converted factory or warehouse, the proportions are all-important, but either way they offer enormous potential for second-hand items that have a presence and personality of their own.

Peeling or restored?
Even the walls of your home may conceal fascinating layers of the past. If you are redecorating and stripping off the old wallpaper has uncovered decades-old paint or wallpaper, why not keep it? Rabih Hage's Rough Luxe Hotel in London's King's Cross does just that so it is like peeling back time, and old and new items sit comfortably together – more like a home than a hotel.

A bedroom in Rabih Hage's unusual London hotel combines the remains of a previous paint discovered behind some wallpaper with a modern sofa and a painted glass lampshade which was already hanging in the room.

Many salvage specialists have in-house restorers who have or can restore an item to pristine condition. However, the whole point about reclaimed items is that they are not pristine. If you have decided to buy an old fireplace or old bricks, presumably it is because you either want to restore or extend an old building or because you like old things. Either way, over-restoration will remove half the point of buying the thing in the first place. Some things need to be restored, of course. A bit of cleaning up, removal of bad stains or marks or a new coat of paint are how you would deal with anything in your home – you wouldn't want to bathe in a rusty bath, for example, and you can't use old radiators or lighting until they have been made safe according to present-day regulations.

An old sofa may need to be re-sprung and new upholstery can make it look smart, but it might be more at home with a simple bedcover or rug thrown over it. What many of us want is an antidote to the freshly-painted, over-polished idea of modern design, not to add to it. If you have bought something that you think needs some sort of remedial treatment, the Conservation Register, operated by the United Kingdom Institute for Conservation (UKIC) has a register of conservation experts in many fields including bronze, wrought iron, terracotta, woodwork, stained glass and stonework. They have produced fact sheets giving general advice on the care and conservation of a range of different materials and objects.

New uses for reclaimed objects

Reclaimed wood was originally grown from trees that had matured over hundreds of years, giving individuality and character. Reclaimed pine is utterly different from, and much harder than new pine. There is a real anxiety about the amount of wood being inefficiently used and thrown away and this is a strong argument for using salvaged wood, which has, of course, already had a long life as an article of furniture or part of the structure of an old building that has given it history and character.

The Global Trees Campaign (a joint initiative between Flora & Fauna International and Botanic Gardens Conservation International) estimate that less than 10 per cent of wood waste is recycled and 3,000 tonnes of reusable timber from demolition of old buildings ends up in landfill or is burned every working day. Woods such as beech, teak, pitchpine, reclaimed parquet floors, maple and oak strip flooring are now being carefully reclaimed and can be found in specialist reclamation yards.

Recrafted from reclaimed

Recrafted items from reclaimed materials are not difficult to find nowadays. There are handmade wooden tables, kitchen units, butchers' blocks, cupboards and flooring made from reclaimed pine; windows and doors from reclaimed pitchpine; hand-carved oak items such as chimneypieces; gargoyles from Victorian stone window jambs; water tanks turned into sturdy low coffee tables; reclaimed Victorian sash windows made into mirrors; and smaller items such as plant stands made from cast-iron stair parts, lamps from industrial bobbins, desk lamps from recycled boiler copper; or you can get bespoke items made to your own requirements. You can often find interesting recrafted items on the Salvo website.

Some specialists in reclaimed timber have workshops where they use their timber to create furniture and then sell it on. For example, Winkleigh Timber Ltd. finds buildings and structures that are due to be demolished from all over the UK, salvages usable timber of many different kinds, takes it back to the yard, where it is prepared, metal-detected using specialised machinery and sorted into sizes and grades ready for use. Some of the timber is then sold for flooring, doors, joinery and so on, but most is made on-site into furniture and sold through the showroom, Winkleigh Pine Furniture. All the furniture is made on the premises using reclaimed timbers. All drawers are dovetailed and tongue and groove backing boards are used for dressers, available polished or 'in the white' ready for painting or varnishing – fantastic for your holiday cottage. Another example is Toby's in Devon, which is a large architectural salvage yard that also makes bespoke kitchens and oak or pine doors from reclaimed wood.

Reproductions and copies

Many salvage yards find they run out of genuine reclaimed original items and offer instead reproductions. This applies particularly to fireplaces, doors, garden sculptures and water features. Most are perfectly clear about which is which and there is usually no difficulty in differentiating between the two. However, if they are being sold as genuine, check that they really are. Reproduction items can be as good as the real thing but not if you imagine you are buying something old.

Reproductions are copies of artefacts, usually those that are no longer made or are becoming rare. In your hunt for genuine original materials and artefacts you will come across many reproductions and many actual fakes. Some older reproductions, perhaps those made in the eighteenth or nineteenth centuries, have a quality and may be valuable in their own right. Modern reproductions, based on original patterns and moulds and using similar materials and techniques, can legitimately take the place of something that is now very rare and/or expensive. However, things that are popular and therefore becoming more difficult to find have encouraged the introduction of reproduction items or even bad copies made of lesser quality materials and possibly mass produced. This makes them more affordable, but less satisfying. Still, you need to know that's what you're buying (especially if recycling is part of your philosophy).

Good quality reproductions can become collectible in their own right, but there are copies made with inferior materials and slightly different proportions that may fit in nicely in a small modern room with a low ceiling but will not look right in a traditional home.

There's nothing necessarily wrong with reproduction doors or furniture. Good reproductions are made using the same materials and the same techniques as the originals would have been and are often handmade and can be valid replacements for what they emulate. Get to know what an original looks like, feels like and weighs. Get to recognise when something in the manufacture is not quite right. Reproduction fireplaces and doors are common.

Get to recognise what's a good copy and what's a poor copy. Lower quality reproductions probably won't hold their value, but if you find something that pleases you and you just want it for your own satisfaction, why worry?

Salvo

Anyone seriously interested in acquiring architectural salvage should know about Salvo, which calls itself the 'gateway to the world of architectural salvage and antiques', and indeed it is. Salvo has a website with a directory of architectural salvage companies who conform to the Salvo Code. Look for the crane logo to check whether a company is a member. The Salvo website also has a list of specific items for sale; a list of 'recrafted from reclaimed' items for sale; information on demolitions about to take place; information on stolen items and a calendar of events of interest to salvage-hunters. It organises the annual Salvo Fair in June and publishes *Salvo* magazine. The man behind Salvo is Thornton Kay who founded one of the first salvage companies, Walcot Reclamation, in the 1970s. 'There were only two others then, LASSCO and Andy Thornton, who sold mainly pub stuff,' he says. He began Salvo full-time in 1991 and the organisation is now an international force in the reclamation world.

A couple of small square coffee tables, created from old galvanised water tanks, share space with a lamp base made from an old fisherman's float at an outdoor architectural salvage fair.

A good-looking Victorian-style reproduction marble fireplace is surrounded by a genuine cast-iron bear, a table lamp, a carriage clock and other reclaimed items in this intriguing architectural salvage centre.

Something to sell?

Second-hand shops can produce surprising pleasures like this metal fish head and tail, which can be used at each end of a dish to display a whole poached salmon to perfection.

- If you have anything to sell you may get a salvage company or local second-hand shop to take it.
- Salvo provides a directory of salvage yards that can be searched by desired location or material. If there are only a few operating in your neighbourhood, don't give up as they will often know someone who can help.
- Specialist reclamation companies may be willing to take large quantities of recycled and antique wood, especially English oak and French oak, as beams, joists, rafters and original floorboards. However, to make it worth their while they sometimes want good quantities of the same species and of one type only, not just a couple of pine shelves.
- Don't be disappointed if you are not offered as much as you had hoped. Dealers usually add between 30 and 60 per cent onto the price. Remember they have to pay for transport and rent on their own premises and need to make a profit.
- If the object needs restoration, expect to be paid less.
- Keep an eye on the market and see what the going prices are for the sort of thing you want to sell. It may be worthwhile getting two or three dealers to quote.
- Certain charities rely on gifts of old furniture and household objects to refurbish and sell on, so before throwing something out, check whether it would be useful to one of those. Emmaus is one such charity. It has branches all over the country and shops selling refurbished goods.
- Sometimes a dealer will specify a period: for example, some may only accept items from before 1940.
- For smaller quantities or individual pieces of furniture or rugs it's worth trying a smaller second-hand, junk shop or emporium. Whether selling to a private buyer or to a salvage company, a good place to start is the Internet. Try Salvo or eBay.
- Advertise in your local paper: this is a cheap way of getting a local buyer who may be willing to fetch the item.

Selling at auction
- You will be asked to put a reserve price on the piece. The auctioneer should be able to advise if you are not sure what a reasonable price would be.
- There are various costs involved such as the cost of a photograph in the auction catalogue (if you want one), the seller's commission (10–15 per cent of the final selling price), transport costs and insurance which are usually subject to VAT.
- Don't try to auction something that has already been rejected by local dealers. Not only do they know what's likely to sell (or not) at auction, but they are the people most likely to be bidding.

Selling via the Internet
- eBay is the most popular selling site on the Internet, accessed by thousands of potential customers.
- Set a reserve price and hope somebody will get the bidding going.
- Choose a short, attention-grabbing title that describes your object in one phrase. Describe it as honestly as possible, always including at least one photograph.
- If you make a habit of selling on eBay, remember if you sell regularly, you will be liable to be taxed on the income you make.

Researching a period or style

The earliest furniture you are likely to find in a salvage yard is probably Victorian, although you may find some Georgian items, particularly building materials. Most Georgian and Victorian furniture is now considered antique, but you might find chests of drawers, chairs or tables or various bits of storage that were intended for the less fashionable parts of the house and have not been particularly well looked after and these can be real bargains. Many pieces of surprisingly sturdy quality were made in the late 1800s and early 1900s for schools, hospitals, museums and offices, which are now beginning to find their way to salvage and reclamation sites.

If you live in a period house – anything from Tudor to Arts & Crafts or country cottage – salvaging materials and furniture for it will mean you can match it up with things that feel at home in it.

In the UK the Victorian Society, the Georgian Group and the Twentieth Century Society can all give information on the period of their particular interest. In the USA contact your local historic preservation society. Many know of salvagers who also specialise in particular building materials. Some non-profit historic societies operate non-profit salvage warehouses and other services for old-time restoration.

There are many museums such as the Victoria & Albert in London, which has a vast collection of furniture and interior artefacts from all periods, or the Geffrye Museum with room sets representing the major periods from Tudor onwards. There is also the specialist Bakelite Museum in Somerset, showing every imaginable thing ever made in that fascinating plastic material.

Charles Brooking has been rescuing original architectural features since he was a schoolboy and now has an impressive collection, some of which is housed at Greenwich University, but a great deal of it is still in several purpose-built buildings behind his home in Cranleigh, Surrey. The Brooking Collection is now the largest archive of original architectural features of its kind in Europe. Here he has large items such as doors, windows and sections of staircases, fanlights and smaller things like doorknobs and knockers, boot scrapers and sample lengths of architrave and skirting mouldings. It is possible to visit his collection, where he will give you an enthusiastic and informed introduction to the fantastic artefacts he holds.

Auction houses are other good places to help get your eye in. They often have a medley of styles and periods on show before each auction and sometimes hold specialist auctions with furniture or other artefacts from a particular period or by a particular designer or factory. Auction catalogues, too, can be very educational.

Look around you when you go out. In spite of modern 'improvements' many traditional homes have been untouched on the outside and still have their original doors and door furniture, so you can get a glimpse of what houses would have been like in their heyday.

A short guide to interior styles

The Georgian passion for classical styles
Interior styles up until the middle of the century were connected much more to their architecture than they are now. Georgian Neo-classical architecture was very much based on Classical Greek and Roman architecture and ancient artefacts were brought home from modern Greece and Rome to complement their homes by young men on the Grand Tour. Nineteenth-century architecture was more eclectic, some of it still influenced by classical architecture but some turning to the medieval Gothic for inspiration. In fact the Victorians revelled in variation. Both eighteenth- and nineteenth-century houses were often built to designs from pattern books by well-known architects and these can sometimes be unearthed in reference libraries.

Classical architecture has had an influence on buildings in England since the sixteenth century. Proud use of classical features such as columns can be seen everywhere in terraced and other houses. There was also a leaning towards Greek architecture led by James Wyatt in the 1780s and 90s. Styles were various and varied with different influences and these overlapped and intermingled. Nevertheless, each century has had a strong representation of recognisable style and can be recognised with a little knowledge.

Victorian invention
Domestic plumbing arrived in the Victorian era. Concern for hygiene and cleanliness at the end of the nineteenth century and the development of a hot water system and the invention of the water closet meant dedicated bathrooms became a feature of large late Victorian houses. However, hot water and a lavatory came very late to most homes. Right up to the end of World War Two many families had to do without running hot water and had to go outside to the loo. When somebody wanted a bath, it would be carried into a warm room and filled with hot water brought up from the kitchen by the servants. I still remember at the age of six being given a hip bath in the living room of the Rectory in Norfolk where my grandfather was the vicar, with a bevy of aproned girls bringing up the water. Understandably, home-owners who could afford a bathroom were proud of it and liked to show off their fine sanitary ware that was often highly decorated.

An imposing Victorian doorway in an end-of-terrace house in London has marbled columns and a glazed fanlight with glazed panels round the door and inset into it, allowing plenty of light into the hall.

A choice of styles and periods can be found in many second-hand shops. Here is a small upholstered Victorian sofa together with various pieces of early and mid-twentieth-century paraphernalia.

This ancient fireplace, seen at Westland, is a true antique from the Tudor or Stewart period and will look its best in a large, sparsely-furnished space where its grand proportions and skilled carving will take pride of place.

This is a typical Georgian front door in a country village, well proportioned with a glass panel above it to light up the interior, with classical columns and a roof to create a practical sheltered porch.

Mid-twentieth-century departure from tradition

New materials, new politics and the intervention of two world wars encouraged twentieth-century home-owners to think again about interiors. They began to introduce things made of plastic, and furniture and fittings originally intended for industrial use, in a style known as 'Hi-tech'.

This is a brief introduction to some of the most popular and recognisable styles that you might find in salvage yards. Many interior and furniture styles take their names from the architecture they were designed to complement. However, interior furnishings changed much more often than their buildings and do not always coincide exactly with the dates of the houses they furnished.

Tudor and Stewart (1500–late 1600s)
Sturdy, often oak furniture often stained to a dark colour, such as chests, refectory tables and carved panelling, but most of this is now only found in antique shops.

Georgian (eighteenth century)
- Georgian is a general term for various styles in English architecture and interiors from the accession of George I to the throne to the death of George IV. Many styles were included during this period including Adam style, Rococo, Neo-Classicism, Gothic Revival and Egyptian Taste.
- Front doors were in solid timber, normally painted black or very dark green and often divided into six panels.
- Furniture was made by companies like Chippendale, Hepplewhite and Sheraton. The main characteristics which held these styles together were respect for good craftsmanship and a leaning towards a classical system of design and proportion, flexible enough to accommodate phases as different as Chinoiserie and Pompeian.
- Shelved recesses, framed with pilasters, were a distinctive feature of the style.
- In grand Georgian houses each room was treated as a work of art in its own right.
- Window bars became slimmer, epitomised by the Adam brothers, Robert and James.
- Stately marble fireplaces, classical motifs, simple panelling; every detail was thought out carefully to complement the decoration.
- In more modest Georgian houses ornament was usually confined to skirting boards, dado rails and door surrounds.

Victorian (nineteenth century)

Furniture:
- As with most things Victorian, there were many designs, ranging from large and important-looking with overstuffed upholstery to little prie-dieu chairs and tiny carved, wall-fixed bookcases suitable for a bedroom.
- Victorian furniture is solid, often dark stained, although nowadays it is often stripped, which gives it a blonde, warm colour that fits in better with modern homes.
- Styles of furnishing were grandiose and varied, ranging from highly ornamented Gothic and Rococo to simpler Arts and Crafts.

Flooring:
- Floors were covered with large Persian carpets in the main rooms and stained floorboards in lesser rooms, covered with Persian rugs.

Doors:
- Front doors were often painted green and might be given grained paint effects. Other popular colours were dark blue, brown, dark red and an olive, often with stained or etched glass panels.
- Decorative glass panels were found inset in hall, kitchen and bathroom doors. The glass could be coloured, patterned or plain with an etched or painted design. Stained glass was popular in front doors and above interior doors.

Bathrooms:
- Originally a bedroom would be sacrificed to make room for a bathroom, so the first bathrooms were comfortable and well-appointed with ceiling mouldings, cornices, perhaps a carpet, a small table of toiletries and room for an armchair. There might be a marble-topped mahogany washstand against one wall.
- Bathrooms were not introduced in most homes until 1870. Where they existed, they proudly displayed free-standing ornate baths, often with claw feet, sometimes made of copper.
- Basins were often decorated with floral patterns and the lavatory would have had a mahogany seat and a highly decorative ceramic bowl.
- Look for the wash jugs and bowls kept on the washstand and filled with warm water by the maid in the morning. Even if one has got broken, the other on its own can be very attractive and useful.
- A well-appointed bathroom might have a heated towel rail that doubled up as a radiator and a free-standing cast iron bath with feet and perhaps even an integral shower with a wide, brass shower head.
- Taps might be brass, nickel, porcelain or brass with a little porcelain disc informing you whether it was 'H' or 'C'.
- By the end of the nineteenth century roll-top cast-iron baths were the most popular. They were white vitreous enamel inside and usually brown on the outside but could be painted in other colours or decoratively painted with marbling or stencilling. The feet were modelled on classical designs such as mythical beasts or ball and claw. They look splendid in large bathrooms where you can appreciate their sculptural qualities but they are extremely heavy, especially when full of water, so if you are thinking of installing one, check that the structure of your building and the floor underneath the bath are strong enough to take it.

Fireplaces:
- A fireplace with a cast-iron carved wood or marble surround was essential. They could be large and imposing or tiny, designed for a maid's room or for the homes of the miners who dug up the coal.

Ceramic tiles:
- Ceramic tiles were very popular, being durable and hygienic, colourful and attractive. They were used indoors and out.

Above left: The Victorians were very aware of both hygiene and decoration. Tiles, both patterned and plain, were used inside and out. These have survived the transformation of this house into a sushi restaurant.

Above right: Victorian doors were often painted green. This one has a brass handle and letterbox (unusually placed symmetrically in the middle) and a larger enamelled number plate.

Left: Lurking in unexpected places are useful narrow pieces of furniture like this Arts and Crafts coat stand found in an architectural salvage yard outside London.

The Victorians were proud of their bathrooms and liked to have decorated ceramic ware. This typical example with its blue floral decoration was seen at an architectural salvage fair in 2009.

A wonderfully sinuous Art Nouveau stove 'Le Triomphe' originally from France, displayed by Lighthouse at the Salvo Fair at Knebworth Park in 2009.

- Many well-known designers designed tiles including William Morris and William de Morgan but there were many anonymous designers who produced various floral patterns, including Art Nouveau designs.

Lighting:

The invention of the gas lamp had a profound effect on Victorian homes. By the 1840s some Victorian homes had gas lighting but oil lamps were still widely used. Brass bedsteads were popular. In the early 1940s my prep school in the North of Scotland, a Scottish baronial mansion, still had a disgusting-smelling gas plant outside the kitchen door. The gas was piped indoors and gas lamps with glass shades were fixed to the wall, which gave out what would be considered a rather feeble light today; these were lit in the evening with a gentle 'pop'. Today, similar lamps can be converted to electricity and do have an old world charm.

- Paraffin lamps were introduced in 1843 but domestic gas lighting was the most important.
- The Victorians hung oil or gas lamps in the centre of a room over the kitchen or dining table, often on a rise and fall system so the light could be lowered to give a more intimate light for eating. Such lights can now be adapted to electricity and give a pleasant general light, or towards the centre of the table, not just suitable for a Victorian home, but for any area where a similar light is needed. They can be very ornate with the look almost of a chandelier, or simple with one glass shade.

Arts & Crafts (1888–1939):
- This late Victorian style, promoted by William Morris in England, was popular in the USA. In fact, New York is the place to look for many Arts & Crafts artefacts. The movement aimed to produce designs for furniture and other household items inspired by 'truth to materials' and 'fitness for purpose'.
- The emphasis was on simplification and honesty of decoration, inspiration from the Middle Ages and the natural world in formal patterns and a return to high standards of craftsmanship.
- Designers used light, clear colours and an airier style in a reaction against what was seen as Victorian clutter.

Art Nouveau (1895–1939):
- Art Nouveau succeeded and dovetailed with the Arts and Crafts movement. Its name came from a shop that opened in Paris in 1895. In Italy it was called 'Stil Liberty' after the London store, and in Germany and Scandinavia 'Jugenstil' (youth style).
- The designs were curvilinear, elongated and often described as 'organic' because shapes found in nature were used.
- Colours were clear and bright, particularly a brilliant peacock blue.
- Bentwood furniture was mass produced by Thonet introducing new possibilities for furniture in homes, public places and offices.
- Tiffany in New York produced Art Nouveau stained glass lamps and the Glasgow architect, Charles Rennie Mackintosh produced many Art Nouveau designs for buildings, furniture and textiles.

Tiffany:
- Louis Tiffany was a New York painter and then an interior designer before turning his full attention to the art glass which made him famous, inspired by medieval stained glass windows in Europe's cathedrals and churches and ancient iridescent glass being unearthed by archaeologists in the Middle East. He used skilled silversmiths and glass artists to produce exquisite iridescent vases, stained glass windows, lamps and lighting.
- The Tiffany Studios Lamp Shop came into being in the 1890s, originally to make use of the offcuts from the stained glass and mosaic workshops to make lampshades for use with candles, oil lamps and the new electric light bulb.
- His lamps have been reproduced and copied ever since and although you are unlikely to find an original – they are very valuable antiques nowadays – you can often find a copy.

Twentieth century

Art Deco (1910–1939):
- Also known as Jazz Modern, this style dominated the decorative arts in the years between the First and Second World Wars. It originated in France and was imported to Britain and the USA.
- Art Deco was influenced by the Bauhaus in Germany and by Cubism, Diaghilev's Ballet Russe and Egyptology.
- Motifs of sailing ships were popular as were sculptural light fittings, particularly of sinuous girls holding light fittings; tasselled cushions, opulence and modernity.
- Art Deco was a popular style for bathrooms which were a great novelty in the 1920s.

Basic and Utility furniture (1940s):
- During the war there was a severe lack of timber in the UK, but also a huge demand for new furniture because so much had been lost due to bombing.
- All furniture produced at the time had to follow designs approved by the government and produced by designers and manufacturers of the day, and was known as Utility furniture.
- Its aim was to supply sturdy, well-designed furniture as cheaply as possible and was made to strict wartime specifications in the tradition of the Arts & Crafts movement, quite severe and unornamented.
- About 700 factories throughout the country were involved in producing it to make transportation easier.
- The scheme closed in 1952 and perhaps because it was all you could get at the time, it quickly became very unfashionable as soon as other alternatives became available.
- Today it seems attractive and well made and because it was, indeed, made to be sturdy, there is quite a lot of it still about.

Retro (1950s to 1970s):
These years saw an enormous reaction to the austerity of the war and post-war years and is full of the spare and beautifully made designs that came over from Scandinavia; all sorts of plastics; a style called Hi-tech, which was a movement to use industrial furniture and components in the home and a living space with no fuss. Materials used were glass, steel, rubber and synthetics, industrial metal stairs, straight or spiral, large room heaters, metal-

A very basic chair that nevertheless has more solid wood and more character than many a new modern design. It only needs a coat of paint to bring it back to life.

This two-storey mews flat in north London is furnished with a huge leather 'croissant' sofa, Mies van der Rohe Brno dining chairs and a Bruno Mattson lounge chair. The mahogany worktop running almost the length of the building is made of reclaimed handrails from a London office block. Design: Retrouvius.

A modern take on Hi-tech: this set of company post-room pigeon holes, seen at Caravan in London's East End, has its own built-in swivel stool and fits in comfortably with the eclectic objects and furniture in the shop.

based tables with glass surfaces, office shelving, filing systems and ergonomically-designed car or aeroplane seats.

There are plenty of second-hand kitchen units from the 1950s and 60s, often in cream and eau de nil or bright red with plastic handles. You can give your kitchen a refreshingly retro look. However, they need thought and care to make them look their best. It's worth trying to find accessories from the same period such as enamelled tea and coffee tins to give a unified look.

Mass-produced dining and kitchen furniture from the 1950s and 60s can be quite cheap in junk shops and can be painted to fit in with modern furniture. Its simple shapes and single colours fit in well with minimalist thinking.

Retro style incorporates more or less anything from 1950 to 1980:
- You can find retro objects at flea markets and in second-hand shops and there is the occasional retro fair.
- In the UK almost anything from the early twentieth century goes as retro, from a Mabel Lucie Atwell illustration cut out from a children's book to some vaguely 60-ish blue and green flower print cotton fabric waiting to be turned into a small curtain.
- Things to look for include 60s' floral lampshades; various tea caddies and biscuit tins; plastic moulded wall pockets.
- Retro fabrics sold on the Internet are usually well described and photographed but may come in very small snippets, enough to use as patches for a patchwork quilt, say.

- Items worth looking for include early plastics such as Bakelite, used for manufacturing radios and other household objects, standard lamps with tasselled shades, aprons and silk and rayon scarves, flowery tea sets and individual items of china, also pottery such as green or brown Denby ware.
- In the USA retro is taken as seriously as antiques and buyers and sellers are knowledgeable and choosy.
- Depression glass, manufactured in the USA, is much sought-after now, after its humble beginnings as a way to get poverty-stricken people to buy items of food during the Great Depression of the 1930s. Factory-made glass objects were made in local factories and given away free with packets of cereal and other everyday essentials. These glass objects are now highly collectible.

Hi-Tech:
- A recognition during the 1960s and 70s that industrial materials, equipment and furniture could give better service in the home than things specifically made for domestic use meant that all sorts of durable, basic items were brought into the home.
- Look for Dexion metal frames that could be turned into shelving, Spur metal upright-and-bracket shelving that could hold the heaviest of books or equipment, metal tables of all shapes and sizes, metal filing cabinets and railway carriage seating.

Chapter Two

Types of Salvage

From the fundamental building blocks of your home to the memorabilia of someone else's life, there is always something fascinating, beautiful and seductive waiting in the wings of the historical stage of the reclamation yard. One of the great things about reclamation yards is the variety they present. Repeat visits will reveal a display of reclaimed items that changes all the time, from traditional building materials to a life-sized knight in shining plastic armour to a folding metal drinking cup in a neat little leather box; there's no end to the surprises in store.

In researching the more you know about particular items, the more interesting they become, and when reintroducing traditional materials or furniture to a traditional home, the more likely you will be to be able to match like with like and put back the true style.

BUILDING MATERIALS

These include stone, slate, marble, bricks and tiles, old beams and rafters – anything that is used in the actual structure of a building. Reclaimed building materials are essential if you live in a listed building or old house and want to preserve its historical integrity. Like second-hand furniture, reclaimed materials are not always in mint condition but if they have already survived for years or even centuries and have been comparatively well treated in the demolition process, they should manage very well for a further few decades at least, resulting in robust, good-looking features with a sense of history. If the Anglo-Saxons reclaimed 500-year-old Roman bricks to build St. Albans Abbey, why shouldn't we make the most of reclaimed bricks too? Try to source your materials locally. For one thing, it is expensive to transport heavy items for long distances and for another, they are more likely to match up with your home. If you want Cotswold stone, you will be more likely to strike lucky in the Cotswolds. Always look for local materials if you are trying to find stone or brick for maintaining or extending your home.

Reclaimed bricks

Bricks differ widely from region to region. England is admired for its mellow red brick buildings and certainly in the south of England and the Midlands from the seventeenth century, bricks became the chosen material for middle-class houses, farmhouses and village churches, often with Dutch gables. So there are plenty of old bricks still around from demolished buildings and walls. If you find reclaimed materials still in their original form, with minimal reprocessing they can be cut to size, adapted, cleaned up or refurbished but will fundamentally retain their original character.

A life-size plastic knight-in-shining-armour (complete with pink plastic face peering out), perhaps from a film or TV programme, guards the door to Dave Dee's emporium in York.

Big blocks of stone, carefully plastic-wrapped and palleted, wait for a buyer beside a reclaimed red telephone box at V&V Reclamation in Heritage Tree Nursery.

Most reclaimed bricks will have remnants of mortar from their original use so the most professional brick reclamation centres will clean up their rescued bricks individually by hand using a brick hammer. Good quality reclaimed bricks only need two workable sides – one bond and one stretcher. Many will have fine creases, characteristic folds and variations in colour that typify old brickwork, adding to their charm. Bricks will be stacked onto wooden pallets and the finished pack covered in polythene. In some cases the salvage company may be able to send you samples (for a small fee).

Reclaimed bricks have often battled with the elements for hundreds of years and the decorative patterns of different coloured bricks in zigzags, diamonds and lozenges have been enjoyed and admired for centuries. You can see this at its best at places like Hampton Court Palace and Queens' College, Cambridge. There are many houses, large and small, that have used warm red brick imaginatively and you can immediately see the difference between traditional bricks and bricklaying and cheap modern work using mass-produced bricks in identical sizes and laid in regular rows with little creative input.

The biggest challenge when buying bricks is matching them up to existing work if you are building an extension or adjoining walls, or if you just want to keep any new building

These reclaimed, cleaned and palleted pink stock bricks in a south of England architectural salvage yard are waiting to be matched up with an existing local wall or building.

in keeping with the look of structures already in place. If possible get a sample or two from the existing brickwork and bring it into the salvage yard to match it up from their stock. Different areas and regions had bricks made out of local clay and local colours and sizes and shapes have a definite quality of their own. In London, the local 'London stock' was a yellowish colour, unlike the pink/red brick found in Surrey or the deep brick-red of the Midlands.

There are good reasons for trying to find matching bricks for a traditional house. Apart from the fact that they will look much better when used in a period house of interest or character, they will contribute to the reuse of useful materials rather than being broken up for hardcore or thrown into landfill.

Buy enough of the bricks you want in the first place because it can be very difficult to match them up later. The rule is to buy 10 per cent more bricks than you have calculated you need to allow for wastage in breakages, etc. Choose a builder who is experienced in using old bricks and lime mortar. It's not only more attractive but will be less damaging to the bricks in the long run. Some yards hold half-bricks in pallets as they are often needed as part of a project.

Brick-laying styles

A bond is the way bricks are laid. Bricks can be laid either lengthways along a wall, or at right angles to it. The long sides are called 'stretchers' and the short sides 'headers'. The most interesting ways of building are to vary the stretchers and headers. Flemish bond alternates the short side of the brick with the long, making a more interesting finish. English bond has stretchers in one row and headers in the next. Or there may be several rows of stretchers and then one of headers. If you have taken the trouble to find bricks that match with existing ones on your property, then matching the way they are laid makes sense as well. Nowadays stretcher bond is the commonest type of brick-laying in which all the bricks are laid lengthways. It is the easiest, quickest and cheapest way of laying bricks, so many modern brick walls are made up of bland expanses of stretcher bond. It's certainly fast and cheap but it lacks visual variety and interest.

Reclaimed bricks

Reclaimed bricks are usually divided simply into two kinds: handmade and machine-made. In handmade bricks all the elements are kneaded together (known as 'tempering' or 'pugging') and this continued to be a manual task until horse-driven pug mills were invented in the nineteenth century. Once the clay was prepared, it would be shaped into sanded moulds and as many as 5,000 bricks could be prepared in a fourteen-hour shift. They were then left to dry in the sun and air for two days, transferred to the kiln where they were initially fired at a relatively low temperature to remove the last of the water content. The temperature was then increased to around 1800°F for about a week.

Handmade bricks

Handmade bricks are more expensive and typically older than machine-made, with more character. They have a rough textured surface and are lighter and softer than machine-made. They were common until World War One when labour shortages made producing them uneconomic. Handmade bricks have slight colour, size and texture variations and therefore produce a much more interesting result than the very uniform look of machine-made bricks.

There are many types of handmade brick. The common ones are soft reds and soft oranges, crease faced and red rubbers, so called because the softness of the surface allows a pattern to be 'rubbed' in using a hand file or special tool. Red was the most popular colour for bricks until the middle of the eighteenth century. The red colour comes from iron in the clay which oxidises during firing.

Reclaimed roofing tiles and slates

Roofing tiles and roofing slates are the two materials used on nearly every roof in Britain. Tiles are made from baked clay, like brick. Tiles, like bricks, are either machine or handmade and in the machine-made side of things there are hundreds of different brands, many of which are interchangeable. So a visit to choose from the stock available is important. Handmade tiles need to be matched for size, camber (the curve in the tile, if any) and colour.

Common types of brick in the UK

In many counties red is the most usual colour. There are many types of which some of the most common include:

- **Cambridge cream bricks**: buff-coloured.
- **Flettons**: hard, smooth-faced pinkish-red to hard red, cheap and cheerful, mass-produced from the late 1950s.
- **Gault bricks**: creamy white to yellow, hard, smooth-faced bricks from East Anglia. There are also red Gault, with a pink tinge.
- **Lincoln bricks**: orangey-red.
- **Luton greys**: purple with white speckle (also Luton reds); used mainly in Hertfordshire and Bedfordshire.
- **Norfolk bricks**: soft red.
- **Pressed reds**: hard, dense, smooth-faced orangey to dark red, often with a shallow groove; used in various parts of the country.
- **Soft reds**: soft textured, often smooth-faced bricks varying from orange to dark red; sometimes known as red rubbers, because they can be rubbed into shape by hand: used all over England. Those from Kent were specially made to be carved into decorative mouldings. You can see these in the flat arches of cut bricks above the windows of Georgian town houses and skilled craftsmen could even carve Corinthian capitals, flamboyant swags and angels' heads as well.
- **Staffordshire blue**: very hard engineering bricks, dark blue bordering on black, used in various parts of the country, often used to build bridges and factories and for houses close to railways because they were strong enough to withstand the vibration from the trains.
- **Tudor reds**: thinner than normal at 2in to 2.25in thick and are usually used to build fireplaces. They are soft-textured, handmade, orange to dark red with a 2in face, often used in barns. They come from various parts of the country and are among the oldest bricks available, usually 100 to 200 years old – not quite from the Tudor era!
- **Yellow stocks**: London stock bricks are made of yellow London clay and vary from bright canary yellow to tan with tinges of black from the firing. There are also mixed stocks and red stocks which are similar but pinker or redder.
- **Simulated reclaimed bricks**: have been distressed during manufacture to look like old brick. They will conform to modern building standards but rarely have the particular attractive characteristics of genuine reclaimed handmade bricks. New copies never look quite the same, so if you can find reclaimed original bricks, so much the better.
- **Modern machine-made bricks**: are made to meet the British Standard size (215mm by 65mm). Earlier handmade bricks were 8–9in long and 2in high so they do look very different and modern bricks can look really out of place in an older house. Machine-made bricks are harder and heavier and the surface is often smooth and shiny. They are often known as wire cuts because many of them have fine, close lines scored along both wide faces which are from where they were made: a wire much like a cheese-cutter was used to cut the clay from a mould.

Soft red bricks in an Oxfordshire country wall used with similar red coping bricks, covered with yellow lichen, indicating a non-polluted atmosphere.

Palleted red roof tiles, cleaned up and ready for use. These are heavier than slates and should not be used to replace a slate roof unless the structure has been strengthened.

A model of good reclamation: these slates have been removed with care, arranged and numbered and are ready for re-use, seen at Herts Architectural Reclamation and Salvage.

A carved stone bust in the classical style has been placed on an industrial ceramic insulator which acts as an elegant pedestal; seen at LASSCO.

Facts about roofing tiles:
- There are several different sizes of roof tiles, often with the same name. If you are trying to match up tiles it is best to take a sample into the dealer and allow him to match up the size and colour for you. It is valuable to make a personal visit so that you have an input in choosing the correct colour. If you can't visit, you may be able to send your samples and ask the company to choose a suitable match.
- There are three main types of roofing tiles: handmade nib with a rustic look, handmade peg, usually smaller, and machine-made nib, with a pressed, compacted consistency and sharper contour.
- Concrete tiles weather to a creamy biscuit or gritty pink colour.
- Peg tiles are the most sought after and are the oldest and richest in character. A peg tile has no 'nibs' or 'lugs' at the top where other tiles would sit over the roofing batten, but has only two holes (often square in the oldest examples) where the tile was originally held in place with wooden pegs.
- Roofing tiles are slim, narrow and vulnerable so that when calculating quantities it's important to take into account that some will be damaged in transport and others will get broken while being laid, so you should calculate 10 per cent more than the quantity originally worked out.
- Roofing tiles can vary widely in colour and appearance due to age and origin and can weather differently depending on their surroundings.

Facts about slate

Slate is a natural common stone in varying colours from greeny-grey to almost black. Slates are nowadays often replaced by tiles when traditional roofs are being refurbished but they are much heavier than slates and can cause the frame of the house to bow out – another good reason for sticking to original materials.

- Most of the slate used in the UK comes from Wales which has probably the largest slate quarry in the world, although there is also slate in Westmoreland and Cornwall. Welsh slate is usually in shades of purple, blue and grey. In Cornwall it is a rusty green.
- Slate comes in regular sizes, and there are at least twenty different sizes in the UK. It is laid in staggered rows, like roof tiles or bricks in a wall and each is largely covered by the one above, so quantities must be carefully calculated. Don't try to do this yourself: get a builder or roofer to do this complicated task.

Building stone

Granite is a very hard, coarse-grained rock characteristically used for building in Scotland and also in Cumbria, Devon and Cornwall and Eire. However, sandstone is also found in Cumbria. Limestone is easily worked. There are various types and a wide choice available in Britain. The Cotswolds in the West of England is where to look for that mellow yellow stone that looks so attractive in the traditional houses locally, but Cotswold stone has now become quite scarce so you need to know who stocks it and where to look.

Most of the stone you see in Yorkshire itself is a yellowy buff colour and that's what most people think of as York stone. In fact, York flagstone is available more often in many shades of grey sitting on many different kinds of rock in this large county. You can buy stone window frames from old castles or wooden ones from Victorian homes.

Decorative stone

There are innumerable sculptured stones to be found in salvage yards including corbels, friezes, stone heads and gargoyles, porches and window frames and fire surrounds. Carved stone has been used for roofs, fireplaces, as busts, as classical decorations on pillars and columns, as pediments and as garden sculpture. Magnificent stone fireplaces find their way over to Britain from Europe, especially from France. Roof corbels can be put back onto traditional roofs, but such stone can be added to large spaces like converted warehouses where its substance and proportions can complement the building.

Structural wood

Would you like a barn of your own? If you are lucky enough to have a plot of land, you could build a new house in traditional style, using a barn frame. Or if you have a very large space in a converted warehouse, you could use oak beams from an old barn to give it character.

Reclaimed wood can be found in the form of beams, floorboards, specific types of flooring, panelling or timbers for panelling, even railway sleepers, often sourced from chateaux and castles in Britain and France. Old beams are special for their character, patina, figuring and individuality. Some may be over 100 years old. Reclaimed oak beams can be hollowed out to conceal modern RSJs, if you are considering an extension or refurbishment of a traditional building.

All reclaimed timber will require some sort of finish once it has been laid. It can be sealed, waxed or oiled. Most suppliers will advise on what would be the best finish for the particular wood you have chosen.

INTERIORS

Doors

The most important feature of your home from the outside is probably the front door. This sort of door was made in different woods including softwoods until well into the twentieth century. Pine is still used for shed doors and doors inside holiday cottages where they indicate simplicity and rural tradition.

- If you can find the right size of original salvaged door to fit your existing entrance you will be lucky. There are three dimensions to a door, the height, thickness and width. The thickness can vary from 30mm to 45mm.
- Period doors are available in various sizes and materials including stable doors (which are cut in half so you could open the top and keep the bottom closed to stop the animals getting out – good if you have small children today).
- Georgian and Victorian doors may have two, four or six panels.
- From the nineteenth century some doors had glazed panels replacing the wooden panels at the top to let in a little light. Often the original glass is still in place, but bevelled, frosted or coloured glass can be inserted into any door.

Three decorative doors embellished with coloured leaded glass, seen at the Arc Reclamation stand at an outdoor architectural salvage fair in 2009.

A stripped pine door with simple white ceramic door handle and fingerplate. Like many stripped doors, this one has warped slightly during the stripping: an indication not to remove any crossbars or other fixings which can help keep the door in true.

It's always worth hunting around: this painted glass window is said to have come from the London Palladium theatre. It was one of the few non-reproduction items in a Brighton architectural salvage yard.

- Hanging a reclaimed door is a job for a specialist joiner, especially if there are locks to be fitted and the door needs to be trimmed to size. Look for reclaimed and salvaged doors in a reclamation yard locally where you are more likely to find a door the right style for your house.
- When buying pine doors check that they are not warped, especially if they have been stripped. The process can often warp the door. You may not mind that, but if you do, check the door carefully. Pine doors are often stripped nowadays which suits many modern homes, but this would have shocked their original owners who would have considered it embarrassing to flaunt such a cheap wood in this way and would always have painted it.

Reproduction doors

The demand for doors far outstrips the availability of suitable salvaged doors which is why there are so many reproduction doors available. So, if you are determined to use a salvaged door, either use your salvaged doors for an extension you are building, to match the style of your house, or be prepared to alter the door opening to fit your reclaimed door.

Windows

- You can embellish interior or exterior windows with stained glass from public houses, churches or domestic homes.
- Sash windows are very difficult to come by, but some reclaimed wooden shutters can still be found that have been torn out of Victorian houses.
- Occasionally you can find a salvaged UPVC window or door frame which may be suitable for the building you live in.

Stained glass

- It is still quite possible to pick up Victorian leaded glass within windows or doors.
- Separate pieces of glass can be fitted into a larger window or hung in front of a window as a piece of art. If the window doesn't fit exactly, you can add or subtract a piece to make it fit.
- Curved or buckled glass should not put you off, because you can often find a way of dealing with the problem. Tap your fingers on the glass and if it doesn't rattle, the lead is still holding it well and the window is OK. If the panes do rattle, that means the putty has dried so sections of glass are loose in their lead channels and will need stabilising.

Wooden flooring

Timber flooring has been used for centuries. It has an outstanding natural beauty that varies between each individual species of timber in its own unique way. Reclaimed wood flooring is sourced from buildings being renovated or demolished: they might be Georgian or Victorian, from homes or schools, convents, manor houses, gymnasiums, squash courts, hotels or theatres. In most cases, the flooring has simply outlived the building it was originally fitted in and if treated in the right way will continue to serve its purpose for many years to come.

Floorboards

Floorboards from the eighteenth and nineteenth centuries will have had a lot of hard wear and may even have been sawn through in several places when central heating was installed in a building. After that the perfectly good boards may be practically unusable from an aesthetic point of view. However, enough may have survived the heating expert's vandalism intact and you may only have to replace a few boards. The challenge is to get a good match. Otherwise, you might want to replace the whole lot and give yourself the pleasure of a wonderful, warm coloured, textural and historic floor by having the whole lot redone.

Woodblock and parquet

- Typically associated with Victorian and Edwardian properties, woodblock or parquet flooring is usually laid in classic herringbone patterns but other patterns are available too, including the popular parquet de Versailles.
- Old parquet develops a rich golden honey-brown colour over the years and this can be imitated by ageing new oak, but doesn't achieve the same depth of colour.
- The most common types of wood used for parquet are oak and pine. Reclaimed pine is probably the easiest kind of second-hand wooden flooring to find. You might find it in skips, household recycling centres or salvage centres.

- Parquet is tricky to fit and the cost of laying it can be more than the cost of the wood itself.
- Think about the size of the boards. A large, open-plan room would look best with long boards and so would a hall, landing or corridor. However, if you have a small or awkward space, shorter lengths would be better. The width too should be considered. Do you want a chunky, rustic look or would a slimmer size be more elegant?
- Nowadays floors are usually carefully taken up to minimise damage to the timber. Signs of its previous life will nearly always show in reclaimed floorboards. There may be marks from years of paint, and oxidisation marks from metal fixings, and so on.
- The timbers often available include English oak, karri and jarrah (eucalyptus), Rhodesian and Burmese teak, keruing, olive and Canadian maple. They are usually tongue-and-groove strips in random lengths with hidden nails. Most will need a light sanding and refinishing and are suitable for either domestic or commercial situations.
- You can often find woods such as maple and beech which are pale and lighter giving an airy, modern feeling.
- Really wide antique elm and oak boards are now very rare and therefore expensive.
- Wide pitchpine floorboards in long lengths can be machined down to any thickness required. Pitchpine may be up to 160 years old and unlike normal soft pine is very durable, being used extensively during the nineteenth century for boat-building, flooring, construction and furniture. The 'pitch' refers to the resin content within the timber.
- Mahogany is difficult to find now but does add a particularly warm glow to a room.
- The resin and oil content of old timber usually prevents attack from woodworm, but sometimes small areas may be discovered and you need to check that they have been treated.
- Any decaying exterior should be stripped off the wood which is then cleaned, de-nailed, and scanned with a metal detector and checked for colour continuity, then sawn into boards and planed or moulded for tongue-and-groove or square edging. Reclaimed timber is thus reprocessed into high quality flooring up to 10in wide, reproducing an authentic period floor often in pitchpine, reclaimed oak and Oregon pine.
- Flooring from re-milled Victorian joists is often cheaper than new and also makes the most of the character of the mature wood. Reclaimed boards may have small splits and pinholes visible: 'imperfections' that can in reality add to the character of a piece.
- Wood tends to deepen in colour with age so it is ideal for older properties, and that's particularly noticeable with pine which becomes a lovely rich warm colour.

Floor and wall tiles and paving

Quarry tiles make sturdy and good-looking floors for kitchens or utility rooms. They were used from the seventeenth century until the late nineteenth century and there are still plenty around and many similar floor tiles can be found, brought over from France. European tiles may not exactly match those that would have been used in Britain, but they have the same qualities and can certainly be thought of as appropriate for most period homes and look good almost anywhere.

Ceramic tiles

Ceramic tiles became very popular during the Victorian period and many designers and manufacturers produced them for exterior cladding to buildings and for surfaces all round the home, from walls and floors to fireplaces. They were hard-wearing, hygienic, easy to

Examples of reclaimed flooring from Antique Oak Flooring Co., from top left clockwise: pine boards; oak parquet; iroko parquet; oak boards; parquet de Versailles; re-sawn oak.

clean, colourful and patterned in an enormous variety of designs from the delicate and floral to bold geometric designs including Islamic inspiration and naturalistic birds. Numerous factories sprang up to manufacture them and Minton's encaustic tiles used a technique that interlaid different colours fusing the different clays together.

Ceramic tiles are to be found in the Houses of Parliament and many other important buildings of the late Victorian period. Art Nouveau designs abounded with their undulating patterns; the famous peacock tail in its glowing turquoise. William Morris and William de

A selection of typical Victorian decorated tiles seen at an architectural salvage fair. Tiles were very popular and there are dozens of designs to choose from.

Morgan famously produced designs in vivid colours but nearly every illustrator and designer had a hand in designing tiles.

- Use reclaimed tiles as splashbacks in the kitchen, over the whole wall in the bathroom, as a decorative frieze together with white ceramic tiles on the wall next to the bath or in a shower cubicle, round the oven or a traditional stove.
- The Victorians used tiles galore and there are still plenty to be found, although those by famous designers such as William Morris or William de Morgan are difficult to come by and usually very expensive. Pretty floral patterns are still around by the dozen though.

Wall panelling

Panelling can include the simple tongue-and-groove boards, often used in schools, domestic bathrooms and New England cottages. It was usually fitted up to dado level and painted a different colour to the rest of the wall. It provided an insulating and attractive finish. Old carved panelling can be very expensive, but you can often find individual pieces to hang on the wall, much like a painting. Victorian reproductions of linenfold panels can be found and used to match older panels or as decorative features in their own right in almost any style of home. They would fill in a staircase, instead of spindles, for example, if you didn't want the open look or were afraid of a child pushing its head through the gaps.

Heating

Fireplaces and stoves

During the eighteenth and nineteenth centuries many homes had a fireplace in every room. Smaller houses might have them only in the main rooms. They were the main way of providing heat and also the focal point of the room. The hob grate was the most common kind of fireplace. It had three or four bars across the front to hold the coal and might have two iron plates on either side for kettles and saucepans. They were manufactured by many companies including, famously, Carron and Coalbrookdale. After 1840 fireplaces had metal plates fixed across the chimney which helped to regulate the amount of smoke and create less draught. Later Victorian fireplaces were often made of cast-iron for reception rooms because they could be so big, heavy and ornate. Arts and Crafts fireplaces in the later nineteenth century were smaller and simpler, often with wooden surrounds.

Where there was no fireplace, there might be a portable paraffin stove. These were often highly ornate and brightly coloured – very attractive additions to any interior. You can still find these today. They can be attractive purely as centrepieces to an interior.

In Europe and America the wood- and coal-burning stove in decorative cast-iron was a much-used alternative to the open fire for room heating. In England they were mostly used in the entrance hall and it wasn't until the early twentieth century that the Cozy stove with its little array of mica windows in front was introduced to British living rooms.

Stoves and ranges

Victorian and early twentieth-century cast-iron stoves and ranges are charming to look at and there are people who still use them, except in high summer, when they turn the kitchen into an oven. However, they are hard work to keep up and not particularly clean to use. They

---

Did you know?

- Very occasionally a fireplace may come on the market, dating from before the seventeenth century. These are understandably very expensive, but deserve to enhance a really gracious home.
- There are still hundreds of sizes and styles of solid fuel fireplaces waiting to be taken home and loved from the time when coal was the main fuel in Britain and mining was a necessary and thriving industry.
- When choosing a fireplace, scale is an important factor. It doesn't work to try to fit a grandiose marble structure in a small upstairs bedroom, but a modest cast-iron Victorian fireplace would look charming.
- You can find tiny fireplaces, designed for bedrooms, maids' rooms and the miners' own homes which can fit in well in modern boxy rooms.
- Modest fireplaces from middle-class homes and large and ornate fireplaces from great mansions can be found for almost any interior.
- The width and height of a fireplace should fit in with the proportions of the room. Many traditional fireplaces can look good in modern settings.
- In modern houses ceilings tend to be lower, and a fireplace should be proportionally lower to allow for this.

do make very attractive centrepieces though, and can be used as display cabinets or simply as sculptures in a large enough kitchen. Smaller room-heating stoves are available still in seemingly dozens of shapes, sizes and designs. They too can be used for heating, but they are also just as interesting to use as decoration and focal points.

Radiators

Cast-iron radiators were introduced to larger houses in the nineteenth century as a simpler, cleaner and more effective alternative to coal fires. These days, just one coal fire can be more expensive to run than a well-designed central heating system. If you want truly authentic central heating for a period house, there's a wealth of period cast-iron radiators available from salvage and reclamation yards sourced from demolition contractors, builders, old offices, schools and church premises. There are long ones, tall ones, radiators with two or three columns and some with art nouveau patterns stamped into the metal.

Did you know?
- Cast-iron radiators provide a constant, gentle heat rather than the rapid hot-cold switch produced by conventional steel designs. This quality makes them popular for older properties as they tend to retain warmth more efficiently, helping to counteract damp and condensation.
- Some salvage companies offer a choice of thermostatic or manually-operated radiator valves in brass or chrome finish.
- Reclaimed radiators can be used in conjunction with other radiators and forms of heating.
- Free-standing Victorian style column radiators do take up space and are particularly suitable for interiors in conversions of warehouses, barns and attics.
- Some small, seemingly humble domestic radiators are very attractively finished with incredible detailing on the valves and working parts. They are strong in design and really act like pieces of sculpture in the home, as opposed to modern slim ones that try to meld into the background.
- If you pick up an old radiator in a disorganised yard, you may have to find someone to clean it up, convert it and make sure it can be used with a modern heating system.
- Because of the difficulty and expense of bringing old radiators into the modern world, many companies now offer replica models which are exact copies of salvaged radiators, which can be guaranteed for up to ten years.

Staircases

Staircases are among the more impressive and seductive things you might find in a comprehensive salvage yard. Grand wooden staircases, humble wooden staircases and cast-iron circular staircases can all be found in reclamation yards, in various states of repair. You can also find individual components such as a handrail that can be adapted for an existing staircase. They may come from old hotels, blocks of flats or even period houses.

Did you know?
- Newel posts, banisters, handrails, panelling, spindles, treads and risers can all be discovered, either to repair an old staircase or to create a new staircase of your own devising.

- One interesting newel post can alter the look of an otherwise very ordinary staircase.
- Newel posts are usually sturdily made from high quality hardwoods, shaped at the top and moulded at the sides for an easy grip.
- The post can be finished with a simple rectangular or tapered handgrip, but may be topped with various shapes such as balls or pineapples, for example.
- You might have to add to or reduce its height – its purpose is to support people going up or coming down the stairs, so it should be a comfortable height for the hand.
- Handrails that have lost their spindles are quite easy to find and reproductions are often indistinguishable from the originals.

Sanitary ware

Did you know?

- If you live in a hard water area, remember the dark colours quickly become discoloured by the hard water deposits and are hard to keep clean-looking.
- Before World War Two most lavatory pans were biscuit-fired, that is fired, glazed, then fired again. This produced clearly defined shapes and edges. After the war toilets were made of vitreous china which is only fired once and produces softer, less defined results. So you can often recognise the age of a piece by its crispness or softness of outline.
- White porcelain is used for toilets in most homes today but the Victorians often added transfer floral patterns to their water closets and basins, which were often moulded into fancy curved shapes with decorative pedestals.
- French sanitary ware is often more sinuous in shape and much decorated with blue or pink floral patterns.
- In the 1970s and 1980s coloured porcelain was popular, anything from turquoise to pale pinks and blues to deep olive or brown. It is tempting to tear these out today, but they can be the inspiration for some really creative bathroom design.

FURNITURE

Domestic furniture

Seating is among the most rewarding things to look for. From church chairs to children's chairs, wing armchairs, railway seats to garden benches, there is an immense choice of interesting, unusual, comfortable (or sometimes uncomfortable) seating.

Almost any type of wood could be used to build furniture but some woods have always been favoured for their beauty, durability and workability. Before 1900 most furniture was made with oak, walnut, mahogany, rosewood and fruitwoods; also rare wood veneers and inlays were popular. American Colonial furniture depended on the availability of local woods and was often made of maple, oak, walnut, birch and cherry. As these woods became scarcer, furniture was made with woods such as ash, pine and poplar. Wooden furniture could be finished in various ways: with varnish, penetrating resin, shellac, lacquer, wax or oil. All these are designed to protect the wood and bring out its natural characteristics.

Other furniture items worth looking for are storage of all kinds including wardrobes, dressmaker's dummies (good for displaying necklaces and scarves), cabinets in many sizes and styles, designer furniture, office furniture, storage trolleys, metal furniture, and plastic items including compartmented trolleys and moulded wall pockets.

Upholstery

There are some wildly exotic reclaimed upholstery pieces to be found. Do they come from plush offices that wanted to display conspicuous consumption? Have they come from some film set? Who knows, but if you have an enormous converted warehouse or barn, perhaps these are just the thing to make a statement in a large space.

Reclaimed or antique?

There's often a fine line between what is simply salvaged or reclaimed and what is antique, and there are various rather vague terms used which can be confusing. Antique is normally considered to be something that is at least 100 years old. Vintage originally referred to the year a wine was produced but in the second-hand market is usually considered to mean something that is 50 to 100 years old. Collectible is a generic term for anything that people collect. Pieces by well-known designers of the time or made by well-known manufacturers are now quite collectible and often expensive, but everyday items can often be found in car boot sales, flea markets and salvage fairs. Retro refers generally to items manufactured during the 1960s to the 1980s. In the USA retro is probably more valued and better appreciated than in the UK.

You may be lucky to find antique objects in second-hand emporia or auction rooms going at a good price, but on the whole in salvage yards you will be looking at things that are either rather eccentric, not old enough to be considered true antiques or a bit too battered to sell as antiques.

Provenance

If you do find something you think is 'special', its provenance may be important – probably less so in salvage but all the same a bar in your living room that once graced the Dorchester Hotel is bound to be more valuable and give you more of a frisson of pleasure than one out of some unidentified pub. You may find items labelled 'ex-Glyndebourne' or, in the case of church furniture, which church the item came from.

Establishing provenance is helpful in preventing illegally-obtained architectural antiques. Thieves will go to great lengths to steal garden statues, for example, and it can be helpful if they can be recognised and there is proof of where they came from. Almost anything of any worth may be stolen and many items are sold abroad, never to be seen again. If you buy an object and it turns out to be stolen, you will get no compensation and might even be prosecuted for receiving stolen goods.

Most architectural salvage is perfectly bona fide, especially if you buy from dealers who are members of SALVO and follow the Salvo Code (see page 157). Provenance can sometimes be established through sales receipts from previous owners, looking at old photographs, newspaper clippings or texts connecting a person to a piece of furniture.

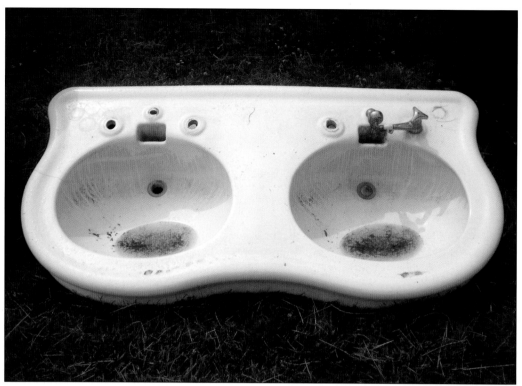

This double ceramic basin in white comes from a French exhibitor at an open-air fair in 2009. It would be a very practical addition to a family bathroom.

A basic utilitarian cupboard made of planks with a padlock in place of a handle would be fit for dozens of purposes. It could be repainted and tarted up with smart handles and hinges or allowed to keep its basic character.

A beautifully made solid wood, narrow chair seen at an outdoor salvage fair, which would sit elegantly in a small bedroom or a narrow hallway.

A Gothic church pew would be too long for many homes, but in a narrow hallway or a large conservatory could come into its own.

A primarily blue-and-red kilim rug looks great on bare boards or on a fitted carpet. Either way, it should have a carpet felt under it to protect it and prevent it slipping or creeping.

Non-domestic furniture

Church items

Manufacturers of church chairs also used to make everything else you would need for your church including altar frontals, umbrella stands, the lectern, pews and other seating, even completely prefabricated church buildings that could be shipped out to the colonies. And they all issued catalogues. Aside from that, a local church might get its own architect to design furniture especially for the church. Because so many churches are redundant, or being refurbished at long last, old church furniture is fairly abundantly available and it does offer all sorts of possibilities for the creative home-owner.

The Act for Promoting the Building of Additional Churches 1818 meant that £1m of government money was made available for new churches. Many of the huge churches in cities like London and Birmingham are the results of this Act and money from the Act helped pay for the high quality nineteenth-century church furniture we can find in salvage yards today.

A number of churches were demolished every year during the twentieth century: something like 10,000 chapels and churches were sold and about seventy are still put up for sale every year. They may be demolished or converted into some other use, perhaps turned into flats, offices, studios or charity premises. Large pews are often taken out and replaced with more flexible seating systems such as industrial chairs. In larger churches and cathedrals worn out ornamental stonework and carved wooden and stone items may be sold to make room for new ones. Many of these things end up in salvage yards or second-hand stores.

Church furniture is often of very good quality, sturdy, well-made and of the best materials: floors, for example, were often made of mahogany or oak parquet and carvings were in first-class stone. Apart from the pews, chairs and structural or decorative stonework, there are stained glass, statues, altars, crosses, doors, windows, lecterns, fonts, lighting, candlesticks, tables, panelling, prayer desks and pulpits and columns. Such items are usually more suitable for larger homes, particularly perhaps converted barns, warehouses or even converted churches themselves, but some can be absorbed into smaller gardens. Of course, they can be the perfect answer to furnishing a bar, restaurant or shop.

Industrial furniture

Old factories, warehouses, offices, public transport vehicles, hospitals, schools, pubs, restaurants and hotels can be fruitful sources of sturdy and highly usable furniture and features. Some of them may well need adapting, but some can be slotted straight into the home where they will give a sense of style and strength. Rows of seats from a theatre can go into a dining room or out into the garden; cupboards can be cut down to size and metal office furniture repainted or used as is, in all its gritty grey.

Carpets and rugs

Although new handmade carpets and rugs can be found very cheaply today, good and interesting reclaimed hand-woven Persian, Anatolian and other rugs can still be found. These are based on the great tribal, village or factory-made continuations of age-old weaving traditions. In the vast area stretching from Turkey and Iran (Persia) right across the Caucasus to India and China rugs of robust quality and unique designs have resisted years of wear to

Did you know?

- Church designs towards the end of World War Two were strongly influenced by the Government-inspired Utility scheme lasting for ten years from 1941.
- They are fairly neat and slim and will fit into all sorts of areas from a child's room or a bedroom, to an office desk area, as hall chairs, kitchen or dining chairs and because they are so sturdy, designed to put up with a lot of punishment, are good for pubs and restaurants too.
- They can be real value for money; the timber might be elm, beech or sometimes American ash or oak.
- Modern chapel chairs are now finished with an acid catalyst lacquer, one of the most hard-wearing finishes you can get today, but previously chairs would simply be waxed, oiled or shellacked.
- The ones you are most likely to find will be Victorian, probably made in High Wycombe, which became the chair-making capital of the world and the classic church chair was the most famous product of the trade.
- Church chairs have become popular for new restaurants.
- Some salvage yards will already have treated their church chairs for woodworm and made any necessary repairs, although you should always check for yourself.

adorn our homes. Almost all early oriental palace carpets are now safely stored in museums but there are plenty of lovely second-hand rugs available at very reasonable prices. Rugs are woven painstakingly and with centuries of skill – choosing and buying one should not be hurried either.

Western carpets such as Aubusson and Savonnerie, rugs designed by William Morris during the Arts and Crafts movement in the nineteenth century, Art Deco and Art Nouveau designs can still sometimes be picked up, though they are now collectibles and are often expensive.

Most hand-woven rugs will fit into almost any interior scheme but there is a fantastic satisfaction in finding one that fits into your own scheme as though it had been made for it. Many shops will allow you to take a rug home and try it out for a week or two.

Did you know?

- Oriental carpets and rugs with a pile are made using the knotted-pile technique.
- Kilims are made by the flat-weave technique (basically the same technique used to weave the great European tapestry wall hangings found in stately homes). They have been woven by nomads and permanently settled tribes for centuries.
- The Turks and Iranians are the best-known weavers of kilims and traditional designs changed very little over the centuries.
- Prayer rugs are small rugs made using the flat-weave technique, often available at very reasonable prices and these make good bedside rugs.
- In general, old carpets in good condition are more valuable than new ones.

These two Hanovia health lamps seem to be chatting together. They could be brought up to present-day standards, fitted with domestic bulb-holders and re-wired using period style braided flex.

Household textiles

For obvious reasons, household textiles do not last as long as say, bricks. However, you can sometimes find horse blankets, Welsh double weave blankets, bed and table linen, and cotton prints in the form of old clothes, aprons or old scarves in silk or rayon. With a bit of ingenuity these can be turned into patchworks, curtains or throws.

A curious three-headed combination of 50s Anglepoise lamps, discovered in a junk shop, is used to good practical purpose in this kitchen designed by Retrouvius.

Did you know?
- Australia is the place to look for second-hand Asian textiles and furniture from places like Indonesia, its near neighbour.
- Vintage hand-woven linen, hemp and embroidery from France and other European countries can include nightshirts, tea towels, sheets and pillow cases, rolls of fabric tablecloths and sacks. Hungarian vintage linen is renowned for its quality, similar to French antique linens.
- Hemp sheets make beautiful curtains, upholstery fabric, Roman blinds and table coverings.
- Hemp curtains using curtain ring clips can be made in a few minutes.
- Sacks and fabric from rolls are good for blinds, chair covers, cushions and upholstery.
- Mattress and cart covers make good heavy curtains, bed covers and huge tablecloths.

Lighting

On the whole, the period light fittings you will come across most often will be Victorian or early to mid twentieth-century.

Tiffany

Tiffany has become a generic term for all lamps and light fittings using coloured leaded glass, whether designed by Tiffany or inspired by his designs. Lewis Comfort Tiffany trained as a painter and then became one of the world's first professional interior designers. He started experimenting with glass as a medium for his painting and followed up by using it in his interior schemes. He redecorated the White House in 1882 and gave a touch of oriental splendour to many a New York and Washington mansion. He designed and made stained glass windows for his father's friends and also for important public buildings. The glass he used was all handmade in different thicknesses and densities and he soon began to design lampshades, often with hand-painted porcelain stands. Tiffany had nearly 200 craftsmen working for him including glassmakers, stone-setters, silversmiths, embroiderers, weavers, gilders, jewellers and cabinetmakers, using natural forms such as shells, tulips, mushrooms and female figures. Alabaster, pewter, beaten copper and acid etching were all used. At the time his work was copied in France, Vienna and Belgium. Tiffany's glass has never lost its appeal and although antique lamps from the Tiffany studio would cost thousands of pounds today, you could hope to find reproductions and interesting salvaged lamps influenced by his designs.

Did you know?
- Reclaimed lighting is a specialist business because the wiring must be brought up to date to conform to modern safety specifications.
- Victorian fittings often had glass shades reminiscent of those used in the older oil and gas lamps. They may be fluted, iridescent, opalescent, tinted or clear glass.
- Early reproduction Art Nouveau sconces such as a hand holding a torch or a curvy woman holding a glass globe can sometimes still be found.
- Lighting from the 1950s, 60s and 70s is widely available, part of the retro look.
- Industrial lighting from factories, warehouses and hotels can have many uses in the home, whether in the form of desk lights or pendant fittings.
- If you buy a period light fitting and it is missing one or two of its glass shades, you will almost certainly be able to replace it with a matching reproduction shade.
- Adam Hill of Retrouvius found several very large glass funnels in an old laboratory, which have been fixed up as pendants over the long table in the showroom (which also came from an old lab).

MISCELLANEOUS

Small, miscellaneous items for the home are the sort of things you might find in a car boot sale, in charity shops, second-hand shops or street markets. They can vary from china and glass, usually odd individual pieces or parts of sets rather than complete dinner or tea services, but you might be lucky enough to find a whole set, to various types of ware for the kitchen. Their appeal to you will depend on how they fit in with your own style. Big enamelled advertisements and posters appear surprisingly often, sometimes from refurbished railway stations or perhaps slipping over from Europe. They can be attractive in their own right but are often turned into amusing and wipeable table tops.

Small household items

Early plastics
Bakelite was invented by Leo Hendrik Baekeland, a Belgian in the USA who patented Bakelite in 1907. It was the forerunner of polystyrene, Formica, acrylic, nylon and polyester. Many products were aimed specifically at the domestic market. If you want to find out more about Bakelite, the Bakelite Museum in Somerset has an enormous collection of Bakelite objects collected by its owner, Patrick Cook, over the last thirty years. Here you will find telephones, electric hot-water bottles (in the shape of traditional rubber hot-water bottles), cups and

---

Did you know?
- You can still find early Bakelite telephones, which were rather angular in shape but they continued to be manufactured right up to the 1960s, by which time they had become a little more rounded.
- The early-look Bakelite phones are now being churned out by factories in the Far East. If you want to check whether one you find is genuine or a reproduction, run your fingers over the numbers on the handset bar: if they are not crisp it is usually a re-moulded reproduction.
- Tins were commonly produced in really inventive shapes until the 1940s. You could get them in the shape of trams, doll's houses, royal carriages or milk churns: for example, there was even a sweet tin in the form of a cricket bat.
- Tins can be just as useful today for holding sweets, biscuits, cereals and other dry foods or anything else small and elusive like sticky tape or coloured felt pens.
- Plastics have a smooth finish, are easy to clean and come in unfading colours, sometimes with a speckled finish.
- Some exciting objects were manufactured for office and even industrial uses, such as desk sets and wastepaper bins.
- Look for posters from the 1920s and 1930s advertising, for example, seaside resorts that you could get to by train, picture frames and kitchen equipment.
- Look for early radios, either as pieces of sculpture or refurbished as working models.
- Look for small decorative cast-iron brackets that make individual shelves much more attractive from below.

A large enamel sign, possibly irrelevant in the twenty-first century, but nevertheless attractive, seen at the entrance to a curtain accessory stand at the Salvo fair.

There's something in here for you if you have the patience to take a close look. The retro lamps give a pleasant light and the music stand is unusually decorative.

Door knockers are available in several intriguing shapes. Here from top left clockwise: a brass hand; a cast-iron plume of feathers; a brass lion; a blue door with simple knocker; a detail of the blue door; an urn.

Door and window furniture

Doorknobs and pull handles were introduced in the late eighteenth century. Few people could afford brass, so for anything other than the really grand mansion, cast-iron is more correct. Try to choose fittings that suit the design of the door. Hunting for the correct ones will take you on a voyage of discovery because although such items are becoming more difficult to find, some salvage yards make a point of collecting them and rummaging through these collections can turn up all sorts of interesting items.

- There might be elaborate escutcheons and fingerplates.
- For indoors painted or plain porcelain fingerplates and doorknobs are charming on any sort of wooden door.
- If you really can't find what you want there are manufacturers producing good reproductions.
- Letterboxes were not introduced until the nineteenth century. Usually they were simply added to the original door wherever they would fit, as often as not destroying its symmetry.

plates. There's a Bakelite dashboard (Hillman Minx 1937), radios, clocks, door handles, and light switches from the twenties.

These materials allowed for the cost-effective production of all sorts of products in lots of colours and imaginative styling. They broke away from the traditional staid styles of previous times and introduced a new age of colour and inventiveness in the home. Radios come particularly to mind, but there were many pieces of household paraphernalia. Mass-produced items from the 1950s and 60s have a definite charm in the modern home, providing colourful or quirky character in a modern setting. The post-war use of injection-moulded plastic ended the splendid age of plastics. Plastics from the 1950s onwards are usually of poorer quality materials, less interesting colours and are generally less robust.

China and glass

Provided you are not looking for 'collectibles' but just things you'd like to have in your home, you can often pick up charming individual pieces or parts of sets where somebody's been having a clear-out. Victorian pieces are sometimes found together with late nineteenth-century and early twentieth-century items and pieces of glass and china from the 1960s and 70s still crop up in unexpected places and usually they are cheap. Companies such as Denby, Midwinter, Rye Pottery, Portmeirion, and Poole Pottery all produced interesting china and pottery. The original green Denby ware is rare now but there was a warm brown version made at the same time which you can still come across sometimes. Studio pottery or pieces by individual potters were popular too, and turn up in second-hand shops and markets.

Did you know?
- Glass sells very well on eBay – anything from Victorian to twentieth-century glass.
- Art Deco is considered antique and rarely found in second-hand shops.
- Twentieth-century Scandinavian glass with its simplicity and clean lines is a 'find'. All things Scandinavian were very popular in England during the 1960s and pieces of glass by manufacturers like Orrefors fit in very well with today's taste in interiors.
- Pretty little everyday glass vases, jugs, plates and salad bowls or old-fashioned glass lemon squeezers, so much pleasanter and easier to clean than plastic ones, still lurk around on charity shop shelves, or in car boot sales or flea markets.
- In the USA Depression glass can be found in fairs and markets, especially in the states where it was made.

IN THE GARDEN

The salvage yard is the ideal place to find things for your garden: from an enormous three-tier fountain to a small birdbath; a pair of lion cubs in stone or a pair of urns in cast-iron; chairs, benches, staddle stones, sundials, ponds and flagstones, railway sleepers and telegraph poles are all to be found. Some of the sculptures are liable to be recently manufactured and distressed to look old, so beware, if that's not what you want.

Telegraph poles

Some salvage yards have quantities of ex-British Telecom phone poles. The metalwork, pegs, insulator rings, plates and other bits may or may not have been removed – usually the uppermost foot pegs or the insulator ring remains. All fittings are attached by square 'coach bolts' which can be removed. Telegraph poles are basically cleaned up tree-trunks and their lengths and diameters vary. A full pole is always over 20ft (7m) and can be as long as 29ft, but as a guideline 23–25ft long is an average length. You may find small ID numbers gouged into the wood and perhaps even a 'lost dog' advertisement pinned to it. If treated with creosote, you can't use them anywhere where there may be risk of frequent skin contact, but they are useful for lengths of really substantial fencing, supports to sit sheds on, pond edging, fence posts or supports for large arbours or walkways.

Stone and concrete

There are many delights to be found among reclaimed garden artefacts from sundials and armillary spheres to garden urns, ornamental stone, planters, stone troughs, arbours, benches, millstones and much more.

Paving stones

Types of reclaimed flagstone available include slate, sandstone, granite and York stone. Paving stones used in York itself are mostly made from the yellow stone, but the most common colour found elsewhere is a medium grey. Paving stones salvaged from old streets have more character than newly-cut flagstones and are usually cheaper. York stone, in particular, can be slippery when wet so shouldn't be laid on a slope.

Did you know?

- All genuine York stone is sold in random sizes.
- The surface area of each slab will vary but slabs are always rectangular or square and don't come in random shapes.
- The thickness can vary quite widely from 2in to 6in.
- An easy, repeating pattern is almost impossible to achieve but with a bit of thought it will become clear how to lay it. The effect, once laid, is aesthetically satisfying and, in a garden setting, usually preferable to the new stone options of regular, repeating patterns with block paving and brick paving, though these can look fine in a driveway.
- Remember, the thicker the flagstone, the less you pay per tonne.
- Try to buy by area rather than by weight.
- There is a lot of difference between the qualities of reclaimed paving. Some is as good as the day it was originally laid, but look out for flaky paving, missing corners, paint or oil stains, roofing tiles sold as paving flags (usually these are less than 25mm thick), very uneven finish and variation of thickness.
- Dealers may sort their flagstones in particular thicknesses, but even so, something classed as 50mm thick may be anything between 40mm and 60mm and this can make them difficult to lay.
- 'Random rubble', suitable for crazy paving, can be found very cheaply. This is a traditional form of paving in some parts of England and when done carefully it can be visually good-looking, but it needs to be laid on a full bed of mortar and is difficult to lay well.

Some facts about railway sleepers

Although creosoted railway sleepers should no longer be used for play equipment or garden furniture (though non-creosoted sleepers pose no problem), they still make good-looking and sturdy garden steps of any length.

Railway sleepers, with their solid no-nonsense quality have always been popular for creating raised beds, garden steps, as the bases for slides, swings and other innumerable uses. There are about twenty different types of sleeper, so they are very versatile. However, reclaimed railway sleepers have often been treated with coal-tar creosote to lengthen their lives or have been given other finishes now considered hazardous to health, and in 2003 European Union rules banned the sale of creosote to consumers. It was feared that this would be the end of the market for reclaimed railway sleepers: luckily, an amendment to the directive says 'the prohibition…does not apply where wood so treated is placed on the second-hand market for re-use'. So we can still buy them.

Did you know?
Creosoted sleepers should not be used:

- Inside buildings, whatever the purpose
- In playgrounds, parks, gardens and outdoor recreational leisure facilities where there is risk of frequent skin contact
- In garden furniture or picnic tables or where they will be near food.

You can use them:

- As garden steps
- To create raised flower or shrub borders, where they provide an excellent, long-lasting and sturdy framework
- To make raised platforms
- As fencing or scaffolding supports
- As driveway edging
- For edging streams
- As jumps for horse-riding
- As the framework for an adventure playground
- As protective posts in car parks.

This reclaimed carved stone plinth would make a fascinating base for a sundial or birdbath, or could stand on its own as a sculpture or a garden waymark.

A circular carved stone pediment elegantly supports the wrought iron roof of a classical-style arbour, complete with stone columns, seen outside LASSCO in London.

Staddle stones (shaped like mushrooms and also known as toadstools or mushrooms) date back hundreds of years. Original staddle stones were made over 200 years ago of local stone to support agricultural buildings such as granaries, acting as stilts to raise them a couple of feet off the ground to try to prevent vermin and water from reaching the grain. Great regional variations exist, since each would have been hand-carved in local stone by a local mason or even a farm labourer. They are attractive used as sculptures or to mark the entrance to a path or a different part of the garden.

You can also find a huge variety of stone urns, cast-iron urns and terracotta urns, each of which will suit different styles of garden.

Cast-iron

Cast-iron is enormously strong and emerges from the smelting in liquid form and can be cast into moulds rather like bronze or silver. Historically its earliest uses included cannon and shot. It is, however, brittle and cannot be bent or shaped at all once it has solidified. It is heavy and durable and can be ornate so it is often used to manufacture chairs, benches, tables, urns, planters and other outdoor furniture which won't be moved about.

Coalbrookdale began to produce the first cast-iron rails for railways in 1768. In the nineteenth century it was noted for its decorative ironwork and made the gates of London's Hyde Park. Today items made in the Coalbrookdale foundry, like garden benches and garden seats, are highly collectible and include serpent and grape designs, convolvulus, oak and ivy, Gothic pattern, fern and blackberry, medallion, horse chestnut, passion-flower, *Osmunda regalis*, osmunda fern, water plant, lily of the valley, medieval, nasturtium, Italian pattern and laurel benches. They were available in permutations of painted or bronze finish with an oak or iron seat and back. The original painted colours were green and brown.

The original Royal Mail letterbox was introduced after 1840 when a universal affordable postage rate was promised. The first letterboxes were hexagonal but a wide variety of other designs soon appeared. In 1859 a cylindrical box was created and other new designs followed.

In the United States cast-iron lampposts have been around since the early nineteenth century. In those days transportation of this extremely heavy material was quite difficult so most towns used local manufacturers to produce them. Styles unique to these small towns and cities were developed across the United States.

Did you know?
- Although all iron furniture requires an occasional touch-up, if it has a good quality coating, it will require less maintenance even if in use for decades.
- It is popular for furniture in public areas because it weighs too much to be easily stolen.
- You can still come across wall-mounted, post-mounted and pillar cast-iron letterboxes. Most of them are still in their Post Office red paint, but you can, of course, repaint them to any colour of your choice.
- Today you can buy postboxes moulded with the royal cipher and crown (VR for Victoria Regina; GR for George Rex; ER for Elizabeth Regina and even ER7th).
- Cast-iron, even if not properly finished, will only rust on the surface. The rust actually becomes a protective coating that prevents the corrosion process from continuing.

Wrought iron

Wrought iron is laminated like plywood and has a tendency to de-laminate over time when moisture penetrates between the laminations: this forms rust which expands the material to many times its original size, causing damage to any adjacent materials.

Although wrought iron has not been manufactured for nearly fifty years, there is a great deal of reclaimed wrought iron available: dismantled bridges, railings and discarded anchor chains being common sources. This can be used where a client specifically requests wrought iron perhaps for restoration or reproduction of an antique.

Miscellaneous garden items

Chimney pots
Thousands of different chimney manufacturers were churning out chimney pots for several hundred years, so there is a huge variety available. Each pot takes its character from its producer and the style of the region in which it was produced. There are fat ones and thin ones, tall ones and squat ones; some seem to have a medieval crown on top, others have little 'pastry' decorations round them. They can be used as plinths for sculptures, as planting containers or simply as sculptures in the garden.

Reclaimed wooden barrels and buckets
Oak barrels come from French wine and brandy makers or Scottish whisky distillers when they sell or upgrade their stock. They can look good in gardens as water butts, planters, seats, water features or even jacuzzis.

Wooden buckets sometimes come over from the continent. They look stylish and have lots of different potential uses, but are quite heavy to lift.

Sundials
Most of the sundials you find in salvage yards will date from the end of the eighteenth century. The dials are usually bronze, copper, brass or stone, engraved with hours and compass points together with the gnomon and are designed to be fixed vertically to a wall or placed horizontally on a pedestal of stone, cast-iron or terracotta.

The armillary sundial is made of a number of circles with the object of indicating the construction of the heavens and the motions of the celestial bodies. Wall-mounted sundials must be fixed to a south-facing wall. Put the sundial in a sunny spot in the garden. Make sure the foundation is solid and level. With the gnomon (the angled shaft) facing north, turn the sundial until the shadow of the gnomon indicates the correct time. For accuracy this is best carried out at midday and in midsummer. For a wall-mounted sundial, set the dial up so that the shadow from the gnomon is over the 12.

Garden furniture
Garden furniture can vary from marble-topped wrought iron tables to stone garden benches, antique bench seats, wrought iron and wooden garden benches.

Victorian gardens were extravagantly furnished with ornate cast-iron benches, chairs, tables; often with naturalistic decoration of woven branches, ferns or vines. Snakes might writhe around table legs and there were curlicues inspired by Greek and Roman statues, urns on pedestals, fountains, sundials, iron and wood trellis, arches, bowers and Chinese pagodas

and Japanese tea-houses. The later Victorian Arts & Crafts movement produced simpler designs in plain wooden benches, terracotta flowerpots, low stone troughs and stone sundials in that informal shrubbery setting that suited the huge number of exotic plants being brought home by the plant-hunters, the rhododendrons and evergreen trees.

UNUSUAL AND EXOTIC

First visits to salvage yards or second-hand shops can be bewildering. There's so much to look at; none of it matches or has any relevance to anything else. It takes time to get your eye in and then, among the fireplaces, staddle stones and church chairs you really went to look at, your eyes begin to light on the unexpected and the entertaining. That's how you may come across theatre props, like life-size plastic knights, spacemen or dinosaurs, plastic or plaster columns, original red Post Office street phone boxes, cast-iron personal letter boxes, sentry boxes (good for a shady bower in the garden), fruit and cigarette machines, vintage lampposts, an ancient petrol pump, ex-British Rail railway seats or galvanised drawers or buckets or animal drinking troughs that have dozens of potential uses.

Chapter Three

Using Salvage

There are so many uses to be found for the things that other people throw away, you could have an entertaining afternoon brainstorming to find the most appropriate or the most bizarre. First of all is the natural idea to put back into traditional houses that which has been torn out or mistreated. In Spitalfields in London's East End there is a pretty well unique house which has survived almost entirely true to its eighteenth-century beginnings against all the odds and among all the modern high-rise buildings surrounding it. Dennis Severs bought this house in the 1970s and restored it himself, working by candlelight, and living in it in much the same way as the early Huguenot weavers he imagined as his family would have done. It had no mod cons and he installed furniture and fittings known to be local to Spitalfields at the time the house was built. Dennis Severs died in 1999 but his house is still occasionally open to the public and if you want a really fascinating feeling of what it might have been like to live in eighteenth-century conditions, go along and experience it. It's dark, it's cold, it's sometimes creepy, but it's the nearest you are likely to get to the true feeling of living in another age. As you go upstairs, the periods change gradually, to finish up with a bedroom of 1914, just before World War One.

You are unlikely to find another experience so genuinely like a time capsule. Most homes have been altered, changed and modernised from the very moment they were built, incorporating the fashions and technical improvements of their times, being extended to house larger families and gradually changing, so it is not necessarily an insult to the house to alter it in keeping with these changes. Provided your changes are sympathetic and provided you appreciate the building's proportions, the quality of the craftsmanship and the specific materials used, you can feel you are doing the house a kindness.

It goes almost without saying that a period home will benefit from period features in keeping with the building's particular period, but if you don't live in a particularly interesting traditional home or if you live in a modern block of flats, reclaimed items can be even more important in providing interest, quality, character and the unexpected. Even if you don't live in a Tudor house, you could find the Tudor style attractive and this style with its heavy furniture and large cupboards and dressers and deep black stained colours, could suit a barn or warehouse conversion but one Gothic style carved chest could equally well adorn a modern minimalist home. There are plenty of items around with a very Gothic look; in particular, salvage collected from old churches and schools. There are pulpits, pews, benches and choir stalls. A stone window frame with a pointed arch could be used as a window or simply to frame a mirror.

Whether you are looking for a specific style to fit in with the period of your home or any style that will brighten up a rather characterless modern interior space or larger-than-life furniture to go in a large studio or warehouse apartment, there are many reclaimed items that will suit your lifestyle.

Sympathetic building

When mass-produced stone cladding tries to emulate a natural local stone, such as Cotswold for example, in the West of England, there is absolutely no mistaking that these are not very good mock-ups of the real thing and it would be better to use a sympathetic natural material rather than a pretence of the original. Handmade bricks, too, have particular local qualities which can be lost if an unsympathetic mass-produced brick is used alongside them.

The yellow stock brick used in all the walls in this local area can be seen on the left of this picture; the bright red machine-made brick on the rebuilt part of the wall is glaringly different

Old walls sometimes collapse or get knocked down by falling trees or driven into by lorries. In many cases, even in conservation areas, new or rebuilt walls bear no relation to the buildings that already exist or the walls adjacent to them. They may be hurriedly replaced in the cheapest uniform machine-made bricks, making them look brash and out of place. It is usually not difficult to combine the salvageable bricks from the wall with similar reclaimed bricks, retaining the slight variations in colour and the method of laying them.

The story of a long, fairly tall wall in an English conservation area shows that it is worth fighting for reclaimed building materials where the result will affect local residents. The wall fell down, the Council agreed to repair it, but the builders chose a cheap meat-coloured red brick and began rebuilding. The local outcry was so great that the wall had to be taken down and again rebuilt using reclaimed local bricks. You can now just spot the bottom row of new red bricks, which was not removed, but otherwise the wall fits in perfectly with its built surroundings and is a piece of work any builder could be proud of. Just round the corner, however, is a similar wall with a new section added in very red machine-made bricks, which really does stand out like a sore thumb.

As a salvage-hunter you may start randomly, being fascinated by anything and everything, then find you are drawn to a particular period or taste. As you know more, your choices become more specific. For some it may be the craftsmanship, for some the nostalgia, for some the simplicity or perhaps a highly decorative quality. The more you know, the better you can search for what you want.

Always ask questions. Many sellers of second-hand objects are well informed about what they are selling. If you can shop at unpopular times you will have more opportunity to talk to the dealer and the more time he will be able to give to your queries and desires. Once you find yourself drawn to a particular era, craftsperson or designer, you can visit museums, exhibitions, salvage yards, read books and magazines, join societies and search the Internet for information and keep asking questions.

Sometimes you will find tremendous bargains; sometimes you may be prepared to pay a bit more for something you particularly want. Be prepared to take your time: buy an item at a time, build up your collection or your style slowly and appreciate each find as it comes your way.

The following are some of the ways in which salvage can be and has been used to produce practical, individual and welcoming homes.

PUTTING BACK THE STYLE

If you are restoring a traditional home, then you will know exactly what you are looking for and you can go to places where you know you will find it. You can phone up suppliers and explain what your house is like and when and where it was built, and they should be able to help you search out any relevant piece. Georgian interiors were influenced by the architecture of the building. They were sparsely but elegantly furnished, showing off the structure of the house. Chairs were often arranged round the walls and there would be paintings on the walls, but they were not full of the clutter so loved by the Victorians, whose compulsive habit of collecting things, from photographs to artefacts, encouraged them to be inventive in ways of storing and exhibiting them.

In Victorian interiors you would find bookcases, glass-fronted display cases, chests of large and small drawers for collections of anything from butterflies to birds' eggs, stuffed animals or family portraits. They also collected purely decorative items so every shelf, every wall, every small lace-covered table and every mantelshelf was covered in objects and every wall covered with wallpaper, every fireplace with carvings, mouldings or tiles. One of the delights of salvage-hunting is finding these old items of Victoriana to display at home.

Using traditional doors

Your front door is the first thing people notice when they visit or walk past your home. If you live in a Georgian or Victorian terraced property, unless the whole street has been vandalised by previous owners, you will see the sort of doors originally installed and that will give you a good idea of what sort of door will be most in keeping.

> **Did you know?**
> - Doors with two panels took over from solid plank doors in the late seventeenth century.
> - By 1700 and throughout the eighteenth century the six-panelled door was the most popular and was also used in Classical style houses in America.
> - Exterior doors were often made in less expensive woods for smaller homes, albeit still expertly made by hand.
> - In modest eighteenth-century houses, when six panels would have been out of proportion, four- or even two-panelled doors were more common.
> - You can still see two-panelled front doors in many narrow terraced houses.
> - One advantage of reclaimed front doors is that they often have the lower two panels flush with the frame and outward curving rails at the bottom of the door, both of which help rainwater to run off, preventing rot.
> - Later and larger doors might have larger panes of glass, sometimes etched or coloured. Larger Georgian doors would have large and elegant fanlights built in above the door.

Putting back the fireplace

It is hard to understand today why so many attractive fireplaces were simply torn out during the last century. After years of stagnation during the war years, when materials, ideas and possibilities were meagre, people suddenly felt the need for change. All things traditional were thought to be old-fashioned and boring. All things new were exciting and, at long last, possible. New became the Holy Grail. Today perhaps we have reached a more balanced attitude and learned to appreciate the best qualities of traditional buildings, while also accepting the simplicity and practicality of modern architecture.

For obvious reasons, original fireplaces of all kinds are much sought after and not always easily available, with the result that companies are now manufacturing reproduction fireplaces in several traditional designs. Many of these are very good reproductions, but even if you can't immediately find the exact original model you're looking for, if you are keen on the recycling aspect of reclamation it should always be possible to find a reclaimed equivalent.

Many of the fireplaces that were torn out in the 1950s and 60s have been salvaged and many of these original fireplaces can still be found in salvage yards. There's every kind of fireplace imaginable from carved stone to classical marble mantelpieces, decorative ceramic tiled all-in-one surrounds to tiny cast-iron grates. Fireplaces in the later eighteenth century's terraced town houses were influenced by the designs of Robert Adam. They were beautifully proportioned, not ostentatious, with subtle detailing at the corners but large enough and elegant enough to attract the eye the moment you enter a room. This sort of fireplace looks surprisingly modern and needs little surrounding decoration, perhaps a painting or a mirror hung above the mantelpiece and a few interesting objects displayed on it.

Owners of larger Georgian homes which have lost their fireplaces might like to look at some of the more extravagant reclaimed Louis XIV, XV and XVI chimneypieces now being brought over from France which are liable to be more ornate than English equivalents and are very able to take their place in a grander environment. Marble was a popular material

Fireplace as a focal point

Traditional homes relied on fireplaces for heating, but when central heating was introduced they were made redundant from a practical point of view.

However, the fireplace had been the focal point par excellence – the 'heart' of the room. With its flickering orange flames, it was also the epitome of comfort on dark, dank evenings. Radiators do not have quite the same attraction and living rooms still need their focus. For many homes today this is provided by a large-screen TV, which hardly has the same charm.

One of the best focal points is still an attractive fireplace, which can be large or small, grand or humble, used or never used – like a piece of sculpture in its own right, providing a fascinating point of interest. A fireplace can be even more attractive with a mirror fixed above it, reflecting other interesting features of the room. The mantel shelf provides a good display area for small decorative items you want to show off. People lucky enough to find the original fireplaces still intact in their homes should hang onto them for dear life. If you are looking for a fireplace for your period home, look for the kind that would have been installed in that particular room when the house was built. The proportions will then be perfect for the room. You may find an original in a neighbour's house which will give you a clue as to what to look for.

for these grand fireplaces. You can find them in reclamation yards specialising in fireplaces or at salvage fairs (sometimes still lurking in a lorry, especially on a rainy day).

Very occasionally you may come across a fireplace from Tudor times; large and ornate with a carved mantelpiece. These are true antiques: seriously grand and rightly expensive, and you're only likely to find them at specialist salvage companies. They ask for a rather special interior, but not a fashionably perfect one. That's not what they would have complemented in their own time.

Mixing and matching

If you are replacing a fireplace in a traditional Victorian terrace, you don't have to buy it in one piece. You can find neat little fire grates in one salvage outlet, add a charming black iron surround with ceramic tiles from another and put them together to form a unique fireplace perfectly in keeping with your home. 'It's a hotchpotch,' said a traditional home-owner who had done just that, but the result is highly successful. You wouldn't know it wasn't designed in one piece. It is important to get an expert to install any original fireplace, but many salvage yards employ installation experts or can advise. The secret of success is to make sure that all the components are of similar proportions and styles. You might want to achieve an Art Nouveau look, or a humbler 'below stairs' for example, or find something a little grander that would go well with an already-existing surround of deep red ceramic tiles. Smaller fireplaces can be perfectly charming. They could be quite severe in design with square moulding and simple lines or they could be decorated with patterns of blackberries and flowers or sinuous Art Nouveau lilies. Fireplaces cause draughts, so screens were popular, not just to divide one part of a room from another, but also to protect people from chilly air coming in through the door.

The standard Victorian cast-iron grate with its little hob for heating water was gradually replaced by the all-in-one fireplace with a cast-iron back panel which helped radiate the heat and allowed for more elaborate designs. They were relatively cheap and cast-iron was seen as an ideal material for kitchen ranges and living room fireplaces in middle-class homes. It allowed many different designs and sizes and often included a small hob for a kettle. Small fireplaces could still be large enough to heat a tiny bedroom, but small enough to need the minimum amount of fuel, necessary ironically, in the homes of the miners themselves.

The traditional bathroom

The Victorians loved decoration in their sanitary ware as much as everywhere else and you can still find highly desirable basins and lavatory pans covered in blue or pink floral patterns. French patterned ceramic ware was often moulded into elegant shapes as well as being decorated florally. These items are finding their way over from France and can really put the style back into a Victorian setting. They can, of course, also add interest to a modern home.

If you want to be true to the Victorian period, your toilet's cistern should be mounted high on the wall with a pull chain to give it enough water pressure to work efficiently. You can still find these cisterns, with their chains, languishing in dark corners of salvage yards. In practice, they take up a lot of what could be useful space, particularly in today's often tiny bathrooms, but old toilets can be combined with modern close-coupled cisterns which means you can site your decorated Victorian loo under a window or under a low ceiling, under the stairs or in an attic.

As for the bath, there are Victorian cast-iron baths of many shapes and styles including some exquisitely glowing copper ones that would take a lot of maintaining to keep in the highly-polished pristine state that they really demand: they were certainly designed for the days of housemaids. Yet roll-top cast-iron baths with feet are imposing, and when restored to their original finish can be a real asset to a bathroom.

The porcelain used for toilets and basins is a white clay with a glazed finish and can be formed into more delicate shapes. Both pedestal and wall-mounted basins can be found, usually in white. Victorian porcelain may have elaborate floral decorations in blue or pink, even in the lavatory bowl. If you want to recreate the feel of an authentic Victorian home, remember that the lavatory would probably have been given a mahogany seat and the cistern a mahogany covering, not just so as to be grand and flaunt the fact that you actually had a bathroom, but also to be demure in the WC part of it. It's easy to recreate such mahogany surrounds, and to open up a mahogany lid and discover a highly decorated floral pattern in the lavatory bowl can be a delightful surprise.

The traditional kitchen

In Victorian times washing-up was done in the scullery, a room off the kitchen which also housed the laundry equipment including the boiler. Washing-up would have been done in an earthenware sink made of porous clay coated in white slip and kiln-fired. During manufacture, after firing, these sinks were given a final finish of thick, clear glaze and then another firing, giving an attractive eggshell white finish.

Heavy white butler's sinks now find their way back into many traditional kitchens. The originals are very much 'what you see is what you get': they are simple in design and there's nowhere, for example, to fit a waste disposal unit. (Still, if you make your own compost in the garden, you won't need a waste disposal unit anyway.) A traditional wooden plate rack over the sink will add to the Victorian feel and provide a drying rack as well as storage for plates and cups. Porcelain and earthenware cannot be reglazed, so damaged butler's sinks are best used as containers in the garden where they make ideal plant containers.

The stove was the heart of the Victorian kitchen, not just for cooking, but for keeping the room warm and drying cloths, clothes and boots. Reclaimed versions can be adapted for electricity or gas and are still in keeping with a traditional kitchen.

Traditional floorboards

Floors are the backdrop to whatever scheme you are planning for your home. Many people living in late Victorian or Edwardian houses in towns and cities throughout Britain would like to retain the original pine (known as deal) floors, but find that when central heating was installed in the mid-twentieth century, the workmen had sawn ruthlessly through nearly all the floorboards, so most or all of them need replacing. Searching on the Internet for local salvage yards is well worthwhile and should bring up several companies who can match up reclaimed boards with existing pine floors.

Matching up original floorboards
- You can take a sample of the original boards along to a reclamation centre where they will match them up as nearly as possible; often cutting them down from old beams they have in stock.
- Reclaimed may not be an exact match, but matching up wood is rather like buying different batches of paint or wallpaper: an exact match is unlikely.
- If there are a few knots more than in the original boards or if the colour is very similar though not exactly the same, these slight variations can be part of the charm.
- Most people add a rug or two to bare floorboards anyway, so the chances of anybody noticing the difference are remote.
- You can find original solid oak boards in gorgeous golden yellow and seventeenth-century oak boards and you may find end-of-run offers for reclaimed oak parquet, but not only are oak boards becoming rare, oak is not necessarily the authentic wood used for boards in most traditional homes.
- Reclaimed pitchpine floorboards in long lengths can be machined to the thickness required and can be found in more generous widths than modern boards.
- Walnut, maple and mahogany floorboards are often available, all of which make absolutely stunning floors.
- Many specialists in reclaimed floors can give a helpful personal service. Don't be afraid to ask. You may have a romantic notion of installing an antique oak floor, but once you have been advised about the cost of oak and the sort of wood appropriate to particular styles of architecture, you may opt for a wood more correctly suited to your home and budget.
- Reclaimed timber is not necessarily a budget answer to flooring, although you may consider it worth paying a bit extra for something so special.
- Floorboards need to be finished when installed, with polish, wax, or matt or shiny varnish.

A charming French ceramic wash-hand basin will add a human touch to the most hygienic bathroom. Taps are often supplied with pieces like this but are not difficult to find anyway.

A second-hand Falcon stove has a similar look to a traditional solid fuel stove. This kitchen has been designed to complement its no-nonsense lines without too many modern appliances.

A reclaimed Victorian cast-iron 'fern leaf' bench looks charming in a bower overhung with a wild eglantine rose. These small benches were popular for town gardens and can be found in various designs.

The traditional garden

You can take your interest in the past right into the garden. In black and dismal Victorian London, for example, where few plants would grow because of all the industrial soot, and where large laurel shrubs were popular because they were about the only things that survived the pollution, control was all important. Flower beds usually consisted of 3ft wide borders round a rectangular back garden. They were edged with specially manufactured edging tiles that could have a rope pattern or crenellated top made in the same sort of colours as bricks. Thus you can find Victorian garden edging in pale 'London stock' colours or dark engineering brick types.

Edging bricks are available second-hand but you might have difficulty finding the colour you want. One dedicated salvager needed a batch of garden edging pieces for his front garden but had difficulty finding the colour he was looking for. 'I wanted to match the pale colour of the few bricks we had found here and they were really hard to trace – most of what you can find is a bright red brick colour or that very dark engineering brick. I researched for hours and in the end had to go to the north of England for the particular colour I wanted. Ironically after we'd put them in, we found dozens of edging pieces buried under some rubble in a corner of the garden. But it is so rewarding when you do find what you want, and now all the bricks in the garden are second-hand.'

The Victorian fashion for cast-iron was carried into garden benches. Cast-iron benches were usually small, very much in proportion with the small terraced house garden they were made for. You may find complete benches or just the frames or backs in salvage yards and these can be put together with narrow-slatted wooden seats, just as they would have been originally. These seats were for effect rather than for comfort, so they do need cushions but they look enchanting in a bower. Several patterns were made including the very pretty Fern Leaf.

LAYERING PAST WITH PRESENT

Perhaps you live in a modern flat or a converted warehouse; perhaps you don't feel constrained to follow a particular architectural tradition. Salvaged items can really liven up a home without a clear architectural style of its own. Modern small houses or apartments with small, square rooms lacking character or any definite focal point can benefit from reclaimed traditional objects and craftsmanship.

Rough Luxe

If you are scraping off decades of old paint or wallpaper, you may find wallpaper from previous inhabitants which has a charm of its own and is a reflection of the past life of the house. So why not leave it there? Give it a new period of life and enjoy it. Old wallpapers can complement all sorts of reclaimed items including lighting, existing fittings and furniture, and even new things you have installed yourself. It will give your interior depth and interest that no entirely new scheme could possibly provide, in the same way that collected items of individual china are usually more interesting than one complete set of one design.

London-based architect and designer Rabih Hage has incorporated the layering approach into his work and introduced the concept for a group of hotels, restaurants and businesses, which he calls 'Rough Luxe'. Rough Luxe is an antidote to the universal sameness of modern luxury hotels and is epitomised in the Rough Luxe hotel in London's King's Cross, a mixture of old and new, furniture and art, combining beautiful colours and fabrics with existing distressed original walls stripped down to much earlier wallpapers.

Rabih Hage has retained many of the chairs and other items that belonged to the Italian family who previously owned the house and has incorporated them into his design throughout the hotel, including a 1970s television set. He has also introduced outside features from the past such as the dining table which was made for him from wood taken from Brighton Pier. These layers of the past create an unusual and unusually welcoming twenty-first-century interior.

His reclamations are always relevant and sympathetic. When the Savoy Hotel was brutally refurbished for £100m in 2007, Rabih Hage bought up some of the 1920s crockery for the Rough Luxe hotel, as a souvenir of a time when people came to London with the sole purpose of staying for a night or two at the Savoy. 'Sometimes you don't have to actually design anything,' he says. 'My rule is that today's design should be in tune with the location and function of the building. It's like a good recipe with a variety of ingredients.' He calls it 'urban archaeology' used with a contemporary way of mixing new and old to get a satisfactory balance. The result is very different from the bland unanimity of modern hotels the world over: it is more quirky, more surprising and much more friendly.

Large converted warehouse spaces will accommodate factory lighting, or railway carriage seats, and converted Victorian houses where the original proportions have been changed during conversion can be improved by introducing reclaimed decorative items and furniture, a mixture of past and present. These are spaces in which you can decide on your own style, be it English country cottage, retro, French provincial or completely eclectic. Your salvage hunt will be less specific and more likely to unearth happy surprises: indeed, one of the most satisfying aspects of using salvaged items in the modern home is being able to create something really unusual and individual. Even mass-produced items like cast-iron radiators or moulded cast-iron brackets can be mixed with a collection of other things that may or may not be of the same period. Choose items you like and the combination will reflect your character and tastes quite clearly.

If you are creating a fantasy in a modern apartment or a converted building you can let your imagination run riot. As there is no domestic past to revert back to, you can opt for the grandiose or the extremely simple; for an enormous French farmhouse stone fireplace or a 60s black metal wood-burning stove with the flue running up through the ceiling. That's one of the wonderful things about salvage; the possibilities are quite literally endless and you can be as creative as you like.

Industrial and government salvage

Offices, churches, factories, public buildings, pubs and hotels are being refurbished and demolished all the time. They can provide hundreds of unusual and often handsome pieces of furniture and other items which sometimes need a little imagination but can be put to very good use in a domestic environment.

Something particularly worth looking out for is second-hand commercial and industrial design. As old factories are refurbished and old hospitals demolished, a whole host of curious and interesting objects find their way into the reclamation world that can be usefully reused, not just in restaurants and hotels, but very much in private homes. Designed to last a long time and to be abused without cracking up, they are often more practical and more robust than anything specially made for the domestic market, and often have that sculptural quality that practical items acquire through being simple, ergonomic and durable.

Industrial and office possibilities
- Cast-iron radiators from factories and warehouses fit in with the layering philosophy very well. Their sturdy, strong shapes are well suited to large, uncompromising spaces such as basements, old warehouse or loft conversions. They can be small or large, highly decorative, Art Nouveau or very plain. They can be left plain, matt or shiny or painted in pastels or bright colours. According to those who have installed them, they hold onto their heat more efficiently than modern radiators, and they have that sculptural presence associated with an old-fashioned range or Aga cooker – a kind of 'friend of the family'.
- Office suppliers often have a large collection of second-hand equipment whose fit-for-purpose design means they are more comfortable than dainty-looking things made especially for the home office.
- Other industrial things to look for are shelving systems such as Spur, which will hold a wall full of the heaviest books; taps made for hospitals, designed to be easy and quick to

A small white 1990s TV set has been retained in this newly-designed Rough Luxe Hotel bedroom. It is an example of the architect's intention to provide a more interesting and human environment than the universal sameness of hotels worldwide.

The unconventional entrance to the Rough Luxe Hotel in London's King's Cross is a welcoming surprise: a mixture of second-hand furniture, 'found' objects, 'discovered' wallpaper, modern art and warm colours.

The dining room in the Rough Luxe Hotel has an undeniably 'private house' feel about it. With its collection of chairs, its modern artwork and its library wall, you could well be dining in a family room at someone's home.

An all-metal industrial table can take its place comfortably in the smallest living room, provided the proportions are right. This one looks very much at home with a white background and white furnishings and a standard reading lamp.

A renovated cast-iron radiator has a solid, reliable look, in keeping with the sturdy wooden chairs and tiled floor in a family kitchen/dining room.

turn on and off; wooden laboratory worktops, metal shelves, filing cabinets, drawer systems and lockers.

- It takes years for a rail company to refurbish its rolling stock, but gradually it happens, and old seats and other features find their way into the reclamation yards.
- A couple of railway carriage seats side by side will make a very comfortable seating area whose upholstery is often in perfectly good nick as it was made to withstand the bums (and feet) of dozens of passengers a day. You can always put them in the children's room but don't dismiss the idea of making them the centre seating area of the living room. Their upholstery is well designed, colourful and very durable indeed. With a collection of retro furniture from the 1960s or 70s they could certainly hold their own.
- There are some wildly exotic upholstery pieces around. Do they come from plush offices that want to display conspicuous consumption? Have they come from some film set? Who knows, but if you have an enormous converted warehouse or barn, perhaps these are just the thing to make a statement in a large space.
- Commercial office furniture can be highly practical in the home office, even if it's in the corner of your living room, demarcating the different areas.
- Second-hand office filing systems, flooring, cupboards and upright-and-bracket shelving systems can be as practical in the home as in an office and will last pretty well for ever.
- Metal office bookcases with adjustment holes in the sides make it possible to alter the shelf heights to fit your belongings. If you like the industrial look, you might keep the grey or grunge green colour you will find them in, but you can, of course, paint them white for a surprisingly gracious look or any bright colour for a child's or work room or kitchen.
- Hospital equipment might not sound very desirable but it is designed to be easy to use and tough: both advantages that modern domestic equipment often misses out on. Taken out of their discomfiting environment, hospital sinks, taps, and other items suddenly become the very thing you need; good-looking, sensible and long-lasting.
- Turning a church lectern into a stand for your mammoth cookbook or plant encyclopaedia does not take too much imagination – and what a splendid addition to your kitchen furniture that would make.

School layering

It's not just office and factory equipment which can be useful in creating your own style. Many items from elderly schools can be just what's wanted at home.

- Old school pianos can be very good buys. Older ones were actually made of oak and these make fine pieces of furniture, while being sturdy, perfectly playable, and still tunable and pieces to be proud of.
- School desks, cupboards, coat hooks and chairs also have these qualities and the advantage of being made of solid wood, and designed to stand up to everyday school rough and tumble, something really hard to come across in new furniture.
- Rows of coat hooks from the locker room can be fixed up in your hall and painted.

Gothic and outsize layering

Churches can provide the Gothic look, with their pointed arches, stained glass, heraldic emblems, carving and gargoyles, dark wood furniture and screens, taking their inspiration from medieval stone or carved woodwork.

- Wrought iron candlesticks have obvious uses in the home; carved screens from various parts of a church can be used as wall panels, or portable screens; hymn boards make good message boards, or postcard holders. Of course, all these things can also be used purely decoratively and will bring to life a large interior that needs some visual identity.
- One obvious use for church furniture today is in pubs, shops and restaurants, playgroups, cafes, church or village halls and waiting rooms, where the large size of many items will relate well to the space in the building.
- Pews can be used as they are or cut up into smaller seating, but are good-looking, sturdy and of solid wood. With a little invention, all sorts of uses can be found for such furniture.
- Even in domestic situations, a full-sized pew can have its uses. It might provide simple seating in a large conservatory, for example: giving it great presence and even acting as a potting table, perhaps.
- Church chairs are sturdy, well made, not too space-consuming and make good dining, kitchen and individual chairs throughout the home and are often used on stage in the theatre when a lot of uniform seating is required.
- Pews make excellent garden benches or even dining room benches.
- Some pews are extremely long and a 7ft pew will seat four people easily, but check that it won't swamp your space and you can get it through the door.
- If a pew is too big, cut it down and make a much smaller bench, with spare wood for shelving or a window seat or new stair treads.
- Be aware of scale. If you are confident, you can introduce very large objects into your home or garden.

Miscellaneous layering

- Mirrors, large urns, enormous enamelled advertisements that once graced a railway station can all look great in an environment where they can be king. And of course, if you are furnishing a large converted space such as a warehouse, large items are exactly what you need to fit in with the scale of the rooms.
- Small-scale fireplaces are particularly suitable for small modern living rooms where they provide a fascinating focal point and the mantelpiece acts as a shelf for small objects. Their subtle decoration can be in various styles and you can often find flowers or geometric patterns included in the moulding.
- Instead of a fireplace, think of introducing one of the marvellously decorative small enamelled stoves, often finished in jewelled colours that go really well with a modern eclectic look.
- Old-fashioned sinks can be fitted into any piece of furniture – a new worktop, or an old wooden sideboard.
- An angled lamp from IKEA may look a lot like an original floor-standing Anglepoise, but if you have the real thing, with its magnificent balance and its infinite adjustments, it will add something indefinable but positive to the character of many different styles of interior decoration, making it very much your own.
- If you live in a home with lots of 'things' in it, whether they happen to be books, collections of pottery or indoor plants, you will need shelves to house and display them all. Victorian cast-iron brackets are much more attractive than modern metal brackets and can support shelves in any interior. There are plenty of designs, including cupids or acanthus leaves, and they will add interest without being ostentatious.

Two leather-covered office meeting chairs look neat and comfortable enough to fit into a living room, and are at least as good-looking as most furniture designed for the domestic market.

This splendid oak door deserves a barn-sized building. It doesn't need any tarting up with shiny brass door handles but is imposing enough just as it is.

Narrow metal bookcases intended for offices with adjustment holes in the sides usually come in grey or goose turd green but can be painted. This one has been painted white and fits neatly into the corner of a primarily white-painted room.

Redundant school furniture is often under-estimated but this solid oak upright piano will last for years, has a good tone and will give its owner a great deal of pleasure when playing it.

A super-size industrial clock with Roman numerals like this one from a north of England mill can tell the time in any large space, from a kitchen to a loft.

- Quirky but comfortable upright chairs with pink frames and turquoise cushions that might have once graced an ice cream parlour will fit in well with other cheerful and quirky pieces of furniture – these make very good dining or even garden chairs in modern surroundings, and they certainly won't be the same as those of anyone else in your street.
- Red quarry tiles make very good flooring in passageways at the back of a country house leading to a garden door, and are the perfect base for dog baskets and wellies, since they are easy to clean.
- An ornate mahogany lavatory seat, wooden tongue-and-groove panelling round the bath. Victorian tiles around bath and basin. Rag rugs on the floor in place of a bath mat and, if you have room, a large bathroom armoire for bed and table linen, provided the room is well aired and does not get damp.

THE RETRO LOOK

Retro, usually considered to be the period from the end of World War Two through the 1970s, attracts many people today. Artefacts from a time that some people can still remember but are ancient history to others have a peculiar fascination all their own. Trying to recapture that 'look' can become an obsession. If you live in a 1970s house, reintroducing retro furniture can be seen as a form of putting back the style. Flat-faced interior doors stained a dark brown; wood block floors in a dark wood, an interior with an open-plan arrangement of rooms opening off each other round a central staircase – all are typical. Dark teak furniture was popular, often with legs sticking out at an angle.

The period was also remarkable for its sense of discovery and fun. After years of shortages and making do with less than the best, designers, manufacturers and the shopping public went overboard for colour, inventiveness and anything 'new'. During the 1960s various types of moulded plastic became popular, from designer's trolleys on castors with cubby holes for drawing equipment, pens and rulers, which could be wheeled around a work station.

Hard plastic moulded wall pockets for a household's bits and pieces such as pens, paper clips and other paraphernalia were practical and popular in the 1960s. These are not so easy to find these days (whatever happened to them all?), but still provide as good an answer as any to the problem of small items you can't find when you need them in a hurry. So if you see one in a retro fair, snap it up and put it in your child's room, or in the garden shed, or in your own home office. This is a retro piece but it can be used for layering.

The retro bathroom

Retro-seekers might be pleased to find they have bought a home in a 1970s development which retains its original coloured bathroom suite. The first reaction of a young family in York who found a pink bathroom suite was that they would have to tear it out and start again. However, on second thoughts, even though they were not naturally pink-loving people they thought it might all be an interesting challenge. With some inventiveness they turned the pink to their advantage by doing the unexpected. Instead of following the pink-is-sweet formula with frills and furbelows, they went the other way: covered the room in matt terrazzo tiles in a stone colour, added a second-hand rattan chair and some crisp white cushions. Suddenly they had a sophisticated, extremely comfortable bathroom in which the pink takes on a much more dignified look than one might have thought possible.

Discontinued and reclaimed retro sanitary ware

- Bathrooms are constantly being refurbished so there's a lot of reclaimed bathroom ware around, including well-known makes like Shanks, Twyford and Royal Doulton.
- You can give a boxy bathroom a Victorian or retro look in several ways. Install a retro coloured bath in one of the popular colours of the 1960s which included pink, turquoise and amber, or the more positive colours of the 70s such as avocado or brown. Add a bit of furniture, a stool or a wicker chair with cushions, a tiny wooden double shelf unit for toiletries, or a lockable Victorian wooden medicine cupboard in lieu of a modern medicine cabinet.
- A word of warning – dark-coloured sanitary ware can be very difficult to clean, especially in hard water areas.

Other possible 'finds' from the 1960s and 70s include standard lamps with large fabric or parchment shades; teak furniture with splayed legs; mirrors with asymmetrical frames; chunky little television sets with convex screens, if you can get them to work still; canteens of stainless steel table cutlery, and ashtrays.

Reclaiming a 'look'

Some furniture manufacturers from the middle of the twentieth century became household names, particularly at a time when it was difficult to find well-made furniture. Lucian Ercolani of Ercol furniture designed a series of chairs, tables and sofas in the 1950s which were spare and elegant and as appropriate today as they were when originally produced. The range included Windsor tables and chairs, a stacking chair, a butterfly chair, nests of tables and a sofa bed, in pale elm and beech.

The Ercol Studio Couch is a good example; an elegant piece based on the company's successful Windsor chair. It is a timeless design that could act as a spare bed but didn't look like a sofa bed. Today it still fits not only into modern ideas of style, but also into the smaller sized rooms found in most new buildings.

The Ercol Windsor furniture sprang from a commission from the British Board of Trade in 1944 for 100,000 chairs of low-cost design. Lucian Ercolani, founder of the company, found a way of combining modern methods of bending wood with an ancient design of chair, which he was able to produce for only 10s 6d a chair (just under £12 today). The chairs were made of English elm, a pale wood that people found attractive after the rather dark stained oak of Utility furniture. Ercol continued to develop the Windsor chair for decades after the war and it remained popular for its light, contemporary, slim look. This furniture was built to last, in spite of its delicate look, and there are companies specialising in finding and restoring this particular design for people who appreciate it.

You might well find Ercol furniture in second-hand shops or even some reclamation yards, but there is another way. One Studio Couch admirer found a specialist company dealing in second-hand Ercol furniture, drove down to the showroom, collected it herself and had the cushions re-covered in her own fabric locally. (The company will get the furniture re-covered for clients, but she thought this service was rather expensive.)

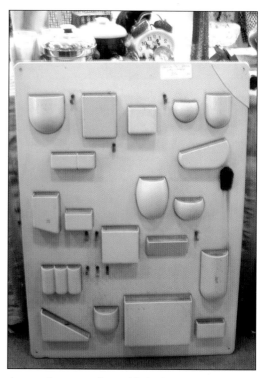

A meticulously-arranged collection of 1950s furniture including an asymmetrical mirror, teak furniture and slightly splayed legs goes together with an electric floor-polisher for the parquet floor. Design by Retrouvius.

A nostalgic set of moulded plastic wall pockets from the 1960s designed to rationalise all those miscellaneous items that get lost in all homes, seen at a retro fair in the west of England.

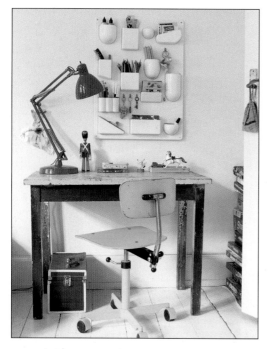

A Swedish interior making good use of a similar set of wall pockets, goes together with a battered painted table, an angled lamp and second-hand desk chair to make a practical corner in a child's room.

A 1960s English Rose kitchen is seen here renovated, painted and looking like new. This stylish design is much in demand nowadays for its versatility and good looks.

A complete suite of bathroom ware in pink or bright turquoise from the 1970s might seem too much to cope with, but if you take on the challenge you can give the pieces a completely modern look.

This reclaimed Ercol studio couch shows off its sleek shape, bentwood detailing and blonde wood with a brand new cover made by a local upholsterer.

The retro kitchen

Kitchens are potential retro finds, too. There is a big run on reclaimed kitchen units from the 1950s; English Rose and Paul kitchens particularly. These were made of aluminium and produced just at the time when kitchens became the must-do refurbishing of homes after the war. Instead of a drab, inefficient little room with a scullery attached, the kitchen became the domain of the good housewife and she wanted to make the most of it. So, apart from the idea that the kitchen could be designed and have a personality and efficiency of its own, it was dressed up with frilly curtains (red and white or blue and white cotton gingham was made fashionable at the time by Brigitte Bardot, who reportedly had them in her kitchen).

These kitchens are remarkably suited to today's modern interiors, having clean lines, bright colours and metallic finishes. Even when you find one in a dilapidated state at some architectural salvage fair or lurking in the reclamation yard, surrounded by boxes, you recognise at once the strength, presence and pure functionality of this early design.

Popular colours for such units at the time were cream and orange and a strong maritime blue. Today's refurbished English Rose and Paul kitchens, once they have been powder-coated or polished and fitted with new nylon drawer runners and catches, can be sprayed in any colour you like. Try a shocking pink, for example. It's still possible to get English Rose accessories: a fridge-freezer and gas cooker, and a substantial service trolley, designed to sit in line with other ER units in its own niche under the worktop, to be brought out when serving tea to guests. One West Country salvage company was offering on its website a 1960s service trolley, describing it as a *très cool* vintage accessory – 'Deliver the tea and scones to guests in true 50s fashion', it suggested. Such accessories are becoming rare, but have a quality all their own and may be sold totally refurbished.

ADAPTATION

One great thing about salvage is that, unless you are specifically looking for period details to complement your home, you can be as inventive as you like with what you find. You can turn a tall table into a coffee table by cutting off the legs to a suitable height and painting or varnishing or finishing it off as you wish. A single coloured paint, crackle glaze or stencilling can be attractive on all sorts of mundane little cupboards or chests to go into a child's room.

If you are doing up a modern or traditional home with no particular wish to be over-authentic, then the salvage world is your oyster. You should go forth with no clear idea in mind of what you want. Keep a very open mind and when you find something you find amusing, interesting, or that you particularly like, get it. Your own taste will ensure that the things you like will somehow go together to create a homogenous whole. So be courageous, be adventurous, use your imagination, take home, adapt, repair, alter, decorate and above all, have fun.

If you are not particularly adept or don't have time for carpentry or making furniture from reclaimed wood yourself, there are plenty of ways of adapting reclaimed items, with a little imagination. There are many recognisable items in salvage yards that can be put to other uses.

If you like something but don't think you have a use for it, be imaginative: think of using it differently, cutting it down, building it up, turning it into separate parts, giving it a different use. Don't imagine that anything has to stay in the same place forever. There is seldom just one 'right' place or one 'right' arrangement, and moving things around from time to time makes you look at them anew and from different angles.

Adapting fabrics

- Old fabrics, whether retro or older, can be used in all sorts of creative ways.
- One of the obvious uses for fabrics that are worn is to cut them up into patchwork pieces, where the small 'good' bits of fabric can be preserved, in the time-honoured way, to make a bedcover.
- Fifties fabrics are not always so easy to come by. Often street markets, flea markets and car boot sales and charity shops are where they crop up most usually in the form of tablecloths, aprons and scarves when somebody's been having a clear out. The designs and patterns have a recognisable quality, individual patterns, often of everyday objects with black outlines and bright colours.
- Retro silk scarves can be sewn together to make curtains, tablecloths are still good as tablecloths, aprons and other clothes can make good pieces for patchwork.
- It is best to find similar fabrics to use together on each piece you make: lightweight cottons from dresses are compatible with each other, but not with velvets or wool. If you want to put together larger patchwork pieces for upholstery, make sure you choose really robust fabrics.
- Objects such as aprons, old-fashioned pinnies, tablecloths, bed linens and reclaimed flour sacks finding their way over from Hungary can all be turned into patchwork or cushions and curtains.
- Silk scarves from the 1960s and 70s can quite often be found in second-hand clothes shops and in street markets and car boot sales. These can be sewn together and turned into lightweight hangings to curtain off a four-poster bed or as a small changing area for trying on clothes.
- Both new and old domestic textiles can be turned into all sorts of unexpected things for the home.
- Charity shops and street markets are adorned with plenty of clothes which can be cut up to make patchwork quilts or tiny stuffed toys or tea cosies, which seem to be coming back into fashion. Patchwork, if the fabric used is robust enough, can be used to cover old upholstery, using larger patches than normal, and possibly in random pieces rather than hexagons or log patterns.

Adapting Indoors

If you find an object you really like but you have absolutely no use for it in your home, think again. There are ideas for both indoors and out that you may not know you have until you find an object and try to find a use for it.

- A ceramic insulator from an electricity sub-station is a very large object and obviously not one you would immediately want to take home. Yet these insulators are very sculptural, super-shiny, the colour of a polished conker, and two of them would make an attractive base for a glass coffee table, or one could become a sculptural water feature in the garden or a plinth for a sculpture. With a bit of imagination and enough space, there are countless unlikely items to make attractive and unusual furnishings.
- If you own a solid wood cupboard that is slightly too deep and slightly too tall for your living room you can take the doors off and use them as trestle table tops elsewhere. The

cupboard itself can be cut down to size and, painted a bright colour, it will provide a child's room with much-needed storage.

- Ceramic floor tiles make attractive splashbacks in a rural kitchen. There are plenty of reclamation companies specialising in original wooden boards who would be able to supply enough for a complete floor or to match up just one or two boards.
- Reclaimed doors placed over low chests of drawers or plain chests can make good children's beds with the storage conveniently underneath.
- Roofing or floor slates can be used as wall tiles or a worktop in a kitchen or shower room. The slate worktop in my own kitchen has lasted twenty years now, and there's not a scratch or mark on it. It's a lovely colour and I've never got tired of it.
- Cast-iron ventilation grilles can be adapted as radiator grilles.
- Rescued timber can be cut down to make a dramatic mirror or picture frame.
- Wall panelling can be cut to size and act as a door for a new cupboard.
- Chapel chairs can make very good bedroom or dining chairs in their own right.
- Pews and pulpits, altars and panelling, lecterns and fonts can be used indoors or out.
- School furniture with lots of non-standard sized cupboards, school desks, coat hooks and more can be turned into storage in odd spaces in the home, such as under the stairs.
- Ornate and enormous mirrors make any room seem larger and lighter, or fixed in the garden can seemingly double the space and offer a better view than exists already.
- Etched glass from old pubs can be used to replace a door panel or the bottom pane of glass in a bathroom to give privacy without losing the light.
- An outdoor vase or urn can be brought indoors to become the focal point of a living room (particularly one where there is no fireplace), or to sit in front of a window on a landing to provide interest. Existing doors can be cut in half to create neater, more manageable doors for new cupboards without losing any of their authenticity. Instead of throwing away an existing door you don't need, why not cannibalise it, cut it up, turn it into a cupboard door, in keeping with the style and proportions of your home?
- You can leave reused doors with their complete panels or replace some of the panels with glass; very useful when you want to be able to check what's in the cupboard without having to continually open the doors.
- Replace mass-produced, boring doorknobs with interesting brass, porcelain or cut-glass knobs. You can find them all over the place, from junk shops to flea markets.
- Redundant wall bars from a refurbished school or gym make excellent storage for various garments, especially shoes with heels.
- Use small crystal doorknobs, made for cupboards, in a row instead of hooks for towels in the bathroom or coats in the hall.
- Change flimsy modern hinges for sturdy second-hand hinges for doors, cupboard doors and kitchen unit doors.
- Washing jugs and bowls can still be found, although most often you will find one without the other. Either way, there are many alternative ways in which they can be used. The jugs make good vases for very large flower arrangements and the bowls can be used for enormous party fruit salads.

Outdoors

- Old chimney pots are available in many different sizes and shapes. They make good planters, adding height and scale to a small garden and showing off the plants particularly well.

Concrete blocks:

- Salvage yards that concentrate on building materials rather than architectural features and furniture may have concrete blocks of various kinds. Some, though hardly decorative in their own right, have a central hole, which makes them ideal for planting herbs through, particularly those which want to escape and take over the garden, such as mint. If buried deep enough, they are completely invisible.
- Very cheap chairs can be taken outside as garden seating.
- Most gardens could do with more seating, so that you or your visitors can sit and enjoy various parts of the scenery.
- Folding chairs can be brought in at night or if it rains and kept in a passage, shed or cupboard out of the way.
- Cane or wicker chairs can live in a conservatory and are light enough to be carried outside when necessary.
- An old pew or a wooden bench from a railway station waiting room can make good seating for a large pub, but that sort of solid, large furniture can also be cut up to make separate small seats for pubs or as garden furniture.
- Set some stained glass into your windows.

SALVAGE AS ART

Be a collector. Enjoy the useless objects that you like. Hang them on walls, place them on wall-to-wall shelving, arrange them on 'occasional' tables, display them in glass-fronted cases (a useful find from salvage yards), and use them every day.

- Decorative plaster mouldings such as ceiling roses are charming and decorative, and can be displayed on a wall or in a display case.
- Pillars and columns don't need to be used structurally. They may come from a church, from a house or even from a theatre production. They may be stone, wood, cast-iron or plaster; plain or painted white; decoratively marbled or otherwise finished.
- A house in north London was spotted recently, its original front door columns delicately marbled in pink on white.
- In a more modern building and especially indoors, you could do what you like with pillars and columns, paint them red, give them touches of gold, or a multi-coloured stippled finish.
- Many Victorian and Edwardian houses had columns by the front door. They added stature and dignity to the front of the house. They were usually painted white, but you don't have to feel constricted by that.
- Columns can make great focal points or decorative punctuation marks in a large room.
- Columns can be used to psychologically divide an open-plan space or mark an interior arched entrance.

A decorative wall built entirely out of reclaimed rubble consisting largely of broken roof tiles and other odd bits and pieces of terracotta building materials.

A plain terracotta chimney pot makes a suitable pedestal for a clay sculpture and nestles well into its garden background. More ornate chimney pots stand well on their own, but this one gives height without detracting from the artwork.

This splendid circular table was handmade from 1½in-thick pine boards reclaimed from a property in Suffolk, so it not only looks good but is really substantial as well and complements the Windsor-style chairs.

A collection of large mirrors made out of reclaimed French doors and fanlights seen at an outdoor fair. This is an inventive way of using old windows and the mirrors will give a trompe l'œil effect of extra space as well as bringing extra light into a room.

- Columns can punctuate the division between two areas of a large room, or can be used as the gateway to a staircase.
- Stone columns can make the base for an outdoor gazebo or you can randomly tumble them to create a classical garden ruin.
- Fragments of columns can make good eye-catching sculpture indoors or out, depending on their size.
- Big industrial ceramic insulators might have been designed specifically as plinths for classical busts or other forms of sculpture. Their sleek rounded lines and their glossy brown colour fit into almost any environment and they are large enough to have a real presence so they attract the eye.
- Chimney pots also make good plinths for sculpture although they are most often used as plant pots.

NEW FROM OLD

Products from salvaged materials

Reclaimed timber products

Some salvage yards have workshops turning reclaimed timbers into furniture, but some craftspeople concentrate entirely on creating new items out of old. Eat, Sleep, Live, for example, is an Internet company using reclaimed wood to produce their own designs of hand-crafted furniture. The wood has been reclaimed from demolished factories, schools, churches, homes and various other 100 to 300-year-old buildings, and would otherwise have been burned or discarded in landfill sites. Their 'Original' and 'Cube' designs are chunky and functional, all in solid wood, and include beds, bedside tables, wardrobes, chests of drawers, dining furniture and mirrors. 'We aim to meet the needs of clients who want their furniture to be individual and elegant in design, offering both functionality and durability. The right choice of furniture should last a lifetime, not a couple of years before it is replaced,' they say. Eat, Sleep, Live also offer reclaimed beech, teak and pitchpine reclaimed parquet flooring, oak strip and reclaimed floorboards.

Another craftsman creates mirrors from reclaimed windows and French doors which are good for large spaces. He also makes mirrors fitted into old tennis racquets and table lamps from old riding boots, among a wealth of inventive and amusing artefacts.

Reclaimed rubber tyre products

Perhaps not exactly architectural salvage, since it comes from your car rather than your home, but at long last the worn out rubber tyre is coming into its own. You can now find a garden table and stool set, and a series of children's swings in the stylised form of various animals. Tyres make sturdy yet flexible planters, usually in slate grey but there's no reason why you shouldn't paint them. They can be used inside or outside, as laundry or firewood baskets, toy storage, and are practically indestructible. These sorts of items are mainly available from websites such as The Recycle Warehouse, Kitsch-U-Like, The Eden Project, the Urban Garden, Green Trading Company and Abundant Earth.

Chapter Four

Practical Tips

There will always be practical considerations when buying second-hand goods. For a start there are no manufacturers' instructions, there may be nothing to guarantee that the product has recently been tested, how to put it together or how to use it. Practical considerations begin before you ever buy anything. It is helpful to go armed with some knowledge about what you are looking for and what you might find.

Many things will need repair or renovation. This may have been done by the salvage company, but some companies sell things as they find them and some items may need a good deal of work before they are usable. Whether you are considering doing this work yourself, or getting a professional to do it for you, you need to know several basic things such as whether it has to conform to safety regulations before you can install or use it.

Most objects could do with small repairs or finishing, which you could certainly do yourself and it is useful to have instructions for doing some of the most common. Reclaimed items will also need cleaning and maintenance and 'less is more' is a sensible approach, but reclaimed things sometimes need a bit of extra care.

BUYING

Safety

Some goods may not comply with modern bye-laws, e.g. on electricity and plumbing. Always get an electrician to check and/or update any electrical goods including lighting and sanitary ware, unless the salvage company has already done so. Any electric or gas fittings may be sold as non-working items, but if you intend to use them it is important to see that they conform to modern standards.

- Old lamps should have the bulb-holder and flex refitted and an earth added.
- Old oil lamps must have a fuel label, e.g. 'paraffin', 'kerosene' or 'petrol'.
- Fridges: laws prohibit re-gassing old fridges but you could have a new gas-compression system fitted (for about £400).
- Fridge door-closing systems were changed in the 1970s after a series of cases when children became trapped inside cast-out fridges. The old clasp handles prevented the fridge being opened from inside. Doors had to be removed before disposal. However, you may be able to get the closing system of an old fridge changed by leaving on the old handle but deactivating the locks and fitting a new seal with a magnetic strip inside. Source Antiques in Bath undertake all types of kitchen restoration and can deal with seals on old fridges.
- Be aware that some materials from demolition or reclamation sites (such as asbestos) are toxic and no longer legal.

If the renovations have not already been done by the architectural salvage company, you will need to know how to clean up, repair and maintain the things you buy second-hand. The wood, the tiles and the cast-iron in this picture would all need attention.

The glass shade over this pendant light fitting will need to be dusted and washed, but it could be used with any modern pendant fitting and already has a modern energy-saving bulb fitted.

This collection of items in Edward Haes' yard in Lancashire gives an idea of the varied items you might find and how essential it is to really explore what's there.

If you fall in love with an interesting old door like this dark baroque one, remember that getting it fitted may be a problem. Try to fit the opening to the door, rather than the door to an opening.

Know your consumer law

There are laws to protect consumers, some of which specifically refer to buying second-hand goods. In the UK consumer rights and responsibilities are clear and include trading standards, faulty goods, scams and illegal street-trading.

The most important law protecting consumers is the Sale of Goods Act which applies to England, Wales and Northern Ireland but not to Scotland, which has similar but different laws. Under the Sale of Goods Act 1979 goods must be 'as described', 'fit for purpose' and 'of satisfactory quality'.

By law, if an object is described in writing as 'original' and it turns out to be a copy, then you have written proof to help you if you want to get your money back. Of course, where reclaimed objects are concerned, fit for purpose may not really apply, since you may want to use the items for a totally different purpose than originally intended.

- In the USA there is no all-covering Sale of Goods Act. Nevertheless, in many situations, including buying on the Internet, consumers do have rights. The law may vary from state to state but there are agencies in every state that can clarify and help with legal problems to do with purchasing goods directly, by phone or online.

Another important law is the Trade Descriptions Act, making it an offence if a trader applies a false statement to any goods. A trade description is an indication of the quality, size or gauge of goods (e.g. 'this rug is 70cm x 90cm'); how they were made (e.g. 'handmade bricks'); what they are made of (e.g. 'solid brass'); or any other physical characteristics. It can be a statement that the goods have been tested or approved by an expert; where they were made (e.g. 'made in France'); when they were made (e.g. eighteenth-century fireplace); who made them (e.g. genuine Coalbrookdale) or any other information about their history (e.g. 'ex-government stock').

Useful points in the law

Second-hand goods

- The Sale of Goods Act does apply to second-hand goods. When considering whether items are of satisfactory quality, you should obviously take into account the fact that they have already been used. For example, you couldn't expect a reclaimed school desk not to have the odd ink mark and scratch, or a 200-year-old fireplace not to have had the odd mark from a poker, unless, of course, it's been skilfully refurbished, in which case you will expect to pay a lot more.

Private sales

- When you buy goods from a private individual you don't have the same rights as when buying from a trader.
- The legal principle of caveat emptor or 'buyer beware' operates here. You have no right to expect the goods to be of satisfactory quality or fit for their purpose, but there is a requirement that they should be 'as described'.

- If you have bought something at a car boot sale with only a word of mouth description, you will probably be stuck with the object whether it's as described or not, so check all goods thoroughly before you buy them.
- Learn to interpret written descriptions. Something described as a 'William Morris tile' should be a tile actually designed by William Morris or produced in his workshops.
- If you do decide to complain about something you've bought, do so as soon as you can, while you still have the memory of the transaction and, importantly, the papers and references, if any.
- When buying fine or antique objects, protect yourself against buying stolen goods by subscribing to Art Loss Register, Trace, or Salvo Theft Alert. If you think somebody might be offering you a stolen garden statue, check these databases yourself.

Tips for salvage-hunting

- Ring the salvage yard or shop before you visit or visit their website to check on their opening hours and find out what they stock.
- Before you set out, measure all the spaces where you would like to put a reclaimed piece of furniture or fitting.
- Carry a notebook and pen with measurements you've made at home and all other useful information. You can keep this for years and always be able to refer to it and check where you got something and for how much.
- Carry your tape measure with you wherever you go, together with a notebook kept especially for the purpose, so that you can look it up five years later if necessary when you've forgotten the name of a supplier.
- Measure doors carefully and buy your door before you create the new opening. It is easier to match an opening to a door than vice versa.
- When choosing bricks, accurate measurements are essential. Make your calculation an average of all the bricks as handmade bricks vary in size. If you can, look at each brick on the pallet. Poor bricks may be hidden in the middle.
- Reclaimed oak is much harder to come by than reclaimed pine, so check how much is available, the size of the boards and the condition. You need to be sure you have enough from the same batch to floor an entire area of your home. The thickness is important, too, if you want a solid, safe floor. All wood comes in boards of different widths so check that as well. The boards should not be split or damaged. They may have knots or a distinct grain, but this will give the floor character.
- Remember that reclaimed stone and slate (and various other items you will find) are still measured in imperial measurements because that was how they were measured when they were first cut.
- Know what you're looking for. Are the building materials appropriate for your period of house?
- Take pictures with a digital camera of furniture or other items you want to match up, and compare them with what you find.

- There's no manufacturer's recommended retail price, so prices can be high or low and it's OK to bargain. When comparing costs, include the cost of restoration, installation and delivery.
- Take time to rummage around, particularly in rather chaotic places. Sometimes the best things are tucked away under newer acquisitions.
- Take a pair of gardening gloves in case you have to rummage.
- Spend time getting your eye in, poke around and move things if necessary, leaving no drawer unopened and no stone unturned.
- If you want to match up materials take samples and/or photographs with you. When looking for something specific (particularly building materials such as wood, bricks or tiles), telephone first and be prepared to e-mail an image over to make it easier to identify what you want.
- Unless you are looking for something specific you will be more likely to find a good bargain if you look in places that will not interest professional dealers. For example, a second-hand shop selling mostly wooden furniture and books will be quite happy to sell the odd china cup or plate, whereas if they specialise in china, the best pieces will quickly go at much higher prices.
- Avoid chairs that need re-caning unless you're prepared to learn how to cane or know someone locally who can do it.
- If you see something that appeals and fits in with your plans, get it while it's still there. Things move fast in the salvage world.
- On reclaimed doors, don't remove hinges, knobs and locks – keep them on the door. Hinges can very often help to hold the door together, particularly if you are going to have it stripped.
- Make friends with the dealer. Dealers are usually expert, knowledgeable and can be very helpful.
- Negotiate – there's no manufacturer's recommended price here. Compare prices between different dealers, unless you find something unusual that you might not find elsewhere or the price is so obviously good that you might lose the purchase if you don't buy straight away.
- Get a receipt in case items turn out not to be what you expected or were told.

Check damage in furniture

- A bargain price may mean that a piece of furniture has one leg shorter than the others or woodworm concealed inside a drawer. Don't buy obviously damaged furniture unless you are an experienced do-it-yourselfer or are prepared to pay for any materials and repairs.
- Look for warping or swelling of wood: check that drawers open smoothly and easily. Warped drawers will not open; worm is expensive to cure and may spread to other wooden items in your home.
- Check that handles, locks and hinges are all of good quality and firmly fixed.
- Check that legs and joints are firmly attached.
- Check that springs in upholstery are sound and won't twang every time somebody sits down.
- Don't buy second-hand foam furniture unless it has a fire-retardant label.
- Look for rust on metal and make sure it is not so badly rusted as to be untreatable.

- Because rare woods are scarce and more expensive than other woods, furniture is sometimes made with a veneer: a thin layer of expensive wood laid over the top of a cheaper wood. Inlays of rare woods were often used to form designs or special effects.
- Avoid veneers especially if you can see the surface beginning to peel away. Old glues were often made of fish bones and were not very reliable. Modern veneers are more durable as the glues are stronger and longer-lasting.
- Look carefully at any veneer that catches your eye. If the base wood has buckled or shrunk the veneer will be impossible to repair, and one of the good things about veneer is its surface perfection.
- Don't buy upholstery if the springs have gone unless there is an upholsterer on-site or you know of one locally. Upholstering is an expensive process, so you should know how much it will cost you before you take the plunge. If upholstery has torn webbing, lumpy springs or a sagging front edge – resist it.

Buying antique baths and sanitary ware

- Antique baths often have the outlet at a low level. You may have to cut a hole in the floor or raise the bath.
- Check that the bath's overflow meets modern plumbing recommendations.
- Can you produce enough hot water to fill a big Victorian bath?
- Check ceramic basins and lavatories carefully for damage and cracks.
- Check that taps, plug, overflow and shower fittings are in complementary styles.
- A cast-iron bath is very heavy, even before you fill it with water. If you want it in an upstairs room, check that the floor is strong enough to support it.
- Baths can be in any condition, showing chips in the enamel or, more commonly, brown stains from dripping taps. These can all be rectified.
- Reclaimed taps are usually in brass, nickel or chrome.
- Reclaimed brass taps are often better quality than modern ones and the technology is pretty much unchanged so if you have a good plumber, you can replace modern taps with reclaimed ones without too much difficulty.
- If there is crazing on an earthenware WC pan or a basin, check that it will actually hold water.
- Check for cracks in basins and any sanitary ware, especially if it's standing outside. Porcelain is not frost-proof, so the chances are it will have cracked during winter.
- Look for basins with the taps still attached for two reasons: brass in old British taps is stronger than modern brass; also, if you have to remove or add taps you may break the basin.

Professional repairs and restoration

Many salvage centres and yards have their own in-house craftsmen working on various aspects of refurbishment. Some will upholster old furniture; others repair and refurbish wooden furniture. You can expect such reconditioned furniture to be more expensive. In others you will find most pieces 'as found'. You may even enjoy their slightly dilapidated state or you might be prepared to polish up an old table yourself. You are more likely to find bargains that way.

Avoid carpet and rug problems

- A carpet suffering from rot, caused by flood damage, for example, will be brittle and small cracks or splits may be seen on the back. Always inspect the whole carpet and if it is under a pile of others or rolled up, make sure you get it pulled out and unrolled so that you can examine it properly. Rolled up carpets can hide all sorts of problems including moth damage, holes, badly repaired patches and rot.
- Look out for white warp threads where the pile has been worn down. Sometimes they may be camouflaged with paint.
- Antique carpets are very likely to have been repaired over the years. If skilfully done, this should not put you off provided you are buying for your own pleasure and to adorn your home rather than as an investment.
- Any carpet will be worn to some extent after fifty years, but provided it doesn't show too much, that should certainly not put you off. Look for rugs that are worn evenly over the whole area rather than having badly worn or damaged patches that will be difficult to repair and certainly will have lost value. Avoid any patches that may have been glued on at the back.
- Borders and fringes may have been ruined by heavy vacuuming and sometimes carpets are repaired by removing the pile back to a convenient line and fraying out the ends into a new fringe, or the outer border may be missing altogether. This may reduce its value substantially but will also look wrong.
- Look out for 'tinting'. This is a cheap way to bring back original colour to a worn carpet. Retouching with leather dyes, waterproof inks or felt-tip pen is known as painting or tinting in the trade and greatly reduces the value (and pleasure) in a carpet.
- Don't buy stained rugs. You won't know what caused the stain and it may be permanent.
- Choose a rug that is big enough so that it will fit completely under a piece of furniture such as a dining table and under chairs when they are pulled out. This is where your tape measure will come in useful. There is nothing so annoying as always to be catching the edges of a rug with chair legs when you are trying to sit down.

When buying an old rug, check the borders and fringes for wear, check the whole carpet for any moth damage and check for patches so worn that the warp threads are showing through.

If an object is antique or you think it may be valuable, don't dream of trying to restore it yourself. If you are unskilled, you could reduce the value of an old object by thousands of pounds. Other items simply can't be restored by an amateur as the process requires equipment and techniques not available at home. This applies to restoring an old cast-iron bath, for example. Some salvage yards have craftsmen working on the premises who may be able to re-upholster an old Chesterfield or repair a lifting veneer or repolish a mahogany dining table. Others have workshops where they create furniture out of reclaimed wood. Some companies are set up specifically to restore and repair specific types of reclaimed items.

Don't be tempted to over-restore. One of the attractions of second-hand things is the life they have lived before and this is marked by the patina they have acquired over the years, by odd knocks and marks, a bit of rust, perhaps; a general comfortable feeling of having had a useful life in the past.

Wear and tear, where antiques are concerned, often adds to the value of an item so to try to make something old look like something new is a mistake. There are plenty of companies who specialise in 'ageing' new products so that they look old. Why not appreciate the truly old whose aging has been caused by true experiences and not just being peppered with shot to give it false age marks?

Don't clean up anything with a patina. Patina is a bloom or lustre which an object acquires with age: a combination of dust, polish, wear and daylight. Much of the value of something like bronze or pewter depends on its patina. However, if you find a wooden dining table that

---

Professional restoration of a cast-iron bath

Some salvage yards specialise in re-enamelling baths to bring back the original finish and others will help find a restorer for you. Re-enamelling services vary from cheap-and-cheerful to expensive and serious. Remember to ask about the position of the waste outlet which may need to be changed.

Restoring an old cast-iron bath to its original perfection is a skilled and painstaking process. Antique Bathrooms housed in an eighteenth-century mill in Devon has a showroom displaying hundreds of baths that have been restored on the premises. The company was set up in 1992 to rescue, restore and sell original antique baths and bathroom accessories and has enamelled baths for the *QE2* and restored baths for Historic Buildings Trusts, stately homes and private homes.

The restoration process is painstaking and time-consuming. It includes stripping the exterior of the bath and its feet to the bare metal, applying two coats of metal primer and perhaps two coats of colour. Meanwhile, the inside of the bath is etched to provide a key for a primer in the original vitreous enamel. Imperfections in the bath's surface are repaired and tap holes can be relocated at this point. An epoxy primer is applied and left to cure for forty-eight hours; the primer finish is prepared for the special mid-coat, which is left to cure for another forty-eight hours. The mid-coat is applied, and then the polyurethane-based enamel topcoat is left to cure for another forty-eight hours. The enamel is hand-sanded and mechanically polished. The whole bath is then waxed and wrapped for delivery or collection. The result is a very desirable period bath in the colour of your choice.

has become scratched or lost its polish, or if you find a chest of drawers with signs of woodworm, these things do need to be treated by an expert. Only with small problems such as the odd scratch or dent, should you attempt to restore an item yourself.

Professional wood stripping

Some reclaimed wood will look better if any paint is taken off and the finish underneath is allowed to be seen. This can apply to mahogany stair rails, for example, or certain pieces of furniture in interesting and attractive woods.

Old doors should be taken to a commercial stripping company. It took me ten years to strip my bathroom door because I was too lazy to take it off its hinges and take it to be stripped. It had been covered in hardboard sometime in the 60s, and it was the glue that was so difficult to remove. Stripping can warp doors slightly, so the shorter time they stay in the stripping solution the better.

WHEN YOU GET IT HOME

By definition, items in a salvage yard come from sites of demolition or disuse and are often damaged, marked, dirty and dusty. As you will have gone to some trouble to find the object you are looking for, it is worth taking similar trouble to make sure it gets the best possible treatment and will look its best. It's not that you are hoping to make it look like new – the whole point of old things is their history and the interest their age gives them, but you do want them to survive and look their most loved and interesting. Cleaning old objects takes much care and you can damage an article quite badly by going at it too fiercely.

Thorough dusting is the most important immediate treatment for most furniture. Take care to remove the dust and not just move it around. Use a clean duster and shake it outside afterwards. Don't forget the legs, dowels and feet. Don't use a feather duster on valuable furniture or veneers because broken feathers can scratch or catch and lift the surface.

Simple home repairs

Preparing reclaimed bricks

If you need a lot of reclaimed bricks for an extension, for example, or large repairs to a wall, get ones that have already been cleaned up by the salvage company. Old bricks are fragile, so have to be cleaned with care. However, if you are just using them for a small project such as the outside pot stand in the garden for example, it's possible to clean the bricks up at home.

1. You will need a brick hammer to remove the old mortar.
2. Place the brick on a soft surface or better still, hold it in your hand to ensure it doesn't chip or crack.
3. With your other hand, gently tap the mortar with the hammer. Old bricks were usually held together with lime mortar which comes off fairly easily. If cement mortar was used it is much more difficult to remove it and you are much more likely to knock bits of brick off with the mortar.

- When using reclaimed handmade bricks in an old building make sure lime mortar is used, not the cement used for twentieth-century building. Modern cements are stronger than old bricks, so the bricks will erode before the cement and this can cause irreparable damage.
- Check that your bricks are suitable for their purpose. Some are not frost-proof and not suitable for outside walls. Suppliers are often very knowledgeable and happy to advise on this.
- Only bricks that were originally joined with lime mortar can be used again, as it can be washed off, unlike cement.

Stripping wood

- You can strip old pine tables and other wooden furniture if you are prepared for the painstaking work, time and effort that this entails. Use a proprietary stripper, according to the manufacturer's instructions. Work in an airy environment and keep the stripper away from any open flame. You can then polish, varnish or paint the object.
- Remove flaky paint or varnish with different grades of wire wool.
- Once stripped, some pieces may benefit from a coat of paint. Old school desks, particularly if for children's use, or a collection of elderly kitchen chairs can be brightened and unified by a coat of paint.

Stripped floorboards

- Reclaimed floorboards, once laid, probably need to be sanded and given some sort of finish. A clear varnish will bring out the warm shades of the natural wood. A varnish with a tint will make it slightly darker. Wax can work well on reclaimed pine. Rubbing it is hard work but the resulting soft sheen is subtle and good-looking. You can also paint or colourwash reclaimed pine, if you don't think you'll miss the natural wood look. White paint will give the boards a 'New England' feel which would suit a basic, minimal look.
- Painted wood such as mantelpieces and fire surrounds, wooden architraves, mouldings, and panelled doors and plaster mouldings too, often have so many layers of paint that they have lost all definition of their carvings or mouldings. If you strip them, that will reveal all sorts of interesting detail. Then add one or two new coats of paint to bring back their original look.

Remedial treatments for elderly wood

Second-hand furniture will almost certainly have been damaged at some time in its life. If the furniture is valuable or the damage is extensive, don't try to treat it yourself – get professional advice. Very often the place you bought it from will be able to give you the name of someone skilled in restoring old furniture, or they may even be able to do the work in their own workshops. For minor damage on less valuable pieces, here are some treatments. With all these treatments do them extremely gently and take your time. Patience will be rewarded but if you rush at it you'll probably make the damage worse. I hope it goes without

saying that you should not try to treat any truly antique furniture yourself. It is very easy to ruin a valuable piece of furniture if you don't know what you're doing.

Woodworm treatment

- Woodworm holes in timber floorboards are not necessarily a bad thing, as long as you don't mind the look of them and, of course, as long as the worm infestation has been treated.
- Woodworm may bore into wooden beams, floorboards or furniture and it can quickly spread to other wooden objects in your home.
- A woodworm infestation is recognisable by small round holes in woodwork or furniture, each about the size of a pinhead and with pale sawdust seeping out.
- Try to look at every bit of a piece: underneath chairs, inside drawers in cupboards and chests.
- Small areas of woodworm can be treated with a DIY woodworm kit. Follow the manufacturer's instructions. Wear gloves when you apply the product and keep it away from your skin, eyes and mouth. It's best to work out of doors and apply the treatment before you bring the object indoors. After treatment, fill any holes with wood filler.
- If you have a large freezer and you can fit the piece in, freezing will kill the woodworm without the use of chemicals. Turn the temperature as low as you can and leave the object overnight.

Black and white watermarks

- Rub the surface with fine steel wool, then re-colour and re-polish. Start with a pale colour and gradually go darker if necessary. Or you can try bleaching with a proprietary wood bleach.
- Rub gently with a paste of salt and cooking oil on a soft cloth. Or rub with very fine steel wool and olive oil in the direction of the grain or rub with metal polish along the grain. Afterwards buff up with a soft cloth.

Cigarette burns

- Apply the same treatments or a paste of mayonnaise or olive oil and cigarette ash. Leave for a while, and then remove the paste and buff up with a damp cloth.
- Small dents on furniture can sometimes be ironed out with a slightly damp cloth and a warm (not hot) iron. Take your time and work slowly and carefully. Try doing this frequently for short periods rather than trying to achieve an immediate result.
- Treat scratches with proprietary scratch remover or rub the scratch with the cut end of a Brazil nut. The oil will conceal the scratch. Some scratches and marks are acceptable in old furniture and even add to their character. Deep scratches may be best filled.

Sticking drawers and loose doors

- Talcum powder can help slide out a drawer, but not if it is too warped or swollen.
- New handles, locks and hinges can enormously improve the look and practicality of many pieces of second-hand furniture.

Filling scratches and dents

- Strip off all old paint or varnish with a wood stripper, carefully following the manufacturer's instructions.

- Rub the wood by hand with steel wool or sandpaper, working in the direction of the grain. Remove all traces of sawdust. Paint, varnish or wax the wood.

Cleaning and maintaining special furniture finishes
You may find all sorts of finishes in reclaimed furniture and some need to be treated with respect.

Carved wood
- Carvings are often very dusty when taken home from a salvage yard. On the whole it's best not to use a feather duster as the quills can damage fine carving and scratch the wood, but dust with a dry decorator's dusting brush, a watercolour brush or an oil-paint brush.
- For deep carving, use a soft toothbrush. This is also useful for removing old caked polish that has lodged in the crevices.

Gilded finishes
- Dust gently using a dry watercolour paintbrush – never rub with a cloth, or the gilding will come off.
- Clean very dirty gilding with a soft cloth dipped in warm turpentine or white spirit. These spirits are flammable so warm them by standing the bottle in a bowl of hot water rather than letting them anywhere near a naked flame or other direct heat.
- Remove stains by gently dabbing with half a raw onion.
- Don't try to retouch any true gilding yourself or be tempted to touch up with gold paint which will give a completely different effect.
- If any piece of gilt seems to be flaking off, get professional advice. Wipe over with a barely damp cloth.

Lacquered (Japanned) furniture, trays and boxes
Japanning suffers from temperature changes and damp atmospheres so keep the piece somewhere dry and warm.
- To clean it initially, wipe it down with a soft damp cloth.
- Remove finger marks with a damp chamois leather and buff up gently with a soft duster.
- Occasionally you can polish the surfaces with wax polish, but remember most people use far too much polish: adding a very small amount of polish very seldom is the rule.
- Once clean, lacquered items should only ever be dusted.

Marquetry and veneers
- Check the surfaces for any bubbling or damage.
- Wipe carefully using a duster with no frayed edges: loose threads are bound to catch in the inlays and leave tufts behind or pull the veneer away.
- Polish with a little furniture cream or wax polish.
- Don't clean any pieces of wood which are damaged or lifting – if wax gets under them it will be impossible to glue them back into place.

French-polished furniture
French polishing was introduced into England around 1820. The technique involves applying shellac dissolved in methylated spirit, and the wood should look satiny rather than mirror-shiny.

Carved and gilded picture frames should be treated with care or you may knock off small bits of carving or wipe off the gilding. Clean with a soft cloth just moistened with turpentine or white spirit.

A carved chest like this may be varnished or wax-polished. If varnished, dust with a soft cloth or paintbrush. If waxed, dust and then buff up gently.

You can repair small sections of leaded glass using a little putty coloured with lamp-black or putty mixed with linseed oil. Wipe off any excess with kitchen tissue.

Dust gathers in the crevices of cane furniture very quickly. After brushing and vacuuming, you can scrub it with salt and water and rinse well. You could paint cane furniture or polish it with furniture polish.

- Dust with a plain duster – nothing oiled or treated. Remove sticky marks with a cloth wrung out in warm detergent solution or with a cloth dipped in vinegar.
- If some of the polished surface has had alcohol spilled on it, try rubbing the area with the palm of your hand. This is slightly oily and will help to replace some of the wax. Apply more wax polish only if necessary.
- Before polishing you can remove any build-up of old polish, often found on veteran pieces, with vinegar on a damp cloth.
- Don't use modern silicone-based furniture polishes on antique pieces.

Wax-polished furniture

Wax polish is created by scrubbing the wood with a mixture of wax, turpentine and colouring, then painstakingly polishing it. The result is a very rich, deep shine.
- Treat as for French-polished furniture, using a clean duster and uncoloured polish.
- Oak and mahogany can be rubbed with a cloth dipped in warm beer.

Untreated wood

Items made from reclaimed wood may be left untreated for you to finish as you please with decorative paintwork, varnish or polish.
- Wipe over the surface with a cloth dipped in vinegar to remove surface dirt but don't leave the surface wet.
- Apply a thin coating of teak oil or linseed oil to hardwood tops using a cloth and rubbing along the grain. This will prevent the wood from drying out and protect it from dampness, stains, etc. Do this only about once every six months.
- Teak and linseed oil are flammable so work away from naked flames and throw away the cloth after use.
- Scrub untreated deal kitchen tables with a clean scrubbing brush and a detergent solution.

Leaded glass

- For simple repairs to stained glass, darken a little putty with lamp-black, use enough to hold the glass piece and just trim off any excess with a putty knife. Or you can mix putty with linseed oil, brush it onto the window panes and wipe off any excess with newspaper or kitchen tissue.
- If the glass is cracked, you might consider that to be part of its character and charm, rather like dents and marks on old wood – part of its history. Unless the glass is actually about to fall out, it's best left alone though you could secure any dangerously loose pieces with epoxy resin glue (such as Araldite).
- If you find a section of stained glass you like that is too small for your window, you can get a wider frame made to fit the space or you can frame it and stand it on a windowsill. Coloured glass always looks best with a light behind it.

Garden furniture

- Cane, wicker and bamboo collect dust easily in the weave, so the first thing to do is brush and vacuum thoroughly.
- If very grubby, scrub with a solution of salt and water, then rinse well. Don't use detergent and dry in the sun if possible.
- You can polish with furniture cream if you wish.

Cedar or other hardwood furniture will withstand most weather and looks good when it's worn. You can still revive it from years of non-use.

- Wipe with a chamois or cloth wrung out in warm water. Rinse with cold water and mop dry.
- Remove stains by rubbing gently with fine wire wool along the grain. Don't use abrasives or scrub – you are not dealing with a kitchen table.

Plastics
Very popular for mid-twentieth-century counter tops, plastic laminates are easily scratched.
- Wipe with a cloth wrung out in a mild detergent solution. Don't use abrasives, chemical cleaners or ammonia.
- Rub mild stains on laminated counter and table tops with a damp cloth dipped in baking soda.
- Rub stubborn stains on laminates with toothpaste or cover them in a paste of baking soda and water and leave for several hours. Then rub briskly before wiping off.
- Popular in the 60s and 70s for baths and tables, acrylic surfaces can become scratched. Wipe with a mild detergent solution to get the general grime off and then rub any scratches with metal polish.

Cleaning and small repairs to upholstery and fabrics

Moth damage

Clothes moths can do an immense amount of damage in a very short time. They attack natural fibres but are not interested in synthetics. Check all fabrics, curtains, carpets and rugs carefully before buying as they may have moth eggs already lurking within their fibres. The eggs will wait for conditions to be right and then hatch out. They like undisturbed places and central heating (ideally a temperature of 15–20 degrees) and a humidity of around 70 per cent. They prefer areas of fabric or carpet that have food or urine on them and they even prefer red wool to black. So cleaning any newly-bought reclaimed rug or fabric is vital. Vacuum both the back and the front. If you think it necessary, spray with a pyrethrum-based insecticide. Carpets kept in dark rooms, or parts of carpets near the wall or under furniture, can harbour moths too. Make sure you vacuum dark corners, under the edges of rugs and under furniture – always taking care not to be too rough with any fringes which can be damaged by vacuuming too enthusiastically.

- Felt, as found on card tables and inside drawers in jewellery boxes, shrinks easily so don't wash it. To clean it at home, make a paste with white spirit and French chalk. Rub well in and let it dry, then brush it off.
- Leather: patch tears by glueing a leather patch large enough to cover the tear. To clean leather, wipe with a damp cloth then apply hide food.
- Torn vinyl: patch with a suitable adhesive.

- Dirty vinyl covers: clean with car upholstery cleaner.
- Braid and decorative trimmings: don't wash. Dry clean by sprinkling with bicarbonate of soda, leave for several hours, then brush off with a fine stiff brush. If it has silver thread, make a paste of methylated spirit and French chalk to remove any tarnish.
- Canvas chairs: scrub with a block of household soap and a scrubbing brush. Afterwards pour buckets of water over the fabric to rinse it thoroughly.
- Glazed chintz: dry clean only.
- Velvet upholstery can be dry cleaned in situ with a proprietary cleaner, following the instructions. Smooth the pile with a soft cloth or a velvet brush.

Bed and table linen and delicate materials
- White cotton or linen damask tablecloths and napkins should be washed in a hot wash. You probably won't be able to remove ancient stains but you should be able to bring the items back to a fairly pristine white. For second-hand coloured linens, use a cool wash and wash same colours together.
- Remove fold marks and other marks from long-term storage by spraying with a spot remover and then wash in hot water while still damp.
- If the marks are very hard to remove, soak the fabric overnight in a mild detergent solution, then wash and give it a gentle spin or stop the machine before the spin starts.
- Drying in the sun will help bleach white linens and cotton discoloured from storage.
- Some of the linen you can find in French markets is unused and a bit stiff and harsh. The more often it is used and washed, the softer it will become.
- Old lace is usually made of cotton. If it is fairly robust, wash it in a warm wash in a bag or pillow case for protection. Pull into shape while drying and iron with a hot iron on the wrong side.
- Very delicate lace should be soaked in warm water and then hand-washed in hand-hot water, just squeezing it between your fingers. Don't wring or twist it. Or pin it onto a linen-covered board and sponge gently with soapy water, and then leave it to dry on the board. Once clean, wash it as seldom as possible. More robust lace such as curtain lace can be washed in hot water.
- Don't vacuum old textiles or embroidery. Cover with warm bran, leave for several hours, then shake off. Embroidery that isn't too fragile can be brushed, very gently, with a baby's hairbrush.

Upholstery
- Accumulations of surface dirt, dust, perspiration and/or hair oil may have damaged the fibres, so the sooner you can clean them up the better. Don't be too rigorous though, because that can damage the fibres too. Be slow and patient: expect it to take not an hour or two but a day or two.
- Pat upholstery gently with a plastic fly-swat or old-fashioned carpet beater (if you're lucky you might pick one up at the same time as the seating) to loosen the dust.
- Vacuum cushions, arm-rests, backs and crevices. A small, hand-held vacuum cleaner is best because its suction is not too strong. Don't use the brush attachments.
- Don't vacuum fringes or embroidery or anything with beads or sequins on. Shampoo the upholstery with a proprietary upholstery shampoo if necessary.

Care of your old rug or kilim
- Vacuum regularly but avoid getting any tassels or fringes caught up in the vacuum cleaner.
- Mop up any spills immediately. The secret of successful stain removal is speed – the sooner you catch the stain the better.
- Check whether the carpet shop you bought the piece from will be prepared to clean the carpet for you from time to time.

Caring for reclaimed plaster moulding
- If mouldings are very dirty, spray with detergent solution in a bottle with a fine spray. Wait for the liquid to penetrate then wipe with a dry cloth and spray again with clear water. Wipe again with a clean, dry cloth. Check that the mouldings are, indeed, washable and that any chips and cracks won't be further damaged by the water.
- Highly decorated plaster mouldings may smudge and streak. Dust them well and then re-paint them if necessary.
- Terry towelling is good for cleaning mouldings because the loops of thread mop up water in the crevices.
- Occasionally dust gently with a cobweb brush or feather duster on a long handle.

Shampooing
You may find that if the seating has been languishing too long in storage, vacuuming isn't enough and you'll need to shampoo it.

- Spot clean any stains at this stage. There are many excellent products for general spot cleaning – since you won't know what caused the stain, follow the instructions on the packaging. Dry foam upholstery shampoos are the easiest to use as they dry to form crystals, drawing out the dirt as they dry. If you want to shampoo cushion covers, don't get the fillings too wet.

Leather care
- Clean dirty areas with saddle soap, using as little water as possible, then buff up with a soft cloth.
- Rub the leather with a small amount of castor oil or neat's foot oil on a cotton wool pad or with your fingertips to prevent it from cracking. Rub it in well and absorb any surplus with a kitchen tissue to make sure it doesn't get transferred to your clothes.
- For pale leather use petroleum jelly (Vaseline).
- Don't wax leather furniture because it won't absorb the wax.
- Salvaged hide may have a rather dried-out look, especially if it's spent time in centrally-heated homes. Apply a proprietary hide food with swabs of cotton wool. Leave for twenty-four hours for the leather to absorb it, then buff up with a soft, clean cloth.
- When using any sort of leather renovator, don't let it get onto any embossed gilding (which you might find on a writing desk, for example) and keep the product away from any surrounding wood.

- Treat a small area at a time using as little water and cleaning fluid as possible so the padding doesn't become wet.
- For robust fabrics rub the entire surface vigorously with a damp towel to take off the foam residue and loosened dirt. Dry with a bathroom towel and don't get the fabric too wet.

Miscellaneous care and maintenance

Maintenance of reclaimed baths
Of course, many reclaimed baths have already been cleaned, refurbished and are as good as new. However, if you find a salvage yard selling baths in a pretty good if not perfect state, they can still be cleaned up at home. Many antique baths, copper ones, for example, are objects of beauty in their own right.

- No matter how grubby your reclaimed bath, don't use abrasive cleaners or very strong bathroom cleaners on it.
- Clean vitreous enamel baths with bathroom cream cleaner applied on a cloth, then rinse well.
- Clean acrylic baths with mild detergent solution. Rub stubborn stains with half a lemon. Rub scratches with silver polish. If necessary, use diluted household bleach or hydrogen peroxide, but don't leave it on. Rinse well.

Most second-hand and traditional pottery just needs washing. Plain ware can go into the dishwasher; anything with a pattern not marked dishwasher-proof should be washed by hand.

Old lampshades are usually best kept dry. Dust them initially, and then try wiping with a damp cloth squeezed out in a solution of vinegar and water. Silk, nylon and rayon can be washed by hand, but remember that the frame may rust or the glue may come unstuck.

Elaborate pieces of glass and china should be washed carefully by hand. Use a plastic washing-up bowl and drain on kitchen towels or another soft surface so there's no fear of knocking them by accident.

- Remove hard water marks with proprietary lime scale remover, or try neat vinegar which usually works just as well.
- Remove rust marks with a proprietary rust remover or use a paste of cream of tartar and hydrogen peroxide and a drop or two of household ammonia. Leave it on for an hour or two before wiping it clean. Then rinse.

China, porcelain and pottery

- Wash fine china and glass by hand in a plastic bowl to prevent chipping. Cover the draining board with a folded tea towel so you won't damage the piece when putting it down to drain.
- Don't soak, rub hard or use cleaning powders or scourers which may damage the glaze and the pattern.
- Cracks in fine porcelain can often be concealed simply by removing the dirt. Cover the crack with a cotton wool pad soaked in a solution of household ammonia or household bleach. Leave for several days, wetting the pad from time to time with more solution. Scrub gently if necessary with a soft toothbrush dipped in the solution.
- China with a raised pattern can be cleaned with an eyebrow or make-up brush kept for the purpose.
- Old tea and coffee stains can be removed cheaply and effectively with a cloth dipped in baking soda.
- Wash old china by hand as it may not be dishwasher-proof. Soaking old china in water may soften the colour and is specially damaging to any gold decoration.
- Earthenware, stoneware and salt-glaze ware won't be harmed by boiling water or soaking. They can be washed in a dishwasher.

Lampshades

- Glass shades: get rid of surplus dust and then wipe with a cloth dipped in a solution of vinegar and water.
- Parchment shades: dust thoroughly and then wipe with a damp cloth.
- Raffia and straw: vacuum gently, then sponge with a just damp sponge.
- Silk, nylon and rayon: wash them by hand, provided the shade is sewn and not glued to the frame and the trimmings are colour fast. Mix up a bowl of mild soap or detergent solution and dip the lampshade in and out. Rinse in the same way in tepid water. Stand the shade on a towel to dry, preferably in front of a fan heater because the quicker it dries, the less likely the frame is to rust. Silk, nylon or rayon which has been glued to the frame should be dry cleaned.

Glass and mirrors

- Fill a bucket or bowl with an egg cupful of vinegar in warm water. Wipe the mirror with a clean lint-free cloth squeezed out in the solution. Then wipe with a clean cloth wrung out in clean warm water and finally, finish off with a clean chamois or lint-free cloth, or better still, with crumpled newspaper.
- Use all proprietary products sparingly or they will produce streaks that can be difficult to remove.
- Take care not to get water between the glass and the frame or onto the backing.

- Modern stained glass is usually quite robust. If a second-hand piece is dirty when you buy it, clean it with a solution of mild washing-up liquid and vinegar and wipe dry with newspaper.
- Antique panes should be washed very gently. Don't use commercial products or detergent.
- Painted glass panels should not be washed. Dust them with a very soft artist's paintbrush instead.
- Wash the insides of vases with warm water and detergent and if necessary use neat vinegar to clean off the green gunge and hard water marks. Leave the vinegar in the vase for five or ten minutes, then clean with a bottle brush, rinse and dry. For narrow-necked vases and decanters shake tea leaves and vinegar in the vase together. Rinse and dry. Or fill with water plus two teaspoons of household ammonia. Stand overnight, then wash and rinse. Or fill with a little sea sand or fine aquarium gravel with a squeeze of washing-up liquid and warm water. Shake well. Leave for a few minutes, shake again. Carry on until the sediment is loose. Then rinse.

Plastics
- In general plastics are easy to clean. Wipe them with a cloth wrung out in warm detergent solution.
- Melamine is a strong, good-looking, tasteless, non-toxic plastic in plain, bright colours used to make plates, cups, tumblers, jugs, and cutlery handles that were popular in the 1960s. It can still sometimes be found in flea markets. Melamine can be safely put into the dishwasher and you can remove tea stains with a little toothpaste or sodium perborate applied with an old toothbrush. Don't use scouring powders or pads which will scratch the surface.

Chandeliers and candlesticks
- Put a dustsheet or polythene sheet under the chandelier to catch the drips.
- Wipe each pendant with cotton-gloved fingers dipped in a solution of vinegar and water.
- Another way is to stand on a firm stepladder and hold a tumbler of hot water and vinegar up to each pendant until it is immersed and then allow it to drip dry.
- There's usually some wax left in candlesticks from previous use. Pour warm water into the candle holder to soften the old wax so you can push it off gently with a soft cloth wrapped around your finger.
- Don't stand weighted or hollow candlesticks in water.

Enamel cookware has a tough finish produced by fusing a special kind of glass onto a metal base. For cooking pans, baths, etc. the base is cast-iron or steel. They may be chipped and rusty. Wash enamel plates, bowls, mugs and casseroles in warm water and detergent. Don't use metal scrapers or scouring powders or anything abrasive, but you can safely use a nylon scourer on pans. Light stains can often be removed by rubbing the enamel with a damp cloth dipped in baking soda.

Care of your reclaimed wood floors
- Apply polish sparingly and infrequently. Buff up in between.
- Liquid wax polish helps to remove dirt and is easier to apply than solid wax.
- Don't wash polished wood floors but after a few years when the polish has built up, you can wipe with a cloth squeezed out in vinegar and water to remove excess polish and dirt.

Narrow glasses, vases and decanters, especially if used to hold flowers, can be cleaned with a solution of vinegar and water. Leave in the vessel for an hour or so, then rinse.

Interesting old brass door furniture can be washed in a detergent solution. Then polish with a proprietary metal polish, following the manufacturer's instructions.

Marble objects and surfaces

Marble is a luxury natural stone which needs very little maintenance. If you find a piece of marble you like, cleaning it is not usually difficult. You can often find marble table tops, fireplace surrounds and other items which may be very grubby.

- Really grubby marble can be wiped with a cloth wrung out in mild detergent solution, but marble is porous so don't use this method more than once or the marble may discolour.
- Dry with a chamois leather so as not to leave streaks.
- Rub any obvious marks with lemon juice or vinegar but don't leave it on for more than a minute or two. It's better to repeat the process several times than to leave the lemon juice on the marble. Rinse and dry immediately.
- If in doubt, get an expert to clean the piece.
- Marble is easy to break if dropped or specially if laid flat as it can break under its own weight. Once safely installed it wears well but it marks easily.
- Alabaster is similar to marble and is often made into lamp bases and ornaments. Treat it as marble and remember that it is porous so don't let any liquid sink in.
- Marble floors are delicate although hard. Coloured liquids such as tea or coffee will soak in very quickly if spilled. Other substances such as lemon juice, vinegar and many household cleaning products will discolour the marble and salt can corrode and pit the surface. Bleach is probably the only thing that will remove a coloured stain. It should be applied with care and not left on for long.
- Abrasive polishing can be used after the bleaching process. It can be done by hand to polish out individual marks and stains, but for the restoration of a complete floor a polishing machine should be used. Get the advice of a specialist marble restoration company before tackling a complete floor.

The most standard of reclaimed baths can become an object of interest if given a cheerful coat of paint and used as a plant container, as has been done in this community garden.

Caring for reclaimed metals

Aluminium: wash aluminium pans in mild detergent water. If it's very dirty when you get it home, add a teaspoon of cream of tartar to 600ml (1 pt) water, bring to the boil and simmer for two minutes. Aluminium cooking pans are dishwasher safe. Getting rid of burned-on grease from aluminium roasting tins is almost impossible and hardly worth the effort.

Brass (an alloy of copper and zinc): if very dirty, wash in a detergent solution. Then use a proprietary metal polish, following the manufacturer's instructions. If you have bought a lacquered piece and the brass has corroded under the lacquer, you will have to remove all the lacquer and either re-lacquer or keep it regularly polished. Very dirty objects such as fire tongs may have to be rubbed with steel wool or very fine emery cloth. Rub the metal up and down, not round and round. You will need patience! Old brass pans should be cleaned professionally if you want to use them for cooking.

Cast-iron: if very rusty, use a proprietary rust remover then dry immediately. To prevent more rust, paint with special rust inhibiting paint or keep oiled with vegetable oil.

Chromium: a soft, usually highly polished silvery metal that doesn't tarnish. Many twentieth-century furniture designs included chrome bases, frames or legs. Very dirty chrome can be washed in warm water and detergent. Dry thoroughly afterwards. A chrome cleaner from a bike accessory shop will do the trick too.

Copper: if you find some desirable copper cooking pans remember that copper forms a greenish surface film which can cause nausea and vomiting, so copper pans must be scrupulously clean. Most modern copper pans are lined with chromium or tin and some even have a non-stick surface, so you'd be well advised to keep your salvaged copper set for show. Copper is an attractive metal, once used in pans for cooking and for bowls; there are even copper baths. However, it tarnishes quickly and dents easily. Old copper is best used for decorative items so don't expect to use it for cooking or anywhere near food.

Pewter (an alloy of tin and various other metals which may include lead, antimony, copper, bismuth and zinc): if your find has been kept in a humid atmosphere, it may have developed what's called a 'hume' with a grey film and tarnishing. If this is the case, get a specialist to deal with it.

Silver: sterling silver contains at least 925 parts of silver to 75 parts of copper. Silver needs constant care. It's at its best when used every day as constant use gives it a rich and mellow lustre. Wear cotton gloves when cleaning silver and treat the pieces gently. Old silver cutlery and tableware has often been worn leaf thin because it was cleaned in the past with home-made abrasive products using whiting. Modern proprietary products should only remove the tarnish.

- If grease gets spilled apply ice cubes immediately to congeal the fat and then scrape it up and clean with a minimal amount of detergent solution.
- Oil and grease stains can be removed with a paste of fuller's earth and soap and water. Place it on the stain and leave for two or three days to draw out the mark.

Applying the polish:
1. Apply polish evenly and lightly to the clean, dry floor with a soft cloth. Allow time for it to soak in.
2. Buff up with a broom head tied up in an old terry towel or with a 'dumper' (a heavily padded weight on a stick), or use an electric floor polisher (available from hire shops). Or you can add to your daily exercise by getting down on your hands and knees and buffing up the floor by hand.
3. Don't apply more polish for another two or three months. Just buff up in between.
4. Build up the surface polish with two or three thin coats rather than trying to apply one thick one. The first coat should cover the whole floor; the next two only the well-worn areas.

Outdoor care and maintenance

- For water features, sculptures and statues that remain outside, you can clean off any debris with a brush and soapy water.
- Never use strong chemicals, solvents or abrasives as this will affect the finish. Once clean, allow to air dry then apply a coat of wax polish with a soft boot brush.
- When using cleaning agents, always be aware of effects on plants and aquatic life.
- Any debris and bits of old leaf or dead flies can be worked out of the more complicated areas of the sculpture with a soft lead pencil. Apply furniture wax, generously working it into features and folds and when dry buff up with a cloth. Water features may benefit from a second application and more frequent attention, especially in hard water areas.
- If left without any protection, bronze will oxidize with time. It may darken, turn green or show streaks of yellow or white depending on the environment. The look of aged bronze is very attractive in a garden so don't try too hard to clean it up.
- Wrought iron: treat with rust inhibitor and paint with rust-resistant paint.
- Stone flags: scrub with a squeeze of washing-up liquid in a bucket of water.
- Natural stone paving is very low maintenance once laid. The pointing is the weakest part and may need to be replaced after a few years. Sweep regularly with a stiff brush. Algae, lichens and mosses tend to colonise stone paving outside and can become slippery when wet, so it may be necessary to remove this with a pressure washer or by swilling the area with disinfectant to kill the algae.
- Painted objects such as old sinks, baths or flowerpots can be repainted if necessary.

Chapter Five

How to Buy Salvage

Salvage-hunting is, above all, an adventure. Whether you are looking for something specific or have no idea what you are looking for, you are setting off on a treasure hunt and you might find the object of your dreams in the unlikeliest of places.

Architectural salvage is all around us, crying out to be reclaimed. Walk up your own street and you may find a desirable Georgian doll's house cast out because its owner has outgrown it or a perfectly good Victorian chair that has simply become a bit shabby. Pick them up, take them home, care for them and enjoy them. Luckily, we have become much more aware of the quality and intrinsic value of original materials and objects, so you may find interesting and available second-hand items in sales, fairs, junk shops, friends' houses or even your own home. However, a main source of serious architectural antiques nowadays is the dedicated architectural salvage company.

Some parts of the country are richer in salvage opportunities than others. London and its surroundings as you might expect has plenty of reclamation possibilities. The south-west of England is also rich in architectural salvage pickings, from wonderful warm Cotswold stone to Art Nouveau tiles and interesting doorknockers. Typical of local companies is Frome Reclamation based in the interesting and largely unspoiled old textile town of Frome. It is a family-run business with thousands of local clay, slate and stone roofing materials in stock. They also have Cotswold stone tiles and reclaimed Welsh slates and a huge selection of chimney pots. They offer garden statuary in stone, marble, iron and terracotta, statues, urns, troughs, staddle stones, rhubarb forcers, borders and edging. You will also find reclaimed boards, bathroom basins, toilets (simple or decorated), doors including early sixteenth- and seventeenth-century up to the 1930s, not to mention ironmongery such as letterboxes, knockers and hinges. In Malvern, nicely placed between the West Country and the Midlands and north of England, Back to Basics organises antiques and collectors' fairs and flea fairs throughout the year. These have a good variety of old items from antiques to retro at quite good prices as dealers come down from the north, where goods are still cheaper than the rich-in-antiques West Country.

Walcot Reclamation in Bath was one of the first reclamation yards, started in the 1960s by Thornton Kay, the founder of Salvo, as a way, he says, of preventing an unfortunate road development in the town. It still offers a wide selection of architectural salvage and has opened a supplementary yard nearby.

Sourcing specific items

Most architectural salvage centres are happy to find what you are looking for. If you need a specific style of lamp, fireplace, brick or tile, for example, or to match up existing floorboards, you may be able to take or send in an example and the company will produce some samples ready for you to choose from. They should also be able to advise you on the suitability of your choice. Even if you are not matching up building materials but want something purely decorative, many reclamation companies will put out a search for you.

Reproduction items

Reproduction items, both good and not-so-good, are sometimes offered alongside the genuinely old. This applies particularly to things that are very popular and have become more difficult to track down, such as fireplaces, doors and door furniture and garden ornaments.

RECLAMATION YARDS

What all architectural salvage companies do is sell some or all of such items as reclaimed and salvaged building materials, traditional fireplaces and furniture, household bits and pieces and garden features so that they can be used again. Different companies vary enormously in what they stock. Some specialise in reclaimed beams or sleepers and bricks, tiles and stone. Most salvage yards supplying reclaimed building materials specialise in local

---

SALVO

Salvo is an organisation dedicated to the reclaiming and salvaging of anything old and worthwhile and to introducing buyers to sellers and promoting an ecological way of doing things. Salvo has its own code, so it's worth enquiring whether the salvage company you are interested in is a member of Salvo and follows the code. Each Salvo Code dealer has a Certificate of the Salvo Code, which is dated for the current year and signed by Thornton Kay, the administrator of the code. Its website (www.salvo.co.uk) contains lists of member dealers, some of whom are based on the Continent, as well as details of sales and some advertisements for specific items with contact details.

The Salvo Code

The Salvo Code Dealer undertakes:

1. Not to buy any item if there is the slightest suspicion that it may be stolen.
2. Not to buy knowingly any item removed from listed or protected historical buildings or from sites of scheduled monuments without the appropriate legal consent.
3. To record the registration numbers of vehicles belonging to persons known to it who offer items for sale, and to ask for proof of identity.
4. Where possible to keep a record of the provenance of an item, including the date of manufacture, from where it was removed, and any previous owners.
5. To the best of its ability and knowledge, to sell materials free from toxic chemicals, excepting those natural to the material, traditional to its historical use, or resulting from atmospheric pollution.
6. To allow its business details to be held on a list of businesses who subscribe to the Salvo Code and to display a copy of the code and their Certificate in a public position within their business premises.

The Art Deco wash jug in the window of this tiny bathroom was found (without its matching bowl) among some items abandoned in the street. The curtain is a second-hand batik sarong from Java.

An architectural salvage fair is always full of interest, history and surprises. These metal boxes were exhibited by a Belgian reclamation company at the Salvo Fair in 2009.

Do you need a restoration knight for your garden? This stone sculpture was found at V&V Reclamation guarding a row of young trees in the nursery.

Highgate Antiques is hidden behind tall black gates, but inside is a wealth of garden ornaments and fountains, as well as stained leaded glass, furniture, clocks and unusual items.

Two small winged cast-iron lion cubs that would grace a small garden or sit on the gateposts of a large one, seen at V&V Reclamation.

bricks and will have a variety. Others also stock panelling, staircases, fireplaces and furniture. Quite a number now also manufacture and sell reproduction panelled doors or fireplace surrounds, sometimes, but not always, using reclaimed wood.

There's often a very quick turnover, especially of popular items, so it's worth visiting at regular intervals as there will always be something newly-acquired and different. The buildings housing all this stuff are often salvaged and interesting in their own right. There are salvage centres in redundant churches, pubs, barns and old mills and there's no question, it does add to the pleasure of the search when it is in an interesting old building.

Every salvage yard has a personality of its own. Some are a chaotic jumble of stacked-up doors, rusty radiators and assorted bricks with a collection of ceramic pedestal basins lurking in a corner. Others are models of organisation, each item categorised, described and priced and probably already refurbished with such precision that they are almost a history lesson in their own right. Others again specialise in the unusual or eccentric and are full of eye-opening surprises. The quality of each place varies; of course, some of them are really just like builders' yards with nobody very knowledgeable to help you with ideas or style but where you might pick up a bargain. Some are places you would go to for inspiration, where you might expect to pay more because everything has been cleaned and restored to pristine condition.

Top of the market

'Reclamation yard' seems a bit of a derisory term for the premises of top-of-the-market companies, who may display their stock in museum-like splendour in historically interesting buildings. Architectural salvage is not really the same as architectural antiques but the two can overlap. When an architectural or garden antique is described as 'fine' it means it is a top of the range item. Some salvage companies specialise in fine items and you can pretty well trust the provenance. Always ask about provenance as the knowledge of an item's history adds value to an antique. Top dealers of fireplaces, for example, include Nicholas Gifford-Mead and Geoff Westland of Westland Antiques. Each offers a choice of very fine and distinguished fireplaces and accessories. Fine architectural antiques are often found in a showroom adjoining a salvage yard or at antiques fairs and auctions.

LASSCO

The Grand Old Man of reclamation yards in England is the London Architectural Salvage and Supply Company, universally known as LASSCO which was founded in the late 70s by Adrian Amos. LASSCO started by stripping doors in Hampstead, then it moved to St Michael's Church in Shoreditch (now the home of Westland Reclamation) and then acquired more yards in Islington and Bermondsey. In 2004 LASSCO bought Brunswick House, an imposing mansion in Vauxhall, built in 1758 of red stock brick. Even if you didn't want any salvage, it would be worth visiting this house which has been renovated down to the bare boards and walls so you can see exactly how the house was built before it was covered with carpets or wallpaper.

Each room is themed so you can go straight to what you are looking for, although it is highly tempting to go through all the rooms anyway: they are so fine in themselves and are laid out with thought and care. In the porch you come across a family of Bakelite wirelesses reflected in two enormous paired mirrors painted with a Scottish highland scene. One room is jam-packed with brass and iron door furniture, everything from hinges and doorknobs to fingerplates. In this room there's a strong smell of soap and you can buy old-fashioned household and garden items such as Silvo and blacking, string and beeswax, mousetraps, raffia, candles and soapflakes.

Downstairs you will find many fireplaces, combination grates, marbled and gilded columns, items made from reclaimed pine (e.g. mirror frames), fluted plaster pilasters, elaborate overmantels, and silver plate by the tableful. There's a room full of doors, anything from pine to painted doors including, when I visited, a set of Art Deco bronze doors crying out for a ballroom to open onto. There are also piles of brightly-polished copper planters and a mosaic sculpture of eagles discarded by a Barclays bank. The end of the room was decorated with a rood screen, presumably from some church, hung with magnificent red velvet theatre curtains.

All through the house you will find reconditioned cast-iron radiators, some small and plain, others wonderfully ornate, rococo versions, some have been renovated and painted in gorgeous plain colours: turquoise, black and cyclamen, for example. There are also numerous prints and paintings including framed botanical illustrations.

In the basement with its arched brick vaults you will find bathroom and kitchen items, rows of pedestal basins, mostly in more generous sizes than you'd find today, including a very colourful transfer-and-hand-painted late Victorian one and some curvy French basins. There are loos with wooden seats, a retro marshmallow-pink basin and toilet with silver-coloured seat and lid as well as a wall of shelving with restored taps. The Bath Room was full of treats including brass and copper bateau baths and handmade basins to match. The kitchen section has wooden plate racks, terracotta flowerpots, kitchen tables and chairs, children's chairs and a toy Triang shop with drawers for the merchandise, a selection of fish kettles, a pyramid empty-bottle holder, fire buckets and ceramic tiles. That's still not the end: upstairs are more rooms with examples of some very desirable wood floors, some new, some reclaimed, some part new with a reclaimed surface including Georgian pine and antique oak. One room contains second-hand furniture of a retro kind, some small Scandinavian chairs, a G Plan bookcase with original Penguin books in it and some Art Deco cabinets, not to mention Victorian framed butterfly collections, chinoiserie screens and panels.

Outside is space round the house for a collection of garden ornaments, industrial ceramic electric insulators, columns, iron spindles, railings, gates, grilles and gazebos, among lots of lavender and herbs planted in containers. This is the very model of a well-run salvage company.

Westland

Westland, based in St Michael's church in London's East End (where once LASSCO used to be) finds, restores and stylishly displays a vast and comprehensive collection of antique and prestigious chimneypieces, antique fire grates, architectural elements and ornamentation ranging through Gothic and Renaissance to Victorian and Art Deco from the British Isles, Ireland, Italy, France, Flanders, Spain and points east, often exotic in concept and style with particularly fine antique fireplace mantels. There are also indoor or outdoor architectural features in the grand manner. They now offer dramatic scenarios where antique panelled rooms, fountains, sculptures, furniture, paintings and chimneypieces are displayed.

The specialists

Many reclamation companies specialise in one particular type of item, such as doors, say, or fireplaces, or building materials or oak beams. If you know exactly what you're looking for, going to a specialist will save a good deal of time, your supplier will be particularly knowledgeable and may have excellent advice as well as a wide variety of the particular thing you are looking for. Some centres stock 'everything' but nevertheless have a leaning towards particular items.

Building materials

Britain is lucky in having a great variety of building stone of all types, colours and strengths. Each quarry will produce not only a particular quality of stone but different parts of the quarry will give different qualities, all requiring careful study if the stone is to be used correctly. Every area in every country has its own specialities. Stone and bricks were too heavy to be moved very far so local stone was nearly always used, creating a definite local character that adds to the charm of a historic building. Local companies like Valley Reclamation in Derbyshire or Masco in the Cotswolds are experienced in demolishing large buildings locally and always have good stocks of local bricks, tiles and stone and can often match these up with local buildings.

Viking Reclamation in Yorkshire specialises in 'quality reclaimed bricks' but if you happen to want a Gothic window for a folly on your estate that's one of the best places to go – they have helped several clients to create 'ruins' to finish off their garden design. They also love that bright red of Post Office pillar boxes and early phone booths, so you'll find plenty of those which can be turned into shower cubicles or sculptures for the garden.

The Cotswold Reclamation Company is a family-run business established in 1994 which specialises in building materials reclaimed from within the Cotswold area, including stones, slates, concrete tiles, handmade bricks, hardwood beams and York paving. They also stock cast-iron baths, basins and sanitary ware, cast-iron radiators and fireplaces. The company manufactures oak and pine doors from reclaimed timber in standard sizes or to order. As a side order they have a warehouse with kitchenalia, ceramics, pottery and glassware and some furniture.

Oak and wood

Antique Buildings Ltd., in the South of England, specialise in reclaiming complete barns or oak beams, floorboards, terracotta tiles and paving from such ancient buildings. They can offer oak-joisted ceilings and inglenook fireplaces. They now have eight such buildings full of unusual reclaimed materials as well as whole barn frames, and show the various features and techniques they might recommend if you want an open-fronted cowshed made into a garage. Although they specialise in oak, they also offer pine, elm and chestnut, and local handmade bricks from Sussex and Surrey.

Several companies offer a design and planning service or can find consultants for a client's existing architects who often have only limited experience in such ancient structures. Frames are painstakingly drawn, numbered and photographed before being dismantled so re-erection is made easier.

Bob Lovell of The Antique Oak Flooring Company has had thirty years in the flooring business and set up his own company in 2002 specialising in reclaimed floorboards. His little showroom in North London is full of fantastic flooring samples, some of great historic interest, such as oak from the Bank of England or mahogany from Chelsea Barracks or star design parquet panels from a 1930s Park Lane apartment in walnut, maple, mahogany and oak – absolutely stunning. There are original Georgian pine vintage solid oak boards in gorgeous golden yellow, seventeenth-century oak boards, very wide pitchpine floorboards in long lengths machined to the thickness required, and you may find end of run offers for reclaimed oak parquet.

In his 12,500sq ft warehouse and sawmill nearby he has stocks of oak from a Mississippi cotton mill, French oak and eucalyptus from Australia, so he can offer an enormous choice of timbers in excellent condition, and if there's something particularly valuable, will probably dismantle it himself. If you are looking for something specific to match up with something in your home, he has connections with several demolition companies who can provide reclaimed timbers.

Parquet or patterned wooden floors are available mainly in the classic herringbone but Victorian Woodworks in Essex has more unusual patterns such as chevron and parquet de Chantilly. They aim 'to bring a sense of environmental awareness to floor design. Salvaged from all over the world, age-hardened woods and exotic timbers draw on a sense of history to create unique focus, feel and depth of colour to any setting.'

Many companies with stocks of reclaimed timber also provide new timber flooring. UK Architectural Antiques in Staffordshire sell three types of floorboards: reclaimed floorboards (usually Victorian square-edged boards), re-sawn floorboards (usually Victorian beams cut into floorboards to your sizes), and new oak floorboards.

Companies such as Reclaimed Ltd. work with the big demolition companies as a way of retrieving fabulous timbers and other items of interest in architectural salvage. Reclaimed has been able to rescue whole consignments of structural timbers and floorboards from buildings such as GEC Marconi in Essex, Royal Arsenal in Woolwich and other noteworthy buildings in and around London.

Fireplaces and heating

Some centres specialise only in fireplaces. Wood- and multi-fuel-burning stoves, so popular in the 1970s and 80s, are back in favour now for very good reasons and there are plenty of those around. There are also brass fenders, fire baskets, marble and pine surrounds, pokers, tongs and other accessories. You can find reclaimed fireplaces in many reclamation yards and companies like Westland specialise in antique, unusual and beautifully reclaimed fireplaces and surrounds. You will find many reproduction fireplaces as well, so if you want an old one, be sure to check.

Doors

Most reclamation yards also have a selection of doors but Period Pine Doors in Yorkshire specialise in reclaimed doors and have a showroom with 4,000 doors in stock at any one time. They have period pine narrow doors, rustic seventeenth-century ledge-and-brace doors, elegant Georgian six-panel doors to the increasingly popular 1930s to 40s-style doors, classic Victorian four-panel doors and a large selection of cupboard doors, door fixtures and fittings, many unique front doors and a range of stained glass and leaded lights. There's a huge stock of old pine doors with many different dimensions and styles, also various beadings. They also have their own workshops where stripping, waxing and restoration are

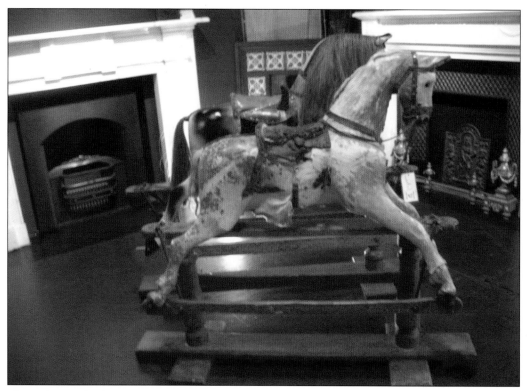

This is the Westland interior where two rocking-horses of different periods show their paces in front of a magnificent display of restored fireplaces.

Doors can be found in most reclamation yards. A good selection can be found in Herts Architectural Salvage and Reclamation, which specialises in building materials and doors.

A brown Doulton lavatory reclaimed by Edward Haes in Lancashire. Some companies specialise in discontinued sanitary ware by various manufacturers in different sizes and colours.

This no-nonsense set of craftsman's storage drawers could be endlessly useful in a child's room, say, or in a garage or large warehouse. The flowery tea set seems very ladylike in contrast.

done in-house and a team of experts replaces stained glass. Their advice to anyone building a house or an extension or converting a barn is to choose the doors before building the door casings, which will give you a wider choice of style and size.

Church and cathedral
Church Antiques in Surrey who specialise in pre-war church furnishings including pulpits, lecterns, prayer desks, chair pews, chapel chairs and church chairs, in fact absolutely anything that once graced a church, cathedral or vicarage, have an excellent online catalogue giving provenance of most items such as 'Liverpool pine pew' or 'Isle of Sheppey pew'.

Restaurant, pub and hotel furniture and fittings
During the 1970s the great thing was to modernise pubs. Original panelling, oak beams, brass fittings, etched glass and mirrors were torn out piecemeal and burned or thrown into landfill. Andy Thornton was the first person to realise that these things had a worth of their own. In the early 1970s he began salvaging old pub fittings and fixtures and selling them to the USA. British breweries soon realised their mistake and began to reinstate the original look for their pubs. Today, Andy Thornton Architectural Antiques Ltd. has the world's largest selection of pub fittings, windows and mirrors, baths and bathroom accessories, architectural metalwork, columns, door furniture, lighting and flooring.

Lighting
W. Sitch is a family-run business in the Soho district of London, set up in 1776. It has an enormous range of antique and reproduction lighting on five floors, and centuries of knowledge and expertise and can renovate and rewire antique light fittings, duplicate originals and replace missing parts. They have a polishing shop where they colour and finish the metalwork of the fittings as well as other items that customers bring in, such as stair rods. The company has worked for the National Trust, English Heritage, Edinburgh Castle and supplied the fittings used in the film *Titanic*, so you are in grand company if you buy anything from them.

Allen's in the USA specialise in authentic gas lamps and early electric fixtures from 1840 to 1910. They have chandeliers, wall brackets, floor and table lamps and appropriate shades. They have lots of lamps by famous makers from Britain and Europe.

Twentieth-century 'retro'
Source Antiques in Bath specialise in twentieth-century antiques and salvage. They have a spectacular range of 1950s kitchen units such as English Rose and Paul Metalcraft, often in startling colours such as brightest rose pink, 'reclaimed, refurbished and recycled to order'. There is even an English Rose fridge-freezer ('sold as a decorative item – don't use until checked by a registered technician'). The company will happily discuss layout plans before you order anything. Here you may even find some of the original Supataps that were *de rigueur* in the 1960s.

Just a few companies specialise in discontinued sanitary ware items (though you may find a few in general reclamation yards as well). Miscellanea in Surrey have an enormous collection of bathroom ware by leading UK and European manufacturers including Armitage Shanks, Ideal Standard, Royal Doulton, Twyfords, Trent, Shires, Allia, Selles, Senesi, Balterley, Sanitiana and more. They have over 100 retro bathroom colours in stock, including pinks, yellows, turquoise blues, and that ubiquitous colour of the 1970s, avocado.

Industrial

Trainspotters in Gloucestershire say 'we rescue, restore and re-use the most stylish elements of the UK's and Europe's recent industrial past'. They sell a very selective range of architectural salvage and period decorative items, especially lighting and reclaimed industrial design and a selection of interesting lighting and workbenches, for example, from East German factories, white metal enamelled downlights from the Dunlop factory in Birmingham, items from the Rover car plant, enormous shop signs, stacking and other storage, plus brass lettering (from the USA). There are clocks, like the polished steel wall clock made in Communist-era Czechoslovakia, original 1920s railway posters, furniture and unusual antique curiosities and one-off finds. It is a source of good 'runs' and quantities of items so if you are involved in the refurbishing of large-scale commercial projects such as pubs, shops, restaurants or hotels, this is a promising company. However, if you have a large kitchen and are just looking for overhead hanging lamps or an Arts & Crafts dining table, they could help you too.

Here you may also find metal desks and lockers, metal filing cabinets, hotel chairs, glass-topped tables with legs made from bollards reclaimed from a dry dock in Portsmouth around 1900, office-style chairs, wooden bentwood hat stands, oak umbrella stands from the 40s and 50s (highly practical for small modern hallways), and adjustable bar stools from the 50s or 60s.

Garden

Garden Art in Hungerford is owned by Travers Nettleton whose office is an old railway carriage on stilts, from which he can spot a likely client and sprint down the steps with a friendly greeting. It's a feast of what he describes as 'High Quality Reclaimed Architectural Antiques, Statuary and Garden Ornaments', which he can send to clients all over the world. There are old stone troughs, enormous metal arbours with or without seats, statues, columns, plinths, garden furniture of various kinds, sundials, stone balls and ponds, mostly, he says, from England but there are some bronze statues from the Far East and many enormous Cretan urns. You might find a large stone gryphon or even find a giant William Pye fountain created in the 1990s. Hidden under a large fairground tent were a couple of gypsy caravans.

Garden salvage is always picturesque but some particularly so. At V&V Reclamation in Hertfordshire the salvage yard is also a well-known tree nursery so that the avenues of young trees are marked by pairs of urns on pedestals and the whole nursery is very much used to complement and embellish the merchandise. Telephone boxes, a sentry box, an old pump and brightly blue-painted street lamps lurk among the greenery, while round every leafy corner are new surprises and delights: a large choice of garden seating, including a wooden three-seater City of London municipal bench, concrete urns and planters are given softer contours among the Japanese maples. There are pallets of paving stones, an old church bell and panelled doors, as well as stoves and grates, ironwork gates and railings and a set of marble garden steps, waiting hopefully for the owner of a terrace to claim them. Items for the garden might include galvanised vessels, watering cans, garden rollers, cast-iron cherubs, fountains and wrought iron garden seats.

Eclectic

Some reclamation companies will take almost any category of architectural salvage from roof tiles and oak beams to ceramic tiles and doorknobs, building materials and stone

Travers Nettleton of Garden Art has his office in this reclaimed railway carriage which is surrounded by large and small items for the garden, from bowers and gazebos to tiny stone troughs.

Cast-iron urns are heavy. Once installed you won't want to move them around, but they make a splendid gateway to a wide garden path.

A beautiful section of Gothic stone wall and coping from Architectural Forum, seen at the Salvo Fair 2009. A piece like this could turn a mere garden into a garden fit for kings.

Architectural Salvage Source has practically everything from bricks to the rural garden house seen here which was exhibited at the Salvo Fair among a wealth of curious and interesting items.

corbels, radiators, fireplaces, furniture, baths, toilets and kitchen equipment right through to cast-iron railings, gazebos, troughs and staddle stones. There are chaotic-looking yards where you can search around among a plethora of rusty and chipped items piled up together, among which you may find exactly what you're looking for. Often fine architectural items are on sale among a whole lot of other things ranging from interesting to tatty, and although some salvage yards specialise in ecclesiastical salvage, many general salvage yards end up with a good selection of pews and church chairs and even in your local junk shop there may be one or two interesting items that started off in a church. Remember, there is a lot of theft from churches, so make sure your source is reputable.

The Architectural Forum in London, owned by Jason Davies, has a smart corner shop with an inviting showroom full of beautifully restored fireplaces, surrounds and radiators. Go downstairs and round the back is a maze of spaces full of as yet unrestored fireplaces and other items waiting to be smartened up and put into the showroom as space becomes vacant: largely fireplaces, fire baskets, stoves, ranges and accessories but also Belfast sinks, tiles, some very interesting radiators with Art Nouveau decorations, gardenalia including urns, statues, decorative metal arches, fountains and, when I was there, a Buddha. Restoration work is done on-site. Jason has been in the business for twenty-five years, starting by selling pine when it was popular in the 1980s. He still does his own sourcing and his shop is full of interesting items with a fascinating history. In 2008, for example, he acquired a set of black marble steps and some large ecclesiastical candlesticks from the seventeenth-century St. Anne's Church in Limehouse (designed by Nicholas Hawksmoore). Although the shop front looks small, there is a huge amount of reclaimed goods here.

Architectural Salvage Source in Hertfordshire has plenty of reclaimed building materials but you might also find a complete set of 1970s English Rose kitchen units, a rustic summerhouse, staddle stones, garden urns, folding café chairs and much more.

MASCo in Gloucestershire have an enormous stock of bathroom goods and 'whiteware'. Others lean more towards building materials and others again concentrate on fireplaces or furniture. MASCo opened a new showroom in 2008 and hold some enormous pieces such as an old bandstand cheek by jowl with porcelain Victorian basins and toilets. Based as it is in the Cotswolds, MASCo holds a lot of limestone fireplaces and Cotswold flagstone, although these are becoming rare nowadays. Steve Tomlin and Debbie Kedge of MASCo can give advice on the best ways of dealing with anything you buy there, from waxing an oak floor to the traditional way of patinating limestone flooring with a mixture of linseed oil and egg white. Many architectural salvage companies are very knowledgeable and happy to advise in this way, and many also carry out restoration and conservation work.

Demolition and salvage

The days when you could get a good bargain direct from a building site because items were otherwise going to be broken up or burned have pretty well gone. You might still be able to find something that way but always phone the site manager first; don't just amble onto the site informally in the hopes of picking something up. Expect to pay in cash and to carry away your purchase yourself.

An interesting development is that some demolition companies have cottoned on to the value of what they are pulling down and now have their own salvage yards. Many others are tied in with a salvage company and deliver relevant items when they are demolishing a suitable building, such as a luxury hotel or a block of flats. This means that bricks are less likely to be crushed and recycled as gravel or hardcore in roads and driveways, but can be reused to match up bricks in a local building. Items are constantly surprising, and very varied, coming as they do from private homes, schools, hospitals, luxury or run-down hotels, railway and underground stations, museums, pubs, shops, restaurants – you might even find seats from 1960s railway carriages or redundant dentist's chairs.

Emphasis on 'green'

Some salvage yards like to emphasise the recycling and ecological aspects of reclaimed materials. Romsey Reclamation in Hampshire, founded by Trevor Halfacre twenty-three years ago, originally started with roofing slates. In the 1990s the company started to import reclaimed wooden railway sleepers, providing the first 'Ground Force' and 'Home Front in the Garden' television programmes with sleepers. It now specialises in all conceivable kinds of building products and operates from an old railway station and sand pit where there are literally hundreds of thousands of bricks, tiles, slates, York stone, wooden railway sleepers, redundant telegraph poles, oak beams, chimney pots and other building delights. The online information (see Directory) on the history and manufacture of 'old' materials is fascinating. To emphasise its 'green' philosophy, the site is surrounded by fourteen acres of natural fields dedicated to wildlife.

Discontinued items

A few companies specialise in discontinued, sometimes unused, items from the 1970s and 1980s. Thomas Crapper & Co., one of the first WC manufacturing companies, sells accurate copies of their old models. Reproductions are available in many salvage yards too. If you're looking for everyday common or garden sanitary ware you may find some very good bargains, although unusual and exotic items may be very expensive.

Combined reclamation yard and design

For those who are looking to introduce old materials or artefacts into a modern interior, there is help at hand. Retrouvius is a partnership between Adam Hills and Maria Speake. Adam researches and unearths interesting and unusual used items and Maria is an interior designer who likes to use these things in her creative use of space. Two enormous reclaimed doors from a bank in St. James's invite you into the front shop with its 12ft-long table top made from a laboratory workbench. Everything possible has been recycled. There are Welsh double weave blankets, oak doors, a range of teak filing cabinets, a 60s rocking chair by Race and a wall of shelves from the British Library. There are school desks, wooden stacking chairs, huge enamelled underground maps and signs, some already turned into table tops. In their projects for clients they have used parquet flooring from St. Mary's Hospital in Paddington, and the marble for the kitchen in their own flat came from their local fishmonger's shop. Upstairs is a room full of ceramic tiles, oak chests of drawers, library steps, bits of leaded glass, large mirrors with baroque carved frames, and bookcases. 'We try not to let fashion and style get in the way of good quality,' says Adam.

accessible to all income levels by offering affordable prices, to create local jobs with living wages and to educate the community about the benefits, both environmental and social of re-use'. Re-use is not such a specific and immediately understandable title as architectural salvage and sometimes these centres are recycling mainly craft materials or old bottles and jars.

However, several do deal in building materials, furniture, fireplaces and all the other things you would expect in an architectural salvage centre including kitchen cabinetry, doors, windows, wood flooring, pedestal sinks, vanities, toilets, carpet, lighting, mantels and 'architecturally significant' items. These centres encourage people to bring in their old materials and equipment and often have pick-up and delivery services. They offer good quality materials at prices well below new retail prices. There is a move in the UK to create a similar network of BMRCs.

SECOND-HAND SHOPS AND EMPORIA

Your local junk shop

These are stores ranging from small corner shops in high streets to 'almost' salvage yards, where you can wander round for hours in a higgledy-piggledy collection of furniture (from cupboards and wardrobes to overstuffed armchairs, lamps, bookshelves, pictures and prints, books – an endless and fascinating jumble). Many of these shops deal in house clearance items but may also take smaller items from demolition contractors such as things cleared from schools or offices, which are often solid, no-nonsense items made of good, solid materials (often from solid oak, something almost impossible to find in modern furniture). If an old school cupboard is not exactly what you are looking for, it can often be altered or adapted to a different use.

These local shops are usually owned and run by people whose stock is as varied and individual as they are themselves. The Cobbled Yard, behind a pub in Stoke Newington, London, is rather bigger than a corner shop, consisting of 1,000 sq ft of showroom with antiques, pine furniture and collectibles. Its success in the five years of its existence has enabled its owner, Carol Lucas, a one-time graphic designer, to open a second outlet, Cobbled Yard 2, directly opposite in a 1960s ballroom. Here you may find all sorts of unusual and desirable things such as double upholstered seats from a 1970s British Rail railway carriage, or curiously-shaped little pink and eau de nil chairs from an ice cream parlour. There are second-hand wardrobes and washstands, occasional tables, chests of drawers and classic early telephones. There may be an Art Deco carpet, Chesterfield sofas, nesting tables. You might find a dentist's chair, various pub stools, enormous signs discarded from Tube stations, 1950s kitchen cabinets, glass-fronted bookcases, mantel clocks, and old electric ceiling fans jostling with chandeliers. Somebody starting up a business might come in looking for velvet curtains, a big round table with chairs, and lighting and folding chairs for a new office space.

Such shops may also offer services such as furniture restoration, upholstery and carpentry on-site and may deliver locally. Local shops like these rely largely on local clients, although their merchandise may come from all over the country. They are particularly busy at weekends but a good time to go is in their opening hours during the week, when you may well have the shop more or less to yourself and will get more of a chance to ask for advice.

Dave Dee in central York is based in an old banana warehouse whose depths reveal a fascinating jumble of furniture, bikes, lighting, theatre props, rugs, picture frames and bric-a-brac.

Paul's Emporium in North London is a tiny corner shop, once a chemist's, where Paul accommodates a wealth of interesting and reasonably-priced furniture including a wide choice of tables (pedestal, drop-leaf, oak, mahogany) and desks, cupboards, panelled doors, display cases, lots of solid wood including old government and council fittings, and smaller objects such as boxes and framed pictures, old photographs and books, and mirrors.

Some second-hand shops may specialise in a particular type of goods, say oak, or pianos. The Piano Warehouse in London is quite daunting at first because all the pianos look so highly polished and new. Some are indeed new, but others have been beautifully repaired. There are no highly valuable and unusual antiques, but I saw several pianos from the 1970s. One attraction about this place is that it will rent you a piano very reasonably for a year so you don't have to fork out thousands of pounds in one go.

Keith Roughton is one of the few furniture shops left in London's popular but increasingly trinkety Camden Market. His large shop space is stocked mainly with large and heavy solid oak furniture. There are chairs, tables, wardrobes, bookcases including glass-fronted, pianos and dressing tables, besides a lot of heavy Dutch farmhouse furniture. The oldest piece dates from around 1840 but most of it is 1890s–1904. They all have the dark varnish sanded so they are a more natural oak colour. Nearly all the wood is oak, although you might find the odd piece in rosewood or walnut.

Highgate Antiques is part second-hand emporium, part architectural salvage yard. There are plenty of unusual items including furniture, fireplaces, stained glass and garden features and behind its black gates are lots of surprises.

Dave Dee's store in an old York warehouse has a very versatile and varied stock from slender chairs to pairs of china spaniels and TV props to bicycles.

This life-size camel puts visitors in the mood for discussing the merits of the different tribal carpets and rugs within the shop.

Paul's Emporium is a model of the good junk shop. It has a variety of furniture from the solid to the good from several periods and many interesting small items, and the stock is always changing.

Seneh Carpets have put out their bargain carpet to entice prospective purchasers into the shop. There is no pressure to buy in such small shops, but a real feeling of customer care.

This display of agricultural galvanised buckets and tubs has been enlivened by the herbs growing in them. Although they can be painted any colour, they look rather fetching in their original gunmetal grey.

Some fairs are famous trading events which bring dealers in from all over the world. From the enormous antiques fair held at Newark, Nottinghamshire to the Shepton Mallet fair in Somerset, held every two months, these fairs are fascinating for anybody interested in architectural salvage and interior design. The breadth of goods on offer is astonishing and there is plenty for non-professionals as well as for dealers. Get there early if you can because the queues may stretch for a long way before the doors open and it may take twenty minutes to file into the space.

The annual Salvo fair 30 miles north of London started off as a trade fair but is now open to the public. Some of the best-known salvage yards show here in the grounds of Knebworth House and you can see some splendid reclaimed items laid out in a field, including fireplaces from France, splendid great doors from Germany and Belgian wooden buckets.

DMG Antique Fairs take place six times a year in four locations: Detling, Kent; Ardingly, Sussex; Newark, Nottingham and Shepton Mallet, Somerset. The Ardingly Fair has up to 1,700 stalls with anything from fine furniture and ceramics to glassware and textiles in a combination of indoor and outdoor stalls. Detling Fair is only thirty minutes from the Channel Tunnel and has an international flavour with many stallholders travelling from mainland Europe to sell their goods, from furniture and ceramics to gardenalia. The Newark Fair is one of the largest in Europe. There are up to 4,000 stalls over eighty-four acres and

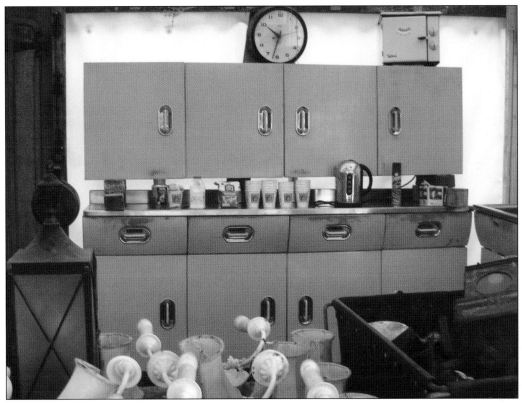

This is an original English Rose kitchen, before renovation, and it's easy to see the attraction of its strong and practical design. This one was exhibited by Architectural Salvage Source and provided staff and visitors with refreshments.

over 200 shopping arcades, forty-four marquees and plenty of outside pitches selling anything from rugs and textiles to paintings, sports memorabilia, grandfather clocks and antique maps. At Shepton Mallet there are four halls with up to 600 stalls of antiques and collectibles ranging from ceramics and paintings to glassware, decorative items and furniture.

Fairs in Twickenham and Woking in Surrey specialise in Art Deco and Art Nouveau, flea and collections markets. They include pottery, porcelain, glass, metalware, lamps, furniture, textiles, ephemera from the Art Nouveau era through to the Deco period of the 1920s to 30s and retro styles of the swinging 60s, as well as items from the 70s which are now becoming of interest, such as Troika pottery.

Indoor bric-a-brac markets and antiques and collectibles fairs take place every month at the George H. Carnall Leisure Centre, Greater Manchester.

Retro fairs are becoming popular and there's an interest in German ceramics from the 1970s. Anything interesting from the twentieth century and anything obviously Art Deco will sell well. Anything that isn't obviously Deco probably won't inspire any interest. Candleholders are popular, as people like them for their dinner parties. There are monthly magazines that list all the fairs regionally. Take a shopping trolley with you. Choose a light one with big wheels. Carrier bags are hopeless if you are buying heavy items.

LOCAL SALES AND FLEA MARKETS

Don't underestimate the value of local newspapers when it comes to finding out what's going in the way of local bric-a-brac sales, church and school jumble sales, auctions, flea markets and street markets. Sometimes local architectural salvage centres and second-hand shops will advertise in the local paper as well.

Car boot sales provide venues in which private individuals can sell things they no longer want. They take place at weekends, often in the grounds of schools or other community buildings or in fields or car parks. Sellers pay a nominal fee for their pitch and arrive with their goods in the boot of their car. Some bring trestle tables to display their merchandise, others simply lay it on a tarpaulin on the ground or leave it in the boot, if there isn't very much, so possible purchasers can peer in and see what's on offer.

What you are most likely to find are small items of furniture, china and glass; in fact the sort of things you might find in a charity, junk or bric-a-brac shop. It's worth bearing in mind that second-hand items may not conform to modern safety guidelines, especially when being sold by private individuals who themselves may not be aware of these regulations. So it's best to avoid anything electrical such as irons or electric fires; foam mattresses or furniture with foam cushions which may not meet modern flammability requirements; paraffin heaters or oil heaters.

These sales take place all over Britain and are popular in France, where the agricultural population is several years behind in modernising and still in the process of turning out its attics of portable bidets and tiny children's wooden clogs. You can still find curious country items such as old copper grain holders, milk churns and other redundant farm equipment.

Entry to the general public may be free or there may be a small charge. Car boot sales can vary enormously in what they offer, depending on the part of the country and time of year. Items on sale are often old books, records, CDs, DVDs, videos, garden plants, stationery and baby clothes. Among this plethora of objects you may find someone with an interesting picture frame or small item of furniture, possibly an interesting old washing bowl and jug or small chest of drawers or perhaps a set of 60s curtains. This is not the way to go looking for specific items, but it can be a way of picking up something very cheaply which fits in with your décor. Seasonal flea markets may happen two or three times a year in local schools or town halls and may be rather like indoor car boot sales or more like an antiques and collectibles fair. Get to recognise the jargon: 'retro' usually means anything from the 1940s onwards; the term 'housewares' means small items like table china and cooking utensils, picture frames and small boxes. 'Household goods' implies larger items like dining tables, chairs, sofas, appliances and so on.

Weekend markets and street markets

These can vary enormously from bright and lively to dead as a doornail with old carrier bags blowing around in a dismal drizzle. The better known the market is, the more expensive it's likely to be. However, even the most unlikely markets will sometimes reveal unexpected prizes, such as the one in a small town whose only interesting stall was a haberdashery one where it turned out the proprietor had a collection of twentieth-century lace well worth looking at. On another stall there were a couple of red 1970s telephones and a rather fetching retro teapot.

Finding a car boot sale

- Keep your eyes open for cars turning off into fields as you drive through the countryside on a Saturday. Advertised times are not necessarily strictly adhered to and in many cases the nature of the site itself makes it possible to get in a bit early for a good look at what's on sale.
- Yellow Pages can also be a way of finding out what exists locally. Look under 'Charity and Thrift Shops', 'Auctions', 'Flea Markets' and 'Salvage & Reclamation'.
- York Sunday Market Car Boot Sale takes place on Sundays.
- York Racecourse Car Boot Sale takes place on Saturdays.
- Rufforth Park Car Boot Sale, Wetherby, York, takes place all year round on Sundays.
- Home Farm Car Boot Sale, Corban Lane, Wigginton, takes place on Sundays from mid-April to October.
- Jumble sales, sometimes called 'give and take days', may be held in local schools and often consist mainly of clothes, old toys and trinkets, but it is surprising how often you can find just one chair or small stool or desk that fits a gap in your home.

Fairs and markets shopping hints

- When shopping in street markets, flea markets or anywhere where the merchandise is likely to be small and cheap, carry your money in cash and in small denominations – change is not always easy to come by.
- Take a selection of packing materials with you – several carrier bags if you are only looking at small items, but a shopping trolley is very useful if you think you'll buy heavy items or buy a lot – then you won't have to keep trailing back to the car with small parcels all the time.
- Get there early for the best bargains (some markets start as early as 6.30 in the morning and begin to peter out at around lunch-time).
- Keep blankets, bubble-wrap and sticky tape in the car for wrapping up breakable objects.

Estate Sales

This usually means all the contents of a home which has to be sold either because the occupant has died or has to move home and doesn't want to, or can't, carry around the clutter of a past life. They may last anything from one to three days. An important estate sale will certainly be infested with dealers – a historic house will be full of interesting, unusual and sometimes rare items collected over the years, especially if it was owned by one family, and professionals will be hoping to find good bargains to sell on, so it's wise to get there early. You won't beat the dealers but may be attracted to something they don't want. I have bought a number of interesting items at estate sales in important houses – an incorruptible set of bathroom scales on one occasion and a carved oak set of bookshelves on another.

Auction Houses

Buying at auction can be a cheap way of acquiring almost anything, provided you are able to curb your own enthusiasm. We're not talking about the really grand auction houses here, but there are many local auctions that have serious antiques mixed with less august items. Some have a whole medley of late Victorian and early twentieth-century things together

A Sunday morning market stall in London's Columbia Road plant and flower market, selling reclaimed and renovated garden implements and kitchen ware.

Part of a collection of tins built up over the years makes a colourful storage shelf. The small 'Bicky House' is an original by the well-known children's illustrator Mabel Lucie Attwell.

This 1950s tablecloth was picked up on a second-hand market stall. Its sketch-like pattern, black outlines and red and yellow colours are typical of the period.

Auction houses can offer many delights. Choose an auction that won't be concentrating just on antiques. Some high street auction houses have retro auctions and others include areas of modest furniture alongside the expensive items.

A second-hand stall in a street market can offer all sorts of delights that may be used as they are or could be adapted to other uses.

with retro radios and other items, some of which are interesting and some exotic and some not much more than rubbish. In a way these are the fun ones because there's no knowing at all what you may find. Some, like Hornsey Auctions Ltd., will open to sell items but not necessarily through an actual auction, so they act more like second-hand shops. Looking in this particular one I found an up-market pine door, nesting tables, lots of dining, pub and individual chairs, a four-poster bed, a rocking-horse, dining tables with barley-sugar legs, a pine dressing table, a wooden trolley, lots of mirrors, masses of framed paintings, prints and maps, a Tiffany-style glass lampshade, a couple of vintage cigarette machines, a wooden fire surround and mantelpiece, oriental rugs, old radios, china and glass – a good place for rummaging.

Auctions are usually categorised, so one may concentrate on furniture, another on textiles, and others may be more mixed. It's wise to go the day before to view the stuff that's going to be on sale so you know whether you want to bid for something or not. If you have chosen a retro style for your home, then you could easily find bathroom scales, kitchen equipment, chairs and tables that would fit into your scheme. Find out if the auction house has a warehouse where things of second-rate quality end up; anything from old-fashioned prams to kitchen units.

If you haven't bought anything at an auction before, it's best to start by bidding for small, non-valuable items while you learn the ropes. Get a catalogue and study it carefully and be aware that the items listed may change by the time the bidding starts.

You can find out about local auctions in local papers and specialist magazines. *Auction News* is a monthly magazine with details of all auctions by official receivers, county courts, Ministry of Defence and the police. Two useful websites in the UK are www.government auctions.com which gives information on auctions of ex-government equipment from houses and cars to furniture and jewellery, and www.ukauctionguides.co.uk which gives information on auctions and lists of local auctions throughout the UK. In the USA www.auctionguide.com is a guide to auctions of all kinds throughout the country.

Typical of auction houses where you may find what could be considered architectural antiques are Criterion Auctioneers of London, which holds auctions in Islington and Wandsworth selling art, antiques and contemporary furnishings. Items are well displayed, described and priced for viewing the previous week so you can decide whether there is anything you want to bid for. Auctions are held every Monday at 5pm; viewing days are Friday, Saturday, Sunday and Monday. There are many true antiques for sale but among them are very reasonable hand-knotted rugs and other second-hand items. The sort of things you might come across are bamboo occasional tables, a steel four-drawer card index cabinet, bedside cabinets, 'set of four honey oak church chairs with solid seats of angular form', 1940s oak tallboy, painted three-panel screens, an Eames chair with its footstool, Victorian glass lampshades, an old gramophone cabinet, log baskets, well buckets, a motley collection of 50s and 60s seating, studio pottery and huge station clocks.

Skips

Underneath the blue plastic that covers the best organised skips at night, you can often find surprising treasures such as fireplaces and floorboards. Keep your eye out for houses being demolished, ripped out or refurbished. There's often a skip outside. It's good practice to ask permission from the people demolishing whether they would mind. Any wood you find might have woodworm, so check carefully and if so, make sure it's treated. It's surprising

Skips can be, and often are, rich in useful items. They don't always appear very inviting but if you peer inside you will often find wood offcuts, or perfectly good furniture and other items.

what people will throw into skips, anything from useful boxes to usable bricks or old chairs. Many people think a Victorian chair is past its sell-by date, but if you can do a bit of joint glueing and upholstery or find someone to do the upholstery, you can find really comfortable and good-looking chairs with a bit of character.

LOOKING FOR ARCHITECTURAL SALVAGE IN EUROPE

Many European countries are now reclaiming and conserving their architectural salvage including Germany, Italy, Belgium and France. All these have interesting reclaimed building materials and furniture and are full of opportunities for those who want to obtain second-hand or reclaimed materials or who enjoy hunting through antique shops. There are various ways to find out where to go.

- Information on French architectural salvage yards can be obtained from www.salvo.co.uk.
- Trocs is a chain of shops selling French antique and reclaimed furniture and furnishings and are a particularly good place to look for plumbing parts and porcelain, doors and mantelpieces. For a list of outlets see www.troc.com.
- Emmaus has a number of second-hand furniture and household shops throughout France. Go to www.emmaus.com to find out where they are.

- German reclamation companies often have interesting doors and window frames. Remember that they will not conform to standard sizes in other countries, so may have to have special openings made for them.
- Belgian companies often have unusual garden items such as zinc containers and wooden buckets, as well as household objects.

USA

Architectural salvage

In the USA people are very aware of the need to save and reuse everything to do with the home, and architectural salvage is springing up in most states. Some specialise in twentieth-century things and what is sometimes called mid-century modern which includes designer furniture from Denmark, Europe and the USA such as Knoll, Sotssas, and Eames. Their websites may simply act as catalogues or you may be able to buy online. Some may have little histories of the buildings their salvage comes from. There is one that specialises in individual beams and other pieces from demolished barns. Some say they are actively purchasing salvage rights to buildings locally. Some not only reclaim but restore as well. Ohmega in California calls its offerings 'usual and unusual building materials' and these include all the usual categories like fireplaces, baths and architectural elements, as well as stained glass and windows, mailboxes, ornamental hardware and much more from around the world. Earthwise in Seattle works with three local non-profit organisations – Earthcorps, Historic Seattle and New World Villages. They concentrate mainly on items from the 1950s or earlier, and you can bid for things online through www.earthwise-salvage.com.

In Washington DC, the Brass Knob is now two separate companies; one specialising in smaller restored gas lighting mantels, stained glass and a variety of decorative items; the other in salvaged house parts (including elevators and fencing and ironwork) from local buildings. Many of the large fairs in the USA offer discount entry coupons if you ask for them.

Some outdoor annual or occasional yard and antique events

- Road lining yard sales: an annual event, known as the 127 Corridor Sale, takes up 654 miles through five states on either side of US Highway 127 and is made up of around 4,000 stallholders, ranging from home-owners to professional dealers or local schools or charities. The traffic is usually hectic and parking can be difficult, especially through the most heavily concentrated areas, but the route is beautiful and the merchandise can be fascinating. Other long yard sales can be found on Highway 11 from Mississippi to Virginia; Highway 411 from Alabama to Tennessee; Highway 80 from Texas to Mississippi; Highway 50 through Indiana; Highway 40 from Baltimore to St Louis; Highway 70 from Memphis to Nashville; the historic Route 66 in Oklahoma; and 200 miles of stalls along Lake Huron. You can find out more details from www.fleamarketjunction.net.
- The three-times-a-year Brimfield Antiques show in Massachusetts is said to be the largest outdoor antiques show in the world with over 6,000 dealers and 30,000 visitors over one week. It takes up twenty-three fields owned by 'promoters' who lease spaces to dealers from all over the world, usually around Memorial Day, the 4th of July and Labor Day. Among a vast range of goods it includes furniture and collectibles from the late eighteenth, nineteenth and twentieth centuries. Parking is a nightmare but there are day-trip buses

from New York and Boston. (Details from www.brimfieldshow.com or Quaboag Valley Chamber of Commerce: 413 283 6149.)

- Farmington Antiques Weekend takes place twice a year, in June and again on Labor Day weekend, at 152 Town Farm Road, Farmington, CT 06032. Here you will find garden ornaments, architectural items, rustic and antique furniture, and vintage table linens as well as smaller items. (www.farmingtonantiquesweekend.com)
- Long Beach Outdoor Antique and Collectible Market is an old-established flea market held on the third Sunday of every month in the Veterans Stadium with an enormous variety of goods from dolls to clothes but including Depression glass, dinnerware, bookcases and other furniture. (www.longbeachantiquemarket.com)
- Springfield Antique Show and Flea Market takes place three times a year in May, July and September at Clark County Fairgrounds, 4401 S. Charleston Pike, Springfield, OH 45502, where you may find fine period furniture, retro 50s rattan and Bakelite as well as paintings and folk art. (www.springfieldantiqueshow.com)

Depression glass

This is clear or coloured translucent glassware made and distributed in the USA during the Great Depression in the form of plates, cups and saucers and jugs in various colours. It was sold in five and dime stores and sometimes given away with a bag of sugar or flour, or a packet of Quaker Oats. Movie theaters and businesses might hand each visitor a piece of glass as a 'thank you' for their business. Over 100 patterns (complete dinner sets were made in some patterns) were made by over twenty manufacturers mainly in clear, pink, pale blue, green and amber but also in cobalt blue, red, black and white. Although not of particularly good quality, Depression glass has become highly collectible since the 1960s. Most of the manufacturers were based in the central and mid-west United States (for example in Ohio, West Virginia, Pennsylvania, Oklahoma) and that is where it is most likely to crop up in flea markets.

INTERNET

The amount and variety of reclaimed salvage you can buy through the Internet is truly astonishing. It's a good way to buy vintage fabrics, which are quick and cheap to send through the post and can be photographed easily. In fact, you can buy almost anything this way, from ten ceramic tiles or a cast-iron door knocker to an old-fashioned red letter box.

Internet auctions

The best known of these is eBay through which you can buy or sell almost anything. Sunday night is the most popular time for Internet auctions, especially for America. There are dozens of categories to choose from.

The auction site on eBay has hundreds of items on sale through private sellers with photographs and descriptions of the objects, and information on the seller. You can either make a bid and hope to make the highest or you might be able to take the 'Buy Now' option. The eBay site has many categories of which Architectural Antiques is a good one to start with. Here you may find locks, clocks, wardrobes, mirrors, beds, cabinets, chests, ceramic tiles and lots more. You can search by material, age or style.

Reclamation yards' own sites

The Internet is an excellent way to discover architectural salvage sources but it can also be a good way to buy reclaimed items, provided you don't mind not being able to examine and handle them in person. You need to be pretty sure an item is what it says it is and in reasonably good condition before committing to it, especially if it's heavy and returning it will be difficult and expensive. If you trust the buyer and know exactly what you are looking for, then it can be quick, easy and possibly a good way to find real bargains.

Edward Haes in Lancashire specialises in reclaiming and renovating furniture and fittings taken from old factories and mills, as well as from smaller properties and homes locally. His website includes light fittings, some wonderful old radiators, furniture, busts, notices and decorative cast-iron agricultural railings and gates. You can get to visit his yard, but only by appointment.

Vintage fabrics on the Internet

The Internet can be a good way of discovering interesting old fabrics. You can often find small offcuts of printed fabrics from the 1940s and 50s, vintage retro textiles from the 60s and 70s, Liberty, Sanderson and Laura Ashley fabrics, William Morris and Arts & Crafts designs, vintage cotton prints, and fabrics for patchwork and quilting.

Sanderson curtains from the 1940s can be good finds; Edwardian religious prints are fascinating; there are so many twentieth-century mending kits and sewing paraphernalia, it makes you wonder how much time was spent mending ladders in nylon stockings. There are offcuts of vintage table and bed linens, lace, embroideries or tiny scraps of vintage fabrics ready to turn into a patchwork or line a purse. Norfolk Textiles is an enterprising shop near Norwich selling vintage textiles including lace, embroidery, table linen and bed linen among a wealth of unusual oilcloths and lining materials.

Reclamation companies' own websites

Most architectural salvage companies now have their own websites which may be a fairly comprehensive catalogue of goods in stock at any one time and may also be a direct buying catalogue. With some of these you can choose an object you want and then get in touch with the company by e-mail or telephone. Others are sales sites in their own right, so you can order online what you want and pay through your credit card or Paypal. Many sites offering specific items automatically take you through to eBay or Amazon to complete your purchase.

Specific salvage centre websites can vary enormously. Many of them now have good, helpful photographs with detailed information, which helps when you don't want to spend an awfully long time trawling through dozens of possibilities and not finding what you want. Some local businesses, although they have websites don't always have the manpower to run them all day and you may wait some time for a reply to your e-mail. However, many are meticulous about replying, courteous and helpful, and may be able to source specific items for you.

Since you are not able to inspect and handle the product yourself, informative descriptions of the object you are interested in are important. Here is the description of an antique chintz fabric from Norfolk Textiles: 'This is a very beautiful fabric; also very old and never used. It was still on the wooden roll when I bought it. It is only 25.5 inches wide, as fabric used to be. Heavily glazed cotton and very crisp, it is a "Roses and Ribbons" design. The colours are very vivid. There are a few very faint marks, due to age, but they really barely notice. The pattern repeat is 40in. I will send this on a roll to prevent creasing. This is being sold by the metre length. There is a 5 metre length at present.' That's a description that tells you what you want to know.

Internet shopping tips
- Speak to the seller on a phone landline before arranging a meeting.
- Some experts advise not to pay by money transfer sites such as Paypal, which may be subject to fraudsters.
- Only buy items from sellers in your area.
- If possible, go and look at the items yourself.
- Find out whether the vendor will deliver, post or send the item or will you have to pick it up, as in 'buyer collects'?
- Find out before you buy, how much delivery will cost. Sometimes the cost of postage can double the amount you spend.
- Remember that if you bid successfully, you are legally bound to honour that agreement.
- eBay is not necessarily the cheapest online shopping site, so compare it with others before going for it to the exclusion of anything else.
- At Internet auctions, bid early in the morning and avoid auctions ending at popular times such as Sunday evenings.
- Don't give your credit or debit card details until you have ascertained that the company has a secure site by looking for the closed padlock sign at the bottom of the screen and look for information about the protection the company has put in place.
- Try to get personal recommendations for companies you have not done business with before. Or get help and advice from specialist organisations such as Trust UK which is endorsed by the UK government and enables consumers to buy online with a certain confidence. You can visit their website at www.trust.org.uk.
- Always print or save the order and keep any terms and conditions that appear on the website in case of any problems later on.

Selling on the Internet

Many people who used to have stalls in local flea markets now find it easier to sell entirely through the Internet, buying at antique fairs and markets rather than selling at them and putting individual items up for auction from the comfort of their own home. Many sellers are simply people with a passion for old things. It can be a way of making a little extra money to boost your pension when you retire. Being online has the advantage of a worldwide audience.

One example of an Internet seller is a retired English social worker who decided to set up an Internet business selling mainly tiles and door furniture through eBay. Small antiques had always been her hobby, so it was really an extension of a previous interest. She has a liking for minimalist, plain items and buys up Art Deco, Art Nouveau and Arts & Crafts ceramic tiles, door furniture and other small items for the home. She finds Deco tiles very popular at the moment, finding they appeal to young people, who find Victoriana too old-fashioned and fussy. She also sells photograph frames, book ends, fingerplates and door pulls.

These nineteenth-century Indian carved wooden columns with their pretty pastel colours could be the basis for a garden arbour. They were found on Edward Haes' Lancashire-based website.

Occasionally she also sells retro stuff from the 1950s and 60s. She finds that most of her sales are abroad, many to the USA.

Sellers must photograph each item and describe it succinctly (and truthfully). Victorian tiles are popular in the USA and selling on the Internet may involve posting items which are heavy and breakable. One seller explained: 'Before you go online you have to pack up the product so you know what the postage is going to be – it often doubles the price of an item. You may sell the tiles for £68 and it'll cost another £50 to post them. Apart from everything else, each object has to be carefully packed, especially if it is heavy and/or breakable such as a bundle of ceramic tiles.'

Internet tips for sellers
- Don't send items before receiving payment.
- Don't accept cheques as payment or part-payment.
- Don't provide personal/banking information to buyers.
- Be realistic in pricing. Find out the going price for other, similar items and price accordingly.
- Be prepared to bargain or accept an offer if it isn't too derisory.

Chapter Six

Information and Directory

GLOSSARY

Antique: an object collectible or desirable because of its age (usually considered to be over 100 years old), its rarity, craftsmanship and quality of materials.

Architrave: a decorated wooden strip that runs round a door, window or panel.

Baluster: one of the short pillars supporting the rail or stone coping round a balcony or terrace.

Bygones: in the reclamation world this usually means items are 'in the style' of something antique or reclaimed rather than being actually antique.

Came: a strip of lead, zinc or perhaps other metals made into channels to hold glass pieces in a pattern (e.g. in a stained glass window).

Ceramic: made of glazed pottery or china.

Chinoiserie: furniture, fabric or wallpaper inspired by Chinese design (often quite an eccentric Western view of what represents true Chinese design).

Collector's item: an object of great interest, value or rarity.

Console table: a narrow table designed to stand against a wall, particularly useful in narrow spaces or hallways.

Cornice: a decorative moulding strip, usually of wood or plaster, which runs round the wall of a room just below ceiling level.

Dado rail: a wooden rail fixed horizontally onto a wall, usually about two-thirds of the way down. The area below is usually panelled or given a different paint or wallpaper treatment to the area above.

Eclectic: a mingling of different styles and inspirations.

Escutcheon: an ornamental protective plate over a keyhole.

Fanlight: a window over a door; often semi-circular with radiating glazing bars.

Finial: an ornamental end to a post, curtain pole, etc.

Fire surround: the 'frame' round a grate, usually of wood, marble or stone.

Firebox: the small chamber in the grate where wood and/or coal are burned.

Focal point: an object or arrangement that attracts attention and becomes the main feature of a room or an area.

Galvanised: iron or steel coated with rust-resistant zinc; used for water tanks, troughs, buckets, baths, etc.

Gilding: application of gold leaf, gold paint or cream to a piece of furniture or frame.

Hi-tech (*see* industrial)

Industrial: describes something originally designed for commercial use (such as flooring, desking or structural systems) used in the home.

Kilim (or kelim): flat-woven (i.e. non-tufted) rug usually made in the Caucasus or the Middle East.

Lacquer: a hard varnish applied in many layers and polished into a high gloss.

Linenfold: wooden panelling carved to look like linen hanging in folds.

Mantel shelf or mantelpiece: a horizontal surface fixed immediately above the fireplace or as part of the fire surround.

Mouldings: decorative plaster or woodwork on cornices, arches and ceilings.

Newel post: the vertical post used to support the beginning and intermediate intervals of a staircase railing.

Overmantel: any architectural structure resting on top of the mantel.

Pavers: thin bricks used for flooring and paving.

Paviour: someone who lays pavers.

Provenance: the source of an item and the history of its ownership.

Quarry tiles: unglazed hard clay tiles, traditionally used on kitchen and passage floors.

Reclaimed: something salvaged and reused in its original form with minimal reprocessing. It may be cut to size, adapted, cleaned up or refinished but it is fundamentally in its original form.

Recycled: any materials taken from waste and reprocessed and remanufactured to form part of a new product.

Reproduction: something reproduced in faithfulness to the form, elements and workmanship of the original.

Retro: styles of the 1950s and 60s, sometimes including the 1970s and 80s or copies reminiscent of those eras.

Sconce: a bracket lamp fixed to the wall.

Shellac: resin secreted by female lac bug in India and Thailand. It is processed into dry flakes, dissolved in denatured alcohol to make liquid shellac, a tough high gloss varnish. In the 1800s it replaced wax finishes and became the dominant wood finish until the 1920s and 30s.

Skirting: a wooden strip running along the bottom of a wall, where it meets the floor.

Spindle: a short, narrow upright piece of wood or metal supporting the rail of a staircase.

Terraced house: one of several houses joined together in a row.

Trumeau: an extra sculpted stone chimney breast that sits over the mantel. It often has a mirror.

Vintage: rather loosely taken to mean an object that is fifty to 100 years old, often applied to an item made after 1900 and before 1980.

DIRECTORY

Always phone before visiting an architectural salvage outlet. They don't always keep 9 to 5 hours.

Bedfordshire

Emmaus Village Carlton (second-hand superstore: reclaimed and restored household goods, furniture, electrical goods, linen, china, books. All electrical goods are tested before being offered for sale)

School Lane
Carlton
MK43 7LQ
01234 720 826
www.emmaus.org.uk

Tomkinson's Stained Glass Windows (dealer in very special antique stained glass: the website is an education in itself with clear colourful images of glass that includes Victorian, Edwardian, French, religious, William Morris, Pre-Raphaelite and Art Nouveau designs. By appointment only)

2 Neville Road
Limbury
Luton
LU3 2JQ
01582 527 866
www.vitraux.co.uk

Berkshire

J. Brant Reclamation (reclamation yard: reclaimed traditional building materials including bricks, wood, doors, furniture, fireplaces, garden benches, stone gates, chimney pots, fountains and gardenalia, phone boxes, street signs, sundials)

Lakeside Garden Centre
Brimpton Common
RG7 4RT
01189 813 882
www.jbrant.co.uk

Garden Art Plus Ltd. (reclamation yard: wide range of interesting architectural antiques and reclamation materials including arbours, fountains, gates, marble, statuary, sundials, temples, troughs and surprises, also reproductions and items made out of reclaimed materials. Will source hard-to-find items)

Barr's Yard
1 Bath Road
Hungerford
RG17 OHE
01488 686 811
www.gardenartplus.com

Bristol

Au Temps Perdu (based in an old church: large and ever-changing collection of antiques and architectural salvage, from eighteenth-century marble fireplaces to Georgian fanlights and garden urns)

28–30 Midland Road
St. Philips
BS2 OJY
07816 934 483
www.autempsperdu.co.uk

Emmaus Bristol (second-hand superstore: reclaimed and restored household goods, furniture, electrical goods, linen, china, books. All electrical goods are tested before being offered for sale)

Barton Manor
Kingsland Road
BS2 0RL
01179 540 886
www.emmaus.org.uk

JAT Environmental Reclamation Ltd. (reclamation yard: reclaimed building materials, stone troughs, oak tubs, iron fencing and gates, chimney pots, Victorian paving)

Belluton
Pensford Hill
Pensford
BS39 4JF
01761 492 906
www.jatreclamation.co.uk

Olliff's Architectural Antiques (reclamation yard: reclaimed period antique items with no reproductions; stock includes antique bathroom sanitary ware, doorways and windows, fireplaces and chimneypieces, garden furniture, gates, railings, lampposts, ironwork, flooring, paving, roofing, architectural stonework, pub furniture)

St. Werburgs Road
St. Werburgs
BS2 9XZ
07850 235 793
www.olliffs.com

Rose Green Tiles & Reclamation Ltd. (reclamation yard: wide range of building and ornamental materials including building materials, cast-iron, fireplaces, chimney pots, flooring, garden features, landscaping, stained glass)

206 Rose Green Road
Fishponds
BS5 7UP
01179 520 109
www.rosegreenreclamation.co.uk

Buckinghamshire

IBS Reclaim (reclamation yard: new and reclaimed bricks, brick-matching service, reclaimed bricks engineered to requirements, garden furniture, roofing products, flooring, stones, cobbles, sets, angles and arches, border and slip bricks, bullnose capping and copings, plinths and stretcher and soldier bricks)

Thame Road
Oakley
HP18 9QQ
01844 239 400
www.ibsreclaim.co.uk

Olney Oriental Carpets (many rooms full of Persian carpets and Turkish kilims, some new and some old, in all shapes and sizes in a 400-year-old house with oak beams and winding staircases)

21 High Street South
Olney
MK46 4AA
01234 712 502
www.olneyrugs.co.uk

Recycled Business Furniture (used office furniture showroom: refurbished and new office furniture)

Unit 1
Pilot Trading Estate
High Wycombe
HP12 3AH
08456 442 612
www.recycledbusinessfurniture.co.uk

Cambridgeshire

Emmaus UK (second-hand emporium: reclaimed and restored household goods, furniture, electrical goods, linen, china, books. All electrical goods are tested before being offered for sale)

Green End
Landbeach
Cambridge
CB25 9FD
01223 863 657
www.emmaus.org.uk

The Hive (antique centre: amazing range of antiques and collectibles from crystal chandeliers from 1920 to Persian rugs, ceramic tiles, china, cutlery and pictures)

Gwydir Street
Cambridge
CB1 2LJ
01223 300 269
www.hiveantiques.co.uk

J. & S.J. Popple Reclaims (suppliers of recycled bricks, tiles, timber and various other recycled building materials such as re-sawn floorboards, slates, beams and other architectural salvage; minimalist website)

58 Coronation Avenue
Whittlesey
PE7 1XE
01733 203 860
www.johnpopple.plus.com

Cheshire

Cheshire Demolition and Excavation Contractors Ltd. (architectural antiques: reclaimed building materials and traditional fireplaces, cast-iron gates and railings, street and garden furniture including red phone boxes, gateposts and tops, reclaimed doors)

72 Moss Lane
Macclesfield
SK11 7TT
01625 424 433
www.cheshiredemolition.co.uk

English Garden Antiques (unusual garden and architectural antiques such as benches, seats and furniture, multi-tiered fountains and smaller lion-head wall fountains, birdbaths, garden lamps, urns, staddle stones, sundials, millstones, planters, stone troughs and metalwork)

The White Cottage
Church Brow
Bowdon
WA14 2SF
01619 280 854
www.english-garden-antiques.co.uk

Great Northern Architectural Antiques (GNAA) (reclamation yard: 40,000 sq ft of indoor and outdoor upmarket architectural salvage from the UK, Europe, America and China including gazebos, gargoyles, fountains, follies, beams, balustrades, baths, beds, door handles, window furniture, Gothic stonework, militaria, railway memorabilia, cigarette cards, juke-boxes, sporting equipment, church items, pub/shop fittings, lighting, ecclesiastical stained glass)

New Russia Hall
Chester Road
Tattenhall
CH3 9AH
01829 770 796
www.gnaa.co.uk

Nostalgia (reclaimed fireplaces: from Tudor to Edwardian including wood, marble, stone, slate, and cast-iron and antique fireplace accessories)

Hollands Mill
61B Shaw Heath
Stockport
SK3 8BH
01614 777 706
www.nostalgia-uk.com

Cleveland

Teesside Architectural Salvage (reclamation yard: all categories of architectural salvage)

18 Rookwood Road
Nunthorpe
Middlesbrough
TS7 0BN
01642 310454
By appointment only
www.teessidearchitecturalsalvage.co.uk

Cornwall

Stax Reclamation Ltd. (reclamation yard: timber, building materials and architectural salvage including granite, cast-iron radiators, chimney pots, urns, planters and troughs, a large selection of stained glass, wood window frames, all styles and ages of bathroom ware)

Avery Way
Saltash Industrial Estate
Saltash
PL12 6LD
01752 849111
www.staxreclamation.com

Cumbria

Old English Timbers (reclaimed flooring: wide range of pine, oak, pitchpine, Oregon pine, hardwoods and beams from derelict buildings such as old churches, schools, hospitals and Victorian mills, used mainly for wood floors, feature beams and oak beams; also new oak wide boards)

Ingswood Cottage
Sandholme
Brough
HU15 2XS
01430 449 996
www.reclaimedfloorboardsuk.co.uk

Semley Reclamation (reclamation yard: reclaimed bricks, tiles, stone, timber, doors, indoor and outdoor furniture, cabinets, drawers and dressers, fireplaces and surrounds, church furniture, beds, oak settles, pews, enamelled advertising signs; there is a workshop that can make furniture to order from reclaimed wood)

Unit 2
Shunters Yard
Station Road
Semley
Nr. Shaftesbury
SP7 9AH
01747 850 350
www.semleyreclamation.com

East Sussex

Best Demolition Ltd. (reclamation yard: reclaimed bricks, stone, roofing materials, fireplaces, stoves and accessories, lighting, iron gates, terracotta roof finials. 'We always take pains to salvage every little thing down to door and window furniture and always have a cupboardful!')

Harcourt Lodge Buildings
Burwash Road
Heathfield
TN21 8RA
01435 862 381/ 866 170
www.bestdemolition.co.uk

Emmaus Brighton and Hove (second-hand emporium: furniture, including beds, wardrobes, sofas, tables and chairs, table lamps, mirrors, paintings, kitchenware, books, fridges and freezers, washing machines, records, clothes, bric-a-brac. All electrical goods are tested before being offered for sale)

Drove Road
Portslade
Brighton
BN41 2PA
www.emmausbrighton.co.uk

Original Oak Ltd. (reclamation yard: oak flooring from period buildings, handmade terracotta tiles, reclaimed Georgian and Victorian pine flooring, oak beams, doors, also new beech, elm, ash and sycamore flooring)

Ashlands
Burwash
TN19 7HS
01435 882 228

Tiger Enterprise Ltd. (surplus building materials yard: from new build and demolition, includes doors, bricks, paving slabs, roof and floor tiles, loft insulation, sanitary ware, concrete blocks)

The Old Gas Works
50 Marina Way
Black Rock
Brighton
BN2 5TR
01273 698 689
www.reuseitdontloseit.co.uk

Traditional Oak and Timber Company (reclamation yard: reclaimed wood including oak beams, re-sawn random width oak floorboards, reclaimed oak doors, also air-dried oak; new handmade ironmongery)

The Old Post Office
Haywards Heath Road
North Chailey
Nr. Lewes
BN8 4EY
01825 723 648
www.traditionaloakandtimbercompany.co.uk

Essex

Anglia Building Suppliers Ltd. (reclamation yard: reclaimed railway sleepers, bricks, paving, roof tiles, lampposts, fireplaces, doors, cast-iron products, church items, gardenalia. Also on site **D.W. Parsons**: fireplace restoration, construction and installation including stoves, linings, gasworks and heating)

Waltham Road
Boreham
Chelmsford
CM3 3AY
01245 467 505
www.angliabuildingsuppliersltd.co.uk

Antiques by Design Ltd. (reclamation yard: wide variety of interesting reclaimed items from England and France, e.g. nineteenth- and twentieth-century furniture, farmhouse furniture and chandeliers; inventive ways of turning reclaimed items into usable domestic objects, e.g. mirrors from tennis rackets, old Citroen grilles, snooker tables, French windows and Norwich Gaol; table and standard lamps from fire buckets, gallon cans, French cavalry boots and oars)

Little Grange Farm
Woodham Mortimer
Nr. Maldon
CM9 6TL
01245 222 771
www.antiquesbydesign.co.uk

Ashwell Recycled Timber Products
(reclamation yard: specialises in tropical hardwoods salvaged from landfill sites, demolition jobs, lock gates and tree felling; hardwood and softwood railway sleepers treated and untreated; crossing timbers, telegraph poles, tree trunks and large construction timbers. Can construct planters, steps and retaining walls, bollards, seating, log benches and signage)

Wick Place Farm
Brentwood Road
Bulphan
RM14 3TL
01375 892 576
www.ashwellrecycling.com

Blackheath Demolition & Trading
(reclamation yard: wide range of reclaimed items in a Victorian granary including bricks, slate, paving, flooring, doors, windows, timber, sanitary ware, fireplaces and accessories, furniture, gardenalia, stained glass and unusual items)

26C Hythe Quay
Colchester
CO2 8JB
01206 794 100
www.blackheathdemolitionandtrading.co.uk

Emmaus Colchester (second-hand emporium: reclaimed and restored household goods, furniture, electrical goods, linen, china, books. All electrical goods are tested before being offered for sale)

Shop: 175 Magdalen Street
Colchester
CO1 2JX
Warehouse: 4 Arthur Street
Colchester
CO1 TTH
01206 768 887
www.emmaus.org.uk

Maltings Reclamation (reclamation yard: reclaimed solid pine doors, stained glass, woodblock floors, Georgian and Victorian floorboards, antique oak, maple strip, reclaimed bricks, spiral staircases, pub memorabilia, lighting, chairs, tables, reclaimed radiators in many styles, fireplaces, chimney pots, gates and railings, railway sleepers, roll-top baths)

Bush House
294 Ongar Road
Writtle
CM1 3NZ
07703 206 161
www.architecturalreclaim.com

Reclaimed Ltd. (reclamation yard: 'proud to be part of the recycling business'; reclaimed industrial joists, rustic timbers and antique structural beams transformed into floorboards and joinery; various grades and dimensions available)

Sewardstone Hall Farm
Sewardstone Road
Chingford
E4 7RH
02085 298 504
www.reclaimed.uk.com

Victorian Woodworks Ltd. (reclamation yard: timber flooring, old oak, pitchpine, planks, tongue-and-groove, wood strip, woodblock, wide floorboards; floors installed, restored, renovated)

Redhouse
Lower Dunton Road
Bulphan
Upminster
RM14 3TD
020 8534 1000
Visit by appointment
www.victorianwoodworks.co.uk

Gloucestershire

ATC Floors & Doors (reclamation yard: reclaimed new and engineered timbers, hardwood and softwood flooring, internal and external doors, skirting, architrave, door liners and door furniture; also a fitting, finishing and restoration service. Also have a branch in Wales)

26 Andover Road
Tivoli
GL50 2TJ
01242 220 536
www.atcfloorsanddoors.co.uk

Cotswold Reclamation Company Ltd. (reclamation yard: reclaimed building materials and garden products)

Unit 2
Sandy Lane Court
Little Rissington
GL54 2NF
01451 820 292
www.cotswoldreclamation.com

Cox's Architectural Salvage (reclamation yard: over 12,000 sq ft of covered warehouse and half an acre of outside yard with large and varied stock of reclaimed building materials and architectural antiques including panelling, pub fixtures, staircases, church furniture, Belfast sinks, fireplaces, ironwork and windows; online shopping available)

10 Fosseway Business Park
Moreton in Marsh
GL56 9NQ
01608 652 505
www.coxsarchitectural.co.uk

Emmaus Gloucestershire (second-hand superstore: reclaimed and restored household goods, furniture, electrical goods, linen, china, books. All electrical goods are tested before being offered for sale)

11 Henrietta Street
Cheltenham
GL50 4AA
01452 413 095
www.emmaus.org.uk

Emmaus Nailsworth Shop (second-hand emporium: reclaimed and restored household goods, furniture, electrical goods, linen, china, books. All electrical goods are tested before being offered for sale)

The Old Coop
Market Street
Nailsworth
GL6 OBX
01453 835 036
www.emmaus.org.uk

Minchinhampton Architectural Salvage Company (MASCo) (reclamation yard: specialist dismantlers founded in 1983 by Steve Tomlin and Debbie Kedge. Large stocks of reclaimed building materials, including Cotswold stone, unusual Georgian and Victorian garden memorabilia, animalia, massive stone features, contemporary sculpture, Coalbrookdale three-tier cast-iron fountains. Proud to 'encourage sustainability through reclamation')

Cirencester Road
Aston Down
Stroud
GL6 8PE
01285 760 886
www.mascosalvage.com

Original Architectural Antiques Company
(reclamation yard: fireplaces, doors and gates,
garden benches, statues, fountains, sundials –
old, reproduction and new. Sell three types of
oak beams, reclaimed, air-dried and fireplace;
finishing service includes power-washing,
cleaning, de-nailing standard on reclaimed
beams; have variety of tinted wax polishes, light
oil finish or traditional whitened and blackened
look)

Ermin Farm
Cricklade Road
Cirencester
GL7 5PN
01285 869 222
www.originaluk.com; www.oakbeamuk.com

Ronson Reclaim (reclamation yard: five-acre
site, once a brickworks, on the banks of the
River Severn; the original kiln chimney still
stands in the middle of the yard. Wide selection
of traditional reclaimed building materials and
architectural features including flagstones and
paving, bricks, roofing materials, building stone,
timber, fireplaces and architectural features
including some from the Bank of England and
Oxford University)

Sandhurst Quay
Upper Parting
Sandhurst Lane
GL2 9NG
01452 387 890
www.ronsonreclaim.com

Trainspotters (industrial reclamation yard:
selective twentieth-century industrial salvage,
including apple boxes, movie posters, and items
such as ceiling lighting from Eastern European
factories. Source good runs and quantities of
items useful for larger-scale commercial
projects such as pubs, shops and restaurants)

Unit 1
The Warehouse
Libby's Drive
Stroud
GL5 1RN
01453 756 677
www.trainspotters.uk.com

Winchcombe Reclamation (reclamation yard:
reclaimed building materials such as half round
coping, bricks, roofing materials, timber,
paving, Cotswold stone, chimney pots, finials,
furniture, external doors, drainage materials,
gates and railings, huge pots, hearth-stones,
outdoor furniture, stained glass, sinks,
decorative ventilation panels, troughs; also
custom-make summerhouses from reclaimed
and new materials)

Broadway Road
Winchcombe
GL54 5NT
01242 609 564
www.winchcombereclamation.co.uk

Greater Manchester

Capital Group UK (reclamation yard: reclaimed
bricks)

Victoria Mills
Highfield Road
Little Hulton
M38 9ST
01617 997 555
www.reclaimedbricks.com

Carnall Fairs (fairs organiser: bric-a-brac and
antiques fairs – up to 120 stalls)

The George H. Carnall Leisure Centre
Davyhulme
M41 7FJ
01617 492 555
Info from www.antiques-atlas.com

Emmaus Mossley (second-hand emporium:
two large floors packed with reclaimed and
restored furniture, household goods, electrical
appliances and bikes. All electrical goods are
tested before being offered for sale)

Longlands Mill
Queen Street
Mossley
OL5 9AH
01457 838 608
www.emmausmossley.org.uk

In Situ (reclamation yard: 2,500 sq ft on two floors – with another building for large items 50m down the road – all types of architectural salvage 'for kitting out old houses, modern warehouses, shops, clubs, bars, restaurant interiors with soul and personality'. Huge range of every imaginable interior fitting and type of furniture including ecclesiastical objects; also reproductions and contemporary items)

252 Chester Road
Hulme
M15 4EX
01618 395 525
www.insitumanchester.com

Wisdom Fireplaces (reclaimed fireplace warehouse: specialises in antique and reclaimed cast-iron fireplaces from the Victorian, Georgian, Edwardian, Arts and Crafts and Art Nouveau periods; also reproduction and contemporary designs)

Unit 4 Haniwells Business Park
Hardicker Street
Off Stockport Road
Levenshulme
M19 2RB
01614 428 259
www.wisdomfirelaces.co.uk

Hampshire

A&A Oriental Antique Rug Warehouse (carpet warehouse: old and new rugs from all over the world. All old and antique pieces are cleaned, restored and photographed)

Unit 7
Abbey Enterprise Centre
Abbey Park Industrial Estate Premier Way
Romsey
SO51 9DF
01794 511 988
www.antiqueorientalcarpets.co.uk

Arc Reclamation Ltd. (reclamation yard: fires and surrounds, many doors, door furniture, furniture, stained glass, garden furniture; workshop, joinery and restoration service)

Unit 1
Upper Downgate Farm
Sandy Lane
Steep March
Petersfield
GU32 2BG
01730 231 995
www.arcrec.com

Emmaus Hampshire (second-hand emporium: reclaimed and restored household goods, furniture, electrical goods, linen, china, books. All electrical goods are tested before being offered for sale)

Bar End Road
Winchester
SO23 9BN
01962 868 300
www.emmaushampshire.org.uk

Ian Parmiter Architectural Antiques (reclamation yard: original architectural antiques, old building materials, little old cabinets, rococo mirrors, advertising signs, doors, furniture, large stock of new and old chandeliers, original and reproduction fireplaces, statuary)

2 Exmouth Road
Southsea
PO5 2QL
02392 293 040
www.ianparmiter.co.uk

Jardinique (reclamation yard: garden reclamation and antiques, architectural antiques going back to the seventeenth century such as sculpture, sundials, urns, troughs, planters, plant stands, ornaments, figures, animals, fountains, birdbaths, hand tools and other gardenalia; also contemporary items chosen for their high quality)

Old Park Farm
Abbey Road
Beech
Alton
GU34 4AP
01420 560 055
www.jardinique.co.uk

Romsey Reclamation Ltd. (reclamation yard: a former sandpit with an enormous selection of reclaimed building materials surrounded by fourteen acres of natural countryside, ecologically sound and full of wildlife)

Station Approach
Romsey Railway Station
SO51 8DU
01794 524 174
www.romseyreclamation.com

Herefordshire

Baileys Home and Garden (reclamation yard: farm complex of reclaimed and created items from various sources which fit in with the company's philosophy of 'repair, re-use, re-think'. In the threshing barn and cowshed are old things, such as furniture, lighting, baskets, boxes, kitchen utensils and china; in the tack room and stable, industrial and other lighting; in the cart shed, industrial furniture. In the workshop they turn 'unloved bits and pieces and recycle them into something useable' (e.g. old textile bobbins into egg-timers or lamp bases, scraps of floorboard as mirror frames or tables))

Whitecross Farm
Bridstow
HR9 6JU
01989 561 931
www.baileyshomeandgarden.com

Leominster Reclamation (reclamation yard with stonework and paving, fireplaces, windows and glass, gates, railing and finials, hardware, bathroom, flooring, timber, shop and pub fittings, doors, radiators, lighting)

North Road
Leominster
HR6 OAB
01568 616 205
www.leorec.co.uk

Hertfordshire

Architectural Salvage Source (demolition company and salvage yard: all types of reclaimed building materials, period doors, panelling, entrance gates, staircases, flooring, stone, railings, fireplaces, cast-iron radiators, industrial items such as metal lockers; matching and valuation service)

Willows Farm Village
Coursers Road
London Colney
St. Albans
AL4 0PF
07960 351 141
www.archsource.co.uk

Emmaus St. Albans (second-hand superstore: reclaimed and restored household goods, furniture, electrical goods, linen, china, books. All electrical goods are tested before being offered for sale)

Unit A
Lee Industrial Estate
Lower Luton Road
Batford
Harpenden
AL5 5EQ
01272 817 297
www.emmaus.org.uk

Heritage Reclamation: (specialises in reclaimed timber from antique oak beams to French oak; also building materials, staircases, radiators, fireplaces, period doors, iron railings, gates and troughs)

14 Wood Lane
Paradise Industrial Estate
Hemel Hempstead
HP2 4TL
01442 219 936
www.heritagereclamation.co.uk

Herts Architectural Reclamation and Salvage (reclamation yard: reclaimed bricks, tiles, slates and stone, doors, fireplaces)

1A Shenley Lane
London Colney
St. Albans
AL2 1NG
01727 824 111
www.herts-architectural.co.uk

A Touch of Class (second-hand garden emporium: three acres and two barns of mostly house-clearance; folding French café chairs, shutters, metal troughs; miscellaneous reclaimed items, e.g. long narrow orange-painted tables-and-benches from the Munich Beer Festival and Olympic Games; will do wood stripping and French polishing)

Orchard View
Bulstrode Farm
Bulstrode Lane
Chipperfield
WD4 9LG
01442 833 808

V&V Reclamation (reclamation yard based in Edward Pearce's Heritage Tree Nursery: stone slabs, wrought and cast-iron gates and railings, cast-iron baths, keystones, black and white marble benches, bricks, flagstones, floor tiles, range of outdoor seating and tables, benches, water features, telephone boxes)

Tree Heritage
North Road
Hertford
SG14 2PW
01992 550 941
www.vandv.co.uk

Kent

The Architectural Stores (reclamation yard: a good variety of restored and usable reclaimed fireplaces and accessories, also radiators, Victorian and Arts & Crafts lights, wrought iron, leaded glass, staddle stones, lion masks, bell pulls and miscellania)

55 St. John's Road
Tunbridge Wells
TN4 9TP
01892 540 368
www.architecturalstores.com

Architectural Treasures and **The Old Radiator Company** (reclamation yard: specialising in reclaimed fireplaces as well as doors and door furniture, also etched and stained glass, architectural ironwork, stone troughs; also over 3,000 reclaimed cast-iron radiators and restoration workshop)

Hallmark Farm
Ashford Road
St. Michaels
TN30 6SP
01233 850 082
www.architecturaltreasures.co.uk
www.theoldradiatorcompany.co.uk

Artisan Oak (reclamation yard: specialises in reclaimed oak including complete frames for barns; can make stairs, skirting, window boards, flooring, doors from reclaimed oak; also stock air-dried and green oak)

Canterbury Road
Molash
CT4 8HN
01233 740 120
www.artisanoak.co.uk

Bygones Architectural Reclamation (Canterbury) Ltd. (reclamation and reproductions yard: vast site with many reproduction, 'authentic style' and distressed items but in the 'bygones yard' are reclaimed fountains, period lighting, radiators, butler sinks, reclaimed railway sleepers, stone and bricks, street signs, lampposts, furniture, roof finials and chimneys, postboxes)

Nackington Road
Canterbury
CT4 7BA
01227 767 453
www.bygones.net

Catchpole & Rye (cast-iron foundry and sanitary ware reclamation yard: range of antique baths and reproduction sanitary ware using old designs and methods)

Saracen's Dairy
Jobbs Lane
Pluckley
TN27 0SA
01233 840 840
www.crye.co.uk

T. Caudwell (reclamation yard: reclaimed building materials, wide variety of bricks including yellow stock bricks produced at Smead Dean Brickworks in the early 1900s, many kinds of reclaimed tiles including concrete, handmade and machine-made, reclaimed stones including York stone, reclaimed slates including Welsh Blue; also a brick-matching service)

The Yard
Yew Tree Cottage
Heath Road
East Farleigh
Maidstone
ME15 0LR
01622 746 225
www.reclaimedbricksandtiles.com

Cottage Style Antiques (second-hand emporium: posh junk shop with lots of fascinating items from other eras including mangles, water pumps, chimney pots, blacksmith's bellows, original cast-iron fireplaces, stained glass, stoves, spirit stoves, foot scrapers, tableware and objects, copper pans, mirrors and lots more)

24 Bill Street Road
Frindsbury
Rochester
ME2 4RB
01634 717 623

DDS Demolition (reclamation yard: building materials, church pews, glass, fireplaces, mirrors, cast-iron railings and hopper heads, corbel stones, library bookcases, pine staircases)

71 Monkton Street
Monkton
CT12 4JF
01843 821 555
www.reclamation-yard.co.uk

Detling Antiques Fair (international fair: held six times a year with English and Continental stallholders selling furniture, ceramics, gardenalia and miscellaneous goods)

Kent County Centre
Detling
Nr. Maidstone
ME14 3JF
Info from: DMG Fairs
PO Box 100
Newark
NG24 1DJ
01636 702 326
www.dmgantiquefairs.com

Emmaus St Martins (second-hand emporium: reclaimed and restored household goods, furniture, electrical goods, linen, china, books. All electrical goods are tested before being offered for sale)

Archcliffe Fort
Archcliffe Road
Dover
CT17 9EL
01304 204 550
www.emmaus.org.uk

Esprit du Jardin (reclamation company, garden antiques: hundreds of antiques spread throughout the owners' Georgian home and shop, including statuary, bestiary, pots, urns, containers, fountains, birdbaths and ironwork)

Waterlock House
Canterbury Road
CT3 1BH
01227 722 151
www.espritdujardin.com

Symonds Salvage Ltd. (reclamation yard: large selection of reclaimed bricks, tiles, stone, slates; hundreds of second-hand doors, antique door furniture, windows including stained and etched glass; you might find stone troughs, postboxes, a hop press; the workshop makes pine and oak furniture, kitchens and doors from reclaimed timber)

Colts Yard
Pluckley Road
Bethersden
TN26 3DD
01223 820 724
www.symondssalvage.co.uk

Lancashire

Emmaus Bolton (second-hand emporium: reclaimed and restored household goods, furniture, electrical goods. All electrical goods are tested before being offered for sale)

Derby Barracks
Fletcher Street
Bolton
BL3 6NF
01204 398 056
www.emmaus.org.uk

Pine Supplies (reclamation yard: specialises in all sorts of pine and reclaimed flooring in various widths)

Lower Tongs Farm
Longshaw Ford Road
Smithills
Bolton
BL1 7PP
01204 841 416
www.pine-supplies.co.uk

Ribble Reclamation (reclamation yard: started as a small landscaping company; now has large stocks of reclaimed materials for home and garden including bricks, slates, flagstones, heads and sills, ironmongery, doors, fireplaces, oak beams, radiators, new and old flooring materials, period baths and garden ornaments)

The Brick House
Ducie Place
Preston
PR1 4UJ
01772 794 534
www.ribble-reclamation.co.uk

Riverside Reclamation Ltd. (stone reclamation yard: lots of reclaimed stone paving, cobbles, setts, bricks and assorted products, cleaned and palletised on site)

Raikes Clough Industrial Estate
Raikes Lane
Bolton
BL3 1RP
01204 533 141
www.riverside-reclamation.com

Steptoe's Yard (reclamation yard: started as a demolition company 'but soon realised that too much valuable and recyclable material was being needlessly discarded' so set up their architectural reclamation yard to prevent good materials being thrown away; specialists in reclaimed stone, timber, cobbles and setts, flooring of all types, doors, cast-iron radiators, Belfast sinks, church pews, steel street lampposts, cast-iron columns, chimney pots, railway sleepers)

Moorfield Industrial Estate
Moorfield Way
Altham
Accrington
BB5 5TX
01254 233 227
www.steptoesyard.co.uk

Leicestershire

Agricultural Barn Conversions (reclamation yard: variety of architectural salvage from all round the Midlands including Georgian and Victorian handmade bricks, cobbles and paving setts, old slates and tiles, reclaimed chimney pots; period bathroom and sanitary ware, reclaimed doorknobs, period fittings and fixtures, hinges, light fittings, taps and ornaments)

Heritage Farm
Sutton Lane
Cadeby
CV13 0AR
01455 290 210
www.abc-reclaims.co.uk

Britain's Heritage Ltd. (reclamation yard: large selection of fully restored antique fireplaces, kitchen ranges, and antique stoves including 1930s and Art Deco shown in four rooms – also a range of reproduction fireplaces)

Shaftesbury Hall
3 Holy Bones
Leicester
LE1 4LJ
01162 519 592
www.britainsheritage.co.uk

Lincolnshire

Lighthouse Emporium (reclamation yard: architectural and garden salvage; good selection of highly decorative solid fuel and paraffin stoves, range of Tiffany-style lighting and other items)

Mill Bank
Fleet Fen
Holbeach
PE12 8QW
07889 050 470

Lincolnshire Antiques & Home Show (large fair held six times a year with 300 stalls selling Lincolnshire antique and collectible furniture, pictures, miscellaneous home and general items)

Lincolnshire Events Centre
Lincolnshire Showground
Grange-de-Lings
LN2 2NA
Information: 01298 27493
www.arthurswallowfairs.co.uk

R & R Reclamation (reclamation yard: huge range of reclaimed and recovered architectural features, beams and timbers, household items and other curious and interesting pieces including sinks, stained glass, parquet, basins, fireplaces, doors, sash windows, chimney pots, troughs, steps, gates, furniture, pub signs, industrial memorabilia, dog carts)

Bluebell Farm
Laughton Road
Blyton
Gainsborough
DN21 3LQ
01427 628 753
www.rr-reclamation.co.uk

London

Andrews Office Furniture (new and used office furniture store: good quality desks, seating, screens, bookcases and cupboards, filing cabinets, lockers, sofas, storage, work stations; seven branches in London; online catalogue – look under 'Quality used office furniture')

Showrooms in Camden, Fulham, Hackney, Romford and Walthamstow
0800 413 704
www.andrewsofficefurniture.com

Antique Oak Flooring Company (beautiful, large samples of antique oak, and other woods, Victorian pine, reclaimed strip, reclaimed parquet, boards reclaimed from the Bank of England, showing woods with different finishes such as oiled, clear wax or lacquer; although specialising in floorboards, you might also find the odd surprise such as pine pew seats or ex-laboratory worktops; informative website)

Sewardson Hall Farm
E4 7RH
02085 017 555
www.antiqueoakflooring.com

Architectural Forum (high street showroom: more space downstairs and at the back with reclaimed and refurbished fireplaces, radiators, doors, architectural items and flooring)

312–314 Essex Road
Islington
NW1 3AX
0207 704 0982
www.thearchitecturalforum.com

Architectural Reclaim Centre (reclamation yard: solid pine doors, stained glass, woodblock parquet, Victorian and Georgian floorboards, cobblestones, reclaimed bricks, slates and tiles, chairs and tables, many styles of reclaimed radiators, fireplaces, chimney pots, gates and railings, railway sleepers, roll-top baths)

83a Stamford Hill
N16 5TP
0208 809 7509
www.architecturalreclaim.com

Caravan (stylish shop: new and old household artefacts and reclaimed furniture and fabrics displayed with imagination and a sense of fun)

3 Redchurch Street
Shoreditch
E2 7DJ
0207 033 3532
www.caravanstyle.com

Cobbled Yard (second-hand emporium with a second warehouse opposite: wide variety of domestic and commercial furniture and artefacts for the home including sofas, chairs, mirrors, old railway train seating, wardrobes, chairs from an ice cream parlour and much more)

1 Bouverie Road
Stoke Newington
N16 OAH
0208 809 5286 or 0208 442 3322
www.cobbled-yard.co.uk

Criterion Auctioneers of London (auction house: auctions include a good choice of second-hand rather than antique furniture)

53 Essex Road
Islington
N1 2SF
0207 359 5707
AND
41–47 Chatfield Road
SW11 3SE
0207 228 5563
www.criterionauctions.co.uk
Auctions every Monday 5pm

Drummonds (architectural antiques showroom: 70,000 sq ft of reclaimed wood flooring, fireplaces, cast-iron radiators, doors and windows, antique door furniture, staircases, floor and wall tiles, antique furniture, antique lighting, antique bathroom ware, garden antiques, gates and railings)

78 Royal Hospital Road
Chelsea
SW3 4HN
0207 376 4499
www.drummonds-arch.co.uk

Emmaus Greenwich, The Second Hand (second-hand emporium: restored furniture, china, glass, electrical appliances, books and other household items sold to help support the Emmaus Community in Greenwich. All electrical goods are tested before being offered for sale)

322 Lee High Road
SE13 5PJ
0208 852 5365
www.emmausgreenwich.org

Emmaus South Lambeth (second-hand emporium: reclaimed and restored household goods, furniture, electrical goods, linen, china, books. All electrical goods are tested before being offered for sale)

9 Knight's Hill
West Norwood
SE27 0HU
0208 761 4276
www.emmaus.org.uk

First Fruit Furniture Warehouse (recycled office furniture warehouse: charity set up in partnership with Green-Works to train and support unemployed or homeless people in which upmarket second-hand office furniture is donated by corporate businesses and stored, recycled and re-sold)

Unit 14
Kierbeck Business Complex
North Woolwich Road
E16 2BG
0207 476 4555
www.firstfruitwarehousing.org

Highgate Antiques (reclamation yard; fireplaces, stained glass, urns, fountains, statues, cast-iron, marble floorings, York stone, antique furniture)

96A Highgate Road
NW5 1PB
07532 197 651

The Junk Shop (Second-hand shop: huge selection of second-hand and interesting items from pictures, prints, porcelain, glass, brass and metalware, toys, kitchenalia, taxidermy and clocks, to wood panelling, standard lamp bases and old books)

9 Greenwich South Street
Greenwich
SE10 8NW
0208 305 1666

Kasra Carpets (oriental carpet shop: second-hand carpets and rugs)

99 Highgate Road
NW5 1TR
0207 424 0318

Keith Roughton (restored second-hand oak furniture 1840s to 1980s – tables, chairs, wardrobes, pianos)

89 The Stable
Chalk Farm Road
Camden
NW1 8AH
0207 482 1498

Lazdan (reclaimed builder's materials: large supply of London stock bricks; various qualities and prices)

218 Bow Common Lane
E3 4HH
0208 980 2213 or 0208 981 4632

London Reclaim Brick Merchants (reclamation yard: over a million bricks in over thirty-five brick types, professional brick-matching service)

Coombe Works
Coombe Road
Neasden
NW10 OEB
0208 452 1111
www.lrbm.com

Nassir Carpets (oriental carpet shop: second-hand carpets and rugs)

28A Highgate Road
NW5 1NS
0207 482 1200

Nicholas Gifford-Mead (restored furniture showroom: specialises in architecturally interesting fireplaces and chimneypieces sourced from Europe and the UK. The stock is 'original or sympathetically restored to realise its true form')

68 Pimlico Road
SW1W 8LS
0207 730 6233
www.nicholasgiffordmead.co.uk

Orientalist (oriental carpet shop: second-hand carpets and rugs)

74–80 Highgate Road
NW5 1PB
0207 482 0555

Paul's Emporium (second-hand emporium: small corner shop with a wealth of interesting, useful and reasonably priced items for the home, ranging from chests of drawers, desks, hall tables and wooden school cupboards to picture frames, pieces of china and 'objects')

386 York Way
N7 9LW
0207 607 3000

Retrouvius (reclamation and design company: showroom and warehouse with two floors of tables, chairs, panelling, tiles, slate and lighting, carefully chosen and often unusual; design service available)

2A Ravensworth Road
Kensal Green
NW10 5NR
0208 960 6060
www.retrouvius.com

Seneh Carpet (oriental carpet shop: second-hand carpets and rugs)
90 Highgate Road
NW5 1PB
0207 482 1632

W. Sitch & Co. (reclaimed lighting showroom: five floors of a nineteenth-century town house crammed with every kind of light fitting, both antique and reproduction. The company has been restoring and rewiring antique metal light fittings since 1776)

48 Berwick Street
W1F 8JD
0207 437 3776
www.wsitch.co.uk

Stoneage Salvage and Reclamation (reclamation yard: variety of reclaimed vintage and reproduction items including doors, bricks, flagstones, gates, lampposts, radiators, flooring, sanitary ware, shutters, stained glass, staircases)

Kings Oak Nursery
Tingeys Top Lane
Enfield
EN2 9BJ
0208 362 1666
www.stoneagearchitectural.com

West 7 Reclamation (reclamation yard: all types of second-hand building materials including old timber, doors and floorboards, structural steel, fireplaces and other architectural antiques)

4 Trumpers Way
Hanwell
W7 2QA
0208 567 6696
www.west7reclamation.co.uk

Westland London (reclamation showroom:
based in the former church of St. Michael's, a
Grade I listed building and worth a visit in its
own right; immense variety of antique fireplace
mantels, architectural elements and
ornamentation, beautifully restored and
displayed)

St. Michael's Church
Leonard Street
London
EC2A 4QX
0207 739 8094
www.westlandlondon.com

Middlesex

Anthemion Ltd. (reclamation yard: founded to
continue the business of Crowther of Syon
Lodge following its closure in 2002. Offers
reclaimed building materials and architectural
antiques, antique garden ornaments, seats, urns,
fountains, chimneys, panelled rooms; can
source objects or make authentic copies)

PO Box 6
Teddington
TW11 OAS
www.ornamentalantiques.com

Peco of Hampton (reclamation yard: reclaimed
fireplaces and doors; stock of over 600 fireplaces
including gas and electric fires, and over 1,000
doors, mostly authentic originals, although they
have recently introduced some reproductions)

139 Station Road
Hampton
TW12 2AL
0208 979 8310
www.peco-of-hampton.co.uk

Norfolk

English Lamp Company (antique lighting shop:
a good selection of antique electric lamps such

as desk lamps with Bakelite, glass or brass
shades, wall brackets in gilt and ormolu finish,
some with glass drops in French style or two-
tier Dutch candelabra with ivory candle tubes
and candle bulbs, also iron handmade interior
and exterior hanging lamps and wall brackets;
also specialises in reproduction of classic lamps
in antique finishes)

The Old Stables
Bayfield Hall
Nr. Holt
NR25 7JN
07769 974 920
www.stiffkeylampshop.co.uk

T.W. Gaze (auction house: auctions of antiques,
rural and domestic bygones, farmhouse and
cottage furniture)

Roydon Road
Diss
1P22 4LN
01379 650 306
www.twgaze.com

Mongers Architectural Salvage (reclamation
yard: sanitary ware, fireplaces, cast-iron
radiators and architectural features, period
doors, door furniture, windows and glass,
garden antiques, reclaimed flooring and timber)

15 Market Place
Hingham
NR9 4AF
01953 851 868
www.mongersofhingham.co.uk

Morways Developments (Demolition company
and reclamation yard: architectural salvage and
barn conversions)

Old Station Yard
Watton Road
Stow Bedon
Attleborough
NR17 1DP
01953 483 914

Norfolk Reclaim Ltd. (reclamation yard and
antique centre: reclaimed building materials
including timber, Norfolk red bricks, pantiles,

floor bricks, floorboards, doors, door furniture
('we try to stock as many original handles,
hinges and latches as possible'), York and
sandstone paving and setts, fireplaces, baths and
sinks, antique furniture, collectibles, gardenalia;
also some reproduction)

Brancaster Road
Docking
PE31 8NB
01485 518 846
www.norfolkreclaim.co.uk

Sutton & Son (second-hand emporium:
collection of what Joe Sutton describes as 'Fine
Tat': mostly 'out of doors' items including shoe
racks, wooden steps and small ladders, chairs,
children's chairs, rocking chairs, watering cans,
forks and trowels; also shows at Newark,
Ardingly and Swinderby)

Unit 1
Grove Farm
Marsham
NR10 5SR
07977 264 749

Northamptonshire

Classic Reclaims (reclamation and builders'
yard: two acres of salvaged building materials,
doors, fireplaces, sinks, chimney pots, taps and
flooring)

East Road
Oundle
PE8 4BZ
01832 270 088
www.classicreclaims.co.uk

Ransfords Building Supplies (reclamation yard:
reclaimed and restored fireplaces in many styles
and materials, stoves and accessories, antique
oak beams, reclaimed oak flooring, doors of
reclaimed pine from 'respectful demolition' to
preparation of recovered material for re-use)

Drayton Way
Drayton Fields
Daventry
NN11 8XW
www.ransfords.com

Rococo Antiques & Interiors (reclamation
yard: Neville Griffiths deals in reclaimed timber,
iron, staddle stones, dragons and gargoyles,
cast-iron masks, radiators, sinks, fireplaces; you
might find a stone arch from a church in
Warwickshire, an Art Deco clock from a Co-op
store, a mustard-yellow shallow sink; also in-
house restoration workshop)

Church Street
Lower Weedon
NN7 4PL
07872 822 609
www.nevillegriffiths.co.uk

Northumberland

Borders Architectural Antiques (reclamation
yard: old garage full of unusual items including
baths, fireplaces, garden statuary, urns and
gnomes, doors and gates, reclaimed
floorboards, large gilt mirrors, chimney pots,
stuffed animals and curios. Also reproduction
brassware and antique-style door fittings and
furniture)

2 South Road
Wooler
NE71 6SN
01668 282 475
www.bordersarchitectural.co.uk

The Old Dairy (reclamation yard:
comprehensive range of architectural antiques,
fireplaces, baths, basins and reclaimed building
materials such as timber flooring and beams,
doors, door furniture, taps, chimney pots, light
fittings and country style furniture; plus
oddments such as old telephones, typewriters,
postboxes and occasional items from France,
e.g. double-ended baths; some new items)

Ford
TD15 2PX
01890 820 325
www.redbaths.co.uk

Jim Railton (auction house: tables, chairs, beds, wardrobes, sofas, ceramics, glass, sporting equipment, electric goods, lighting)

Nursery House
Chatton
Alnwick
NE66 5PY
01665 603 567
www.jimrailton.com

Salvage Tree (reclamation yard: restored staddle-stone granary full of unusual pieces including Deco lighting, industrial lighting, industrial furniture, display furniture, pictures, posters and fairground art)

Mire Meadows
Steel
Hexamshire
NE47 0HA
07738 003 564
www.salvagetree.co.uk

Trunk Reclaimed (recycle workshop and showroom: items made from reclaimed wood; furniture made from solid reclaimed wood, locally sourced and crafted; also restored antique furniture and reclaimed doors and floors)

Whitehouse Farm Centre
North Whitehouse Farm
Morpeth
NE61 6AW
01670 789 222
www.trunkreclaimed.co.uk

Nottinghamshire

Amorosa Enterprises (second-hand emporium: interior design accessories; also African baskets, pots and miscellaneous items)

64a Baladerton Gate
Newark
NG24 1UN
01636 646 861
By appointment only

Newark Antique Fair (antiques fair: Europe's largest international antiques event, held four times a year with up to 4,000 stalls)

Newark and Nottinghamshire Showground
Winthorpe
Nr Newark
Info from: DGM Antiques Fairs
PO Box 100
Newark
NG24 1DJ
01636 702 326
www.dmgantiquefairs.com

Nottingham Reclaims (reclamation yard: reclaimed building materials including bricks, oak beams, original period fireplaces, doors and windows, sanitary ware, parquet and timber flooring, spiral staircases, stone gargoyles and garden features, planters; plus fireplace restoration, door stripping, blasting and finishing services; some reproduction fireplaces)

St Albans Works
181 Hartley Road
Radford
NG7 3DW
01159 790 666
(Open weekends – by appointment only midweek)

Oxfordshire

Emmaus Oxford (second-hand superstore: reclaimed and restored household goods, furniture, electrical goods, linen, china, books. All electrical goods are tested before being offered for sale)

171 Oxford Road
Oxford
OX4 2ES
01865 763 698
www.emmaus.org.uk

Oxford Architectural Antiques (reclamation yard: aims to save and reuse as many items of architectural heritage as possible. Sells fireplaces, sanitary ware, doors from all periods, windows, cast-iron radiators, pine, garden furniture and ornaments, reproduction ironware)

16–18 London Street
Faringdon
SN7 7AA
01367 242 268
www.oxfordarchitectural.co.uk

Pathway Workshop (recycle workshop: artefacts made from reclaimed wood including garden products and furniture including benches, bird-tables, bird-houses, tables from reclaimed timber that would otherwise be burned or used as landfill, made by people with a wide range of disabilities. You can buy the products from the workshop, online, by phone or on eBay)

Dunnock Way
Blackbird Leys
Oxford
OX4 7EX
01865 714 111
www.pathway-workshop.co.uk

Shropshire

Antique Fireplace Company (reclaimed fireplace showroom: restored Georgian, Victorian and Edwardian cast-iron fireplaces, oak, pine, slate and original marble fireplace surrounds)

Prees Green
Nr. Whitchurch
SY13 2BN
01948 840 666
www.oldfireplaces.co.uk

North Shropshire Reclamation and Antique Salvage (reclamation yard: reclaimed bricks, coping, cartwheels, barrels, farm carts, staddle stones, church pews, light fittings, leaded glass, sinks, baths, doors, windows, enamelled advertising signs, who knows what you might find. Some reproduction)

Wackley Lodge Farm
Wackley
Burlton
Shrewsbury
SY4 5TD
01939 270 719
www.old2new.uk.com

Priors Reclamation Ltd. (reclamation yard: 4,500 sq ft of reclaimed flooring, doors and doorknobs, latches in brass, glass, wood and nickel, window latches in pewter and iron, copied from originals)

Unit 65
Ditton Priors Industrial Estate
Ditton Priors
Bridgnorth
WV16 6SS
01746 712 450
www.priorsrec.co.uk

Somerset

Bridgwater Reclamation (demolition and reclamation company: recycled building materials including natural slates, concrete roof tiles, glazed roof tiles, discontinued Marley and Redland patterns, colours and textures; also reproduction doors made locally from reclaimed pine)

44a Monmouth Street
Bridgwater
TA6 5EJ
01278 424 636
www.bridgwaterreclamation.co.uk

Castle Reclamation (reclamation yard: building materials, doors, cast-iron baths, wrought iron arches and railings, stone windows, pillars, staddle stones and steps, weather vanes, millstones, repro furniture, also reproduction items)

Parrett Works
Martock
TA12 6AE
01935 826 483
www.castlereclamation.com

Frome Reclamation (reclamation yard: family business established in 1987 with a large stock of reclaimed materials including roofing, flagstones, bricks, timber, statuary, flooring, fireplaces, baths, doors, stone windows and the occasional miscellaneous items such as phone boxes, tyre covers, a cider mill and stone troughs)

Station Approach
Frome
BA11 1RE
01373 463 919/07729 263 949
www.fromerec.co.uk

Gardenalia (second-hand shop: used and reclaimed garden features and contemporary garden ornaments, furniture and accessories)

4 Mile End
London Road
Bath
BA1 6PT
01225 329 949
www.gardenalia.co.uk

Glastonbury Reclamation (reclamation yard: four showrooms and three polytunnels offering reclaimed building materials usually sourced locally including bricks, stones, tiles and flagstones, beams, flooring, fireplaces and furniture)

The Old Pottery
Northload Bridge
Glastonbury
BA6 9LE
01458 831 122
www.glastonburyreclamation.co.uk

Loran and Co. (recycling workshop: restore or re-fashion antique furniture, lighting and linen in an original and ecological way 'as an antidote to our disposable culture')

Unit 2
Manor Farm
Claverton
Bath
BA2 7BP
01225 447 277
www.loranandco.co.uk

Morris Interiors (producers of high quality hand-painted period-style curtain poles based on French and English originals including distressed and antique paint finishes; stock a selection of antique French fittings, curtain poles, finials, holdbacks and brackets and always have thousands of old curtain rings in stock)

F1 Studios
Anglo Trading Estate
Shepton Mallet
BA4 5BY
(Appointment only)
01749 342 769
www.morris-interiors.co.uk

Shepton Mallet Antiques & Collectors Fair (well-known fair held five times a year with over 600 stalls in four halls and forty shopping arcades including ceramics, glassware, furniture, decorative items)

Royal Bath & West Showground
Shepton Mallet
BA4 6QN
Info from: DMG Antique Fairs
PO Box 100
Newark
NG24 1DJ
01636 702 326
www.dmgantiquefairs.com

Somerset Reclamation (reclamation yard: wide selection of indoor and outdoor items including reclaimed building materials, lampposts, large wardrobes; lots of doors, panelled and glazed; flooring, furniture, staddle stones, hardware)

Hay Street Farm
Ston Easton
Radstock
Bath
BA3 4DN
08450 943 295
www.materials4diy.co.uk

Source Antiques (reclamation yard: specialises in twentieth-century antiques and salvage including Art Deco, quite a lot of French items, huge variety of lighting, galvanised garden equipment such as watering cans, cast-iron multi-fuel stoves, acrylic items, will also design complete interiors using reclaimed materials such as aluminium)

Victoria Park Business Centre
Bath
BA1 3AX
01225 469 200
www.source-antiques.co.uk

South West Reclamation (reclamation yard: reclaimed building materials, specialising in reclaimed Bridgwater clay roof tiles and ridges; staircases, leaded glass, sinks, baths, doors, pews, cast columns, staddle stones, troughs, chimney pots; also new tiles and Spanish slate)

Wireworks Estate
Bristol Road
Bridgwater
TA6 4AP
01278 444 141
www.southwest-rec.co.uk

Walcot Reclamations (now **MASCo Walcot**) (reclamation yard: indoor and outdoor, with reclaimed building materials such as flagstones, paving, flooring, roof tiles, stone, gates and railings, radiators, joinery, doors, chimneys, grates, baths and basins, lighting and mirrors. Also reproduction items including ironmongery, lighting and oak doors.

108 Walcot Street
Bath
BA1 5BG
01225 444 404
www.walcot.com

Wells Reclamation Co. (reclamation yard: family-run business with five and a half acres of reclaimed and reproduction items covering everything from building materials to Delft tiles, including doors, door furniture, ironmongery, furniture and garden features. If you don't want to bother with the reproduction items when consulting the online catalogue, click onto 'salvage')

Coxley
Wells
BA5 1RQ
01749 677 087
www.wellsreclamation.com

Wharton Antiques (dealer and restorer: fine antique stone chimneypieces, garden and architectural ornaments; trading from the UK but also with a permanent base in the Dordogne area of France)

Somerset
England
07974 579 694
By appointment only
www.whartonantiques.com

Staffordshire

Blackbrook Antiques Village (reclamation yard: general indoor and garden reclamation and materials)

London Road
Weeford (Nr. Lichfield)
WS14 OPS
01543 481 450

Cawarden Brick Co. Ltd. (reclamation yard: specialist supplier of reclaimed and period building materials with over 1 million reclaimed bricks and 500 doors in stock plus flagstones, garden features, fireplaces, radiators, doors, flooring, timber and beams)

Springs Farm
Blithbury Road
Rugeley
WS15 3HL
01889 574 066
www.cawardenreclaim.co.uk

Gardiners Reclaims (reclamation yard: building materials, roofing, bricks, railway sleepers, timber and flooring, paving, cobbles, natural stone)

Grove Road Industrial Estate
Grove Road
Fenton
Stoke-on-Trent
ST4 4LG
01782 334 532
www.gardinersreclaims.co.uk

Les Oakes & Sons (reclamation yard: wide variety of architectural ironmongery, roofing, timber, walling, flooring, sanitary ware, doors and windows, fireplaces, radiators, furniture, church furnishings, gates and railings, telephone boxes)

Hales View Farm
Oakamoor Road
Cheadle
ST10 4QR
01538 752 126
www.lesoakes.com

Rayson Reclamation (reclamation yard:
reclaimed building materials, stained glass,
fireplaces, doors, ironwork, gardenalia)

Unit 15
Pillaton Hall Farm
Pillaton
ST19 5RZ
01785 711 495
www.raysonreclamation.com

UK Architectural Antiques (reclamation yard:
architectural salvage and garden antiques, much
of it quite unusual, including pine tongue-and-
groove floorboards, panelling, pub fittings,
church pews, tables, shelving, lamps and
lighting, statues, staddle stones, cast-iron post
and pillar boxes from around 1915;
manufactures window shutters from salvaged
pine)

Hill Farm
84 Hayfield Hill
Cannock Wood
WS15 4RU
07890 728 144
www.ukarchitecturalantiques.com
By appointment only

Suffolk

Heritage Reclamations (reclamation yard:
family-run, reclaimed architectural salvage
company with extensive stocks of architectural
antiques, period ironmongery, building
materials and interior fittings)

1A High Street
Sproughton
IP8 3AF
01473 748 519
www.heritage-reclamation.co.uk

Home & Garden Renovation Centre
(reclamation yard: two-storey warehouse of
architectural salvage, reclaimed building
materials and salvaged period features,
landscaping materials, garden features, gazebos,
patio sets, stone troughs, water features,
wrought iron and wooden gates and some
reproduction)

The Barn
Block Farm
Bradfield Combust
Bury St. Edmunds
IP30 0LW
01284 828 081
www.abbotsbridge.com

Ipswich Roofing (reclamation yard: roofing
contractor with yard of reclaimed timber,
reclaimed bricks and chimney pots, stone and
marble architectural ornaments)

3A Roofing Ltd
The Laurels
Copdock
IP8 3JF
01473 730 660
www.ispwichroofing.co.uk

Tower Reclaim (reclamation yard: specialises in
dismantling and reclamation of antique
building materials and garden items from
country cottages, farmhouses, manor houses,
Victorian workshops and a variety of buildings
from Suffolk and surrounding counties. Wide
selection of interesting and unusual items)

Tower Farm
Norwich Road
Mendlesham
IP14 5NE
01449 766 095
www.tower-reclaim.co.uk

Treesave Reclamation Ltd. (reclamation yard:
reclaimed building materials specialising in
reclaimed wooden floors, architectural salvage
and antiques including cast-iron railings and
radiators, over 300 reclaimed doors, period
beams, metal and stone, windows, bricks, slates
and chimneys, early furniture to twentieth
century, wall panelling, fires and surrounds,
skirting, architrave, mouldings, pine boards)

Unit 16 The Barn
Fysh House Farm
Cuckoo Hill
Bures
C08 5LD
01787 227 272
www.treesave.co.uk

Surrey

Antique Buildings Ltd. (reclaimed buildings: supply dismantled frames and oak beams reclaimed from ancient oak-framed buildings, also wide oak floorboards, handmade bricks, terracotta floor tiles and paving)

Dunsfold
Godalming
GU8 4NP
01438 200 477
www.antiquebuildings.com

Cast Iron Reclamation Company (reclamation yard: cast-iron radiators, radiator covers, cooking ranges, toilet roll holders, fireside irons, towel rails, copper and roll-top baths; radiators are refurbished ready for use)

The White House
8a Burgh Heath Road
Epsom
KT17 4LJ
020 8977 5977
www.perfect-irony.com

Church Antiques and **Good Table** (reclamation yards, sister companies: **Church Antiques** sells ecclesiastical furnishing, domestic antique furniture and fittings from vestries and vicarages including altars, communion plates, brass vases, candle holders, lighting, panelling, organ cases and more. They hire out chairs and pews for functions and to film and theatre companies. **Good Table** sells all sizes of antique-style pine tables, dining tables made from old wood (such as Victorian joists and beams) and reclaimed pine tables)

Rivernook Farm
Sunnyside
Walton-on-Thames
KT12 2ET
01932 252 736
www.churchantiques.com

Cronin's Reclamation (reclamation yard: reclaimed building materials, items from the 1920s, redundant teak laboratory tops, wrought iron gates, garden items, spiral staircases, cast-iron windows with leaded panes, reclaimed and new oak beams)

The Barns
Preston Farm Court
Lower Road
Little Bookham
KT23 4EF
01372 459 991
www.croninsreclamation.co.uk

Drummonds (architectural antiques showroom: 70,000 sq ft of reclaimed wood flooring, fireplaces, cast-iron radiators, doors and windows, antique door furniture, staircases, floor and wall tiles, antique furniture, antique lighting, antique bathroom ware, garden antiques, gates and railings. Also have a branch in London)

The Kirkpatrick Building
25 London Road
Hindhead
GU26 6AB
01428 609 444
www.drummonds-arch.co.uk

Miscellania (discontinued bathroom ware showroom: over 50,000 items of replacement bathroom items from discontinued obsolete ranges in all the old colours and old styles from toilet seats to bathroom sinks, 1960s toilets to complete retro bathroom suites)

Churt Place Nurseries
Tilford Road
Churt
GU10 2LN
By appointment only
01428 608 164
www.brokenbog.com

Smiths Architectural Salvage (reclamation yard: reclaimed doors from early plank doors to 1930s Art Deco, fireplaces, flooring, stained glass, can supply stained glass panels to suit period doors)

Unit 9
The Looe
Reigate Road
Epsom
KT17 3BZ
020 8393 4139 or 07974 781 538
www.smithsarchitecturalsalvage.co.uk

Take Five Fairs (Art Deco and Art Nouveau fairs in Twickenham, Harlequins Rugby Stadium, Middlesex and Woking Leisure Centre, Surrey)

Contact John Slade 0208 894 0218
www.antiquefairs.co.uk

Tyne and Wear

G. O'Brien & Sons (NDC) Ltd. (reclamation yard: reclaimed building materials including roofing, timber, flooring and other architectural salvage)

Cleadon House
Cleadon Lane
East Boldon
NE36 OAJ
01915 377 946
www.gobrien.co.uk

Olde Worlde Fireplaces (reclamation company: antique and reproduction fireplaces including original kitchen ranges and hobs, some reclaimed door furniture plus miscellaneous items from churches, schools and other period properties)

18 Blandford Square
Newcastle upon Tyne
NE1 4HZ
01912 619 229
www.olde-worlde-fireplaces.co.uk

Pure Imagination (reclaimed retro warehouse: specialises in vintage retro furniture, furnishings and household accessories of all kinds including glass, rugs and mirrors, mainly from Scandinavia but including e.g. G Plan items and Arkana moulded chairs and tables)

2 Westoe Village
South Shields
NE33 3DZ
07715 054 919
www.vintageretro.co.uk (for general retro items) www.pureimaginations.co.uk (for items by specific designers, e.g. Bjorn Wiindblad, Nils Thorsson and Lisa Larson)

Shiners (antique and reproduction fireplaces: marble, slate, cast-iron and wooden surrounds; original and reproduction fireplace tiles; restoration and fitting service; also antique and reproduction door furniture)

81 Fern Avenue
Jesmond
Newcastle upon Tyne
NE2 2RA
01912 816 474
www.shinersofjesmond.co.uk

Tynemouth Architectural Salvage (reclamation yard: specialises in antique bathroom fixtures and fittings, interesting basins and sinks, baths and loos, also church items, coats of arms, e.g. reclaimed from North Shields post office)

Corrections House
28 Tynemouth Road
Tynemouth
NE30 4AA
01912 966 070
www.tynemoutharchitecturalsalvage.com

Warwickshire

Emmaus Rugby (second-hand emporium: reclaimed and restored household goods, furniture, electrical goods, linen, china, books. All electrical goods are tested before being offered for sale)

36 North Street
Rugby
CV21 2XD
01788 544 003
www.emmaus.org.uk

Source 4 U Ltd. (reclamation yard: demolition and architectural salvage company concentrating on small barn and outbuilding demolition and yard clearance. They have reclaimed building materials including brick, copings, stone, flagstones, paving, setts, wood, hardware, cast-iron, fireplaces, troughs and sinks. Also new and reproduction; the website allows you to filter products by reclaimed/repro or original)

The Holloway
Market Place
Warwick
CV34 4SJ
01926 498 444
www.source4you.co.uk

West Midlands

Coventry Demolition Co. Ltd. (reclamation yard: reclaimed building materials and architectural salvage)

Ryton Fields Farm
Wolston Lane
Ryton-on-Dunsmore
CV8 3ES
0800 294 8603
www.coventry-demolition.co.uk

Emmaus Coventry & Warwickshire (second-hand emporium: reclaimed and restored household goods, furniture, electrical goods, linen, china, books. All electrical goods are tested before being offered for sale)

Red Lane
Coventry
CV6 5EQ
02476 661 466
www.emmaus.org.uk

West Sussex

Architectural Salvage Sussex (reclamation yard: architectural salvage of all kinds including garden furniture and ornaments, sinks, cast-iron radiators, chandeliers, floorboards, French windows, panelling, pews, railings, door furniture, fireplaces and fireplace accessories)

Tangmere Corner
Tangmere
Chichester
PO18 0DU
01243 774 025
www.architecturalsalvagesussex.co.uk

Ardingly International Antiques & Collectors Fair (antiques fairs: six fairs a year with up to 1,700 stalls in five buildings, arcades and marquees selling anything from furniture to ceramics, glassware and textiles including decorative items from Europe)

South of England Centre
Ardingly
Nr. Haywards Heath
RH17 6TL
Info from: DMG Antique Fairs
PO Box 100
Newark
NG24 1DJ
016363 702 326
www.dmgantiquefairs.com

Bedouin (architectural salvage showroom; diverse collection of antiques, artefacts and architectural objects, 'a mixture of the practical, the beautiful and the curious': you might find French chairs, cast-iron railings, Rover radiators, gate and roof finials, sewing dummies, hat moulds, chairs and sofas, cabinets and cupboards, tables, mirrors and gardenalia)

Unit 4
The Grainstore
Coolham
RH13 8GR
01403 741 742
www.bedouin.uk.com

Brighton Architectural Salvage (reclamation and reproduction showroom: mainly reproduction and contemporary fireplaces and surrounds; some genuine Victorian tiles, cast-iron inserts, reclaimed oak and pine flooring, stained glass)

33–34 Gloucester Road
Brighton
BN1 4AQ
01273 681 656
www.brighton-architectural.co.uk

Brighton Flea Market (second-hand shops and emporia, mainly for small household items)

31a Upper St. James Street
BN2 1JN
01273 624006

Emmaus Brighton and Hove (Second-hand emporia: furniture including beds and wardrobes, kitchenware, books, electricals, records, clothes, bric-a-brac. All electrical goods are tested before being offered for sale)

Drove Road
Portslade
Brighton
BN41 2PA
01273 426 480
www.emmausbrighton.co.uk

Heritage Oak Buildings (reclaimed oak-framed buildings: selection of fine old frames looking for new sites. The company saves, restores, supplies and re-erects antique oak-framed buildings, usually redundant farm buildings dating from the sixteenth century)

Benefold Farmhouse
Petworth
GU28 9NX
07836 250 882 or 01798 344 066
www.heritage-oak-buildings.com

Wiltshire

Beechfield Reclamation Co. (reclamation yard: all types of building materials 'from 100 bricks for a fireplace to 1,800 for a house', stone, beams, paving, fireplaces, sleepers, doors, flooring, sinks, architectural joinery, gates, staddle stones, fountains, stained glass, signs, spiral staircases and gardenalia, miscellania)

The White Horse Yard
Beechfield Road
Hopton Park Industrial Estate
Devizes
SN10 2ET
01380 730 999
www.beechfieldreclamation.co.uk

Sanitary Salvage (discontinued sanitary ware showroom: 7,000 pieces of new and fully refurbished obsolete baths, loos, basins, pedestals, cisterns and bidets, shower trays, shower doors, and a range of baths for disabled people dating from the 1940s to today, including current models)

Cotswold Farm Stables
West Dean Road
West Tytherley
SP5 1QA
01980 863 030
www.sanitary-salvage.co.uk

Worcestershire

Malvern Fairs (antiques fairs and flea markets: regular fairs and events through the year)

Three Counties Showground
Malvern
WR13 6NW
Info from B2B: 077741 147 197 or 07717 725 302
www.b2bevents.info

Yorkshire

Andy Thornton Ltd. (reclamation showroom: specialises in furniture to the hospitality industry; extensive showrooms with the largest stock of architectural antiques and salvage in the UK aimed at pubs, restaurants, hotels etc; also enormous range of modern pub furniture)

Ainleys Industrial Estate
Elland
W. Yorkshire
HX5 9JP
01422 376 000
www.andythornton.com

BBR Auctions (auction house: regular auctions of household items, antique advertising, kitchenalia and brewing equipment)

Elsecar Heritage Centre
Barnsley
S. Yorkshire
S74 8HJ
01226 745 156
www.onlinebbr.com

Chapel House Fireplaces (reclamation yard: fireplaces; converted coach house and barn full of a wide variety of fireplaces from the eighteenth to twentieth centuries; specialises in restoration – no reproductions)

Netherfield House
St. George's Road
Scholes
Holmfirth
W. Yorks
HD9 1UH
01484 682 275
www.chapelhousefireplaces.co.uk

Emmaus Leeds (second-hand emporium:
reclaimed and restored household goods,
furniture, electrical goods, linen, china, books.
All electrical goods are tested before being
offered for sale)

St. Mary's Street
Lincoln Green
Leeds
LS9 7DP
01132 484 288
www.emmaus.org.uk

Emmaus Sheffield (second-hand emporium:
reclaimed and restored household goods,
furniture, electrical goods, linen, china, books.
All electrical goods are tested before being
offered for sale)

Cadman Street
Sheffield
S. Yorkshire
S4 7ZG
01142 720 677
www.emmaus-sheffield.org.uk

Hoyland Dismantling Co. (reclamation yard:
reclaimed timber, stone, slate, Yorkshire paving,
coping, rope-top edging, troughs with some
architectural parts from pubs and churches,
mouldings, brackets and columns, windows and
doors, and some surprises; also new timber,
sleepers and stone)

Tinker Lane Foot
Hoyland Common
Barnsley
S. Yorkshire
S74 0PR
01226 747 221
www.reclaimedtimber.co.uk

Old Flames (Reclaimed fireplace showroom:
antique fireplaces and accessories including
wrought iron firedogs; lighting and
architectural salvage, also reproductions)

30 Long Street
Easingwold
Y061 3HT
01347 821 188
www.oldflames.co.uk

Period Pine Doors (reclamation yard:
specialises in reclaimed doors)

Helderleigh
Easingwold Road
Huby
Y061 1HJ
01347 811 728
www.periodpinedoors.com

Viking Reclamation Ltd. (reclamation yard:
specialists in reclaimed bricks, wide oak
flooring, building materials and architectural
items)

Cow House Lane
Armthorpe Industrial Estate
Armthorpe
Doncaster
DN3 3EE
01302 835 449
www.reclaimed.co.uk

Northern Ireland

CS Architectural Salvage (reclamation yard:
good quality reclaimed building materials
including refurbished cast-iron radiators, bricks
from the early 1800s, reclaimed timber beams,
slate, re-sawn flooring in pitchpine, Oregon
pine and Douglas fir, available in various
widths; also buy old buildings and Bangor blue
slate roofs for stripping)

Unit 19C
Campsie Industrial Estate
Eglinton
Derry
02871 812 999
www.csarchitecturalsalvage.com

Wilsons Conservation Building Products
(reclamation yard: wooden beams, French and
English flooring, French and English baths and
fittings, stained glass, sandstone entrances and
windows, cast-iron and marble fireplaces; also
modern sculptures and gardenalia)

123 Hillsborough Road
Dromore
County Down
BT25 1QW
02892 692 304
www.wilsonsyard.com

Scotland

Auldearn Architectural Antiques (architectural
reclamation yard: wide range of furniture, linen,
china and other household items as well as
furniture workshops)

Lethen Road
Auldearn
Highland
1V12 5HZ
01667 453 087

Edinburgh Architectural Salvage Yard (EASY)
(reclamation yard: original architectural salvage
bought and sold throughout Scotland including
cast-iron all-in-one fireplaces, Georgian,
Victorian and Edwardian fireplace surrounds;
4-panel and 6-panel doors, original cast-iron
radiators pressure-tested with new fittings,
suitable for 15mm pipes, also stained glass,
sinks, doorknobs, shutters)

31 West Bowling Green Street
Leith
Edinburgh
EH6 5NX
01315 547 077
www.easy-arch-salv.co.uk

Emmaus Glasgow (two second-hand shops:
reclaimed and restored household goods,
furniture, electrical goods, linen, china, books.
All electrical goods are tested before being
offered for sale)

Community shop: Emmaus House
101 Ellesmere Street
Glasgow
G22 5QT
01413 533 903

Solidarity shop: 576 Dumbarton Road
Glasgow
G11 6RH
01413 424 4089
www.emmausglasgow.org.uk

Glasgow Architectural Salvage (architectural
reclamation yard: baths, basins, WCs, doors,
door furniture, fireplaces, radiators, sinks,
furniture, gardenalia, lighting, pews, stoves,
sinks, mirrors, skirting and architrave, stained
glass)

Unit 1
Albion Centre
1394 South Street
Glasgow
G14 OAP
www.glasgowarchitecturalsalvage.co.uk

**Hargreaves Reclaimed Wood Flooring and
Architectural Salvage** (reclamation yard: timber
specialists in supply and removal of hardwood
flooring including maple, beech, oak, pitchpine
and exotic woods; also reclaimed panelled
doors, ceramic sinks, cast-iron radiators,
staircases, fire doors, roll-top baths, slates and
other miscellaneous salvage such as pews from a
cathedral in Sheffield)

Douglashill Farm
Cowie Road
Airth
FK2 8LT
01324 832 200
www.hargreavesreclaimedflooring.co.uk

Holyrood Architectural Salvage Ltd.
(reclamation yard: over 8,000 sq ft of Georgian,
Victorian and Edwardian fireplaces, doors,
pews, wood and brass handles, cast-column
radiators and other reclaimed items, mainly
sourced from Edinburgh homes; also range of
good quality reproductions)

Holyrood Business Park
146 Duddingston Road West
Edinburgh
EH16 4AP
01316 619 305
www.holyroodarchitecturalsalvage.com

Wales

ATC Floors & Doors (reclamation yard: reclaimed, new and engineered timbers, hardwood and softwood flooring, internal and external doors, skirting, architrave, door liners and door furniture, and a fitting, finishing and restoration service; also have a branch in Cheltenham, Gloucestershire)

2 Mayhill Industrial Estate
NP25 3LX
01600 713 036
www.atcfloorsanddoors.co.uk

Celtic Antique Fireplaces (reclamation yard: good selection of antique cast-iron fireplaces, both antique and reproduction, plus spares such as front bar sets, hoods, tile sets)

Unit 3
Players Estate
Clydach
Swansea
Glamorgan
SA6 5BQ
01792 476 047
www.celticfireplaces.co.uk

Drew Pritchard Ltd. (reclamation showroom: reclaimer and restorer Drew Pritchard collects a vast array of reclaimed goods ranging from everyday items like floorboards, beams, quarry tiles and doors to character pieces like chandeliers, ecclesiastical remnants and fireplaces, panelling, statuary, urns, country furniture and leather chairs, stained glass and leaded panels)

Llanrwst Road
Glan Conwy
Conwy
LL28 5TH
01492 580 890
www.drewpritchard.co.uk

Gallop & Rivers (reclamation yard: architectural antiques, building materials, ironmongery, paving, interior flooring, garden features, fireplaces and 'all of the architectural items necessary for authentic restoration projects')

Ty-r-ash
Brecon Road
Crickhowell
Powys
NP8 1SF
01873 811 084
www.gallopandrivers.co.uk

Radnedge Architectural Antiques (reclamation yard: wide range of interesting reclaimed doors, around 800 Georgian and Victorian fireplaces, baths, all kinds of garden ornaments, stone window frames, church furniture including pews, columns, lecterns and pulpits, cast-iron radiators, decorated chimneys, flooring, timber, gates and railings)

Dafen Inn Row
Dafen
Llanelli
Carmarthenshire
SA14 BLX
01554 755 790
www.radnedge-arch-antiques.co.uk

Theodore Sons & Daughters Reclamation (reclamation yard: demolition and recycling company with building materials, fireplaces, chimney pots, flagstones, flooring, roofing, posts and supports, sanitary ware, stained glass, windows, door furniture, chapel pews, UPVC windows and doors)

North Road
Bridgend Industrial Estate
Bridgend
CF31 3AQ
01656 648 936
www.theodorereclamation.co.uk

Welsh Salvage (demolition company and salvage yard: specialises in traditional Welsh salvage from Welsh chapels, churches, schools and other period buildings including stone, stone arches, slate and roof tiles, leaded windows and lintels, doors and frames, pier caps, pulpits, fonts, pews and church furniture, organs and pianos, flooring, timber, beams, joists and trusses)

R.M. Rees (Contractors) Ltd.
Rheola
Resolven
Neath
SA11 4DT
01639 711 688
www.welsh-salvage.co.uk

Europe

Architecture et Materiaux Authentiques (French reclamation yard: unique items from restored or demolished French mansions including parquet and floorboards, radiators, fireplaces, staircases and panelling, floor tiles, doors, railings and sanitary ware)

212 rue du Flocon
59200 Tourcoing
Nord (59)
+33 320 680 101
www.a-mat.com

Florian Langenbeck (reclamation yard, historic doors and building materials: entrance and interior doors; doors with glass panes, windows, gates, fences, railings and grilles, cast-iron, stone and wood columns, stone flooring and tiles)

Mülhauser Strasse 8
79110 Freiburg
Germany
+49 761 135 801
www.langenbeck.com

Thomas Knapp Historische Baustoffe (reclamation yard, reclaimed and antique building materials: 15,000 sq m of building materials including bricks, tiles and stone; specialises in ancient oak beams and boards)

Am Bahnhof 1
37627 Deensen
Germany
+49 055 321 320
www.knapp-online.de

Useful Organisations, UK

Bakelite Museum
Orchard Mill
Williton
TA4 4NS
01984 632 133
Open in summer by appointment

Bioregional Reclaimed (Charitable organisation specialising in practical solutions to sustainability; specialises in reclaimed building materials, promotes and facilitates the use of reclaimed materials in place of new)

BedZED Centre
24 Helios Road
Wallington
SM6 7BZ
020 8404 4880
www.bioregional-reclaimed.com

Charles Brooking (reclamation showroom: personal collection of thousands of examples of period architectural details acquired over the last forty years, including doors and door furniture, windows, fireplaces and staircases, and stained glass, skirtings and architraves)

01483 274 203
www.thebrookingcollection.com
By appointment only

Conservation Register (register of conservation experts in many different fields)

c/o Institute of Conservation
0207 785 3805
www.conservationregister.com

Dennis Severs House (restored eighteenth-century terraced house – a time capsule – open occasionally to the public)

Number 18 Folgate Street
Spitalfields
London
E1 6BX
020 7247 4013
www.dennissevershouse.co.uk

The Georgian Group
6 Fitzroy Square
London
W1T 5DX
0871 750 2936
www.georgiangroup.org.uk

The Twentieth Century Society
70 Cowcross Street
London
EC1M 6EJ
0207 250 3857
www.c20society.org.uk

The Victorian Society
1 Priory Gardens
London
W4 1TT
020 8994 1019
www.victoriansociety.org.uk

Canada

Croatian Cultural Centre (regular flea markets and retro markets)

3250 Commercial Drive at 16th Avenue
Vancouver, BC
(Details: www.21cpromotions.com)

Kerrisdale Antiques Fair

Kerrisdale Arena
5670 East Boulevard at 41st Avenue
Vancouver, BC
(Details: www.21cpromotions.com)

USA

Arizona

National Office Liquidators (used office furniture warehouse: enormous range of used office goods with online catalogue)

1430 East Hadley
Suite 110
Phoenix AZ 85034
877 897 1910
www.nationalofficeliquidators.com

California

Ohmega Salvage (reclamation yard: usual and unusual building materials)

2407 & 2400 San Pablo Ave
Berkeley
CA 94702
510 843 7368
Mon–Sat 9–5; Sun 12–5

Olde Good Things (reclamation yard: wide range of architectural salvage, including gardenalia and household objects)

1800 South Grand Avenue
Los Angeles
CA 90015
213 746 8600 or 8611
www.ogtstore.com

Florida

American Salvage (reclamation yard: architectural salvage and reclaimed building supplies)

7001 NW 27th Avenue
MIAMI
FL 33147
305 691 7001
www.americansalvage.com

Illinois

Salvage One (reclamation yard)

1840 West Hubbard Street
Chicago
IL 60622
312 733 0098

National Office Liquidators (used office furniture warehouse: enormous range of used office goods with online catalogue)

1500 S. Western Avenue
Chicago IL 60608
312 878 4593
www.nationalofficeliquidators.com

Kentucky

Covington Re-Use Center (reclaimed building materials)

315E. 15th Street
Covington
KY 41011
859 291 0777
www.covingtonreusecenter.org

Massachusetts

Allen's Antique Lighting (lighting)

Cindy and Chris Allen
43 Under Pin Hill Road
Harvard
MA 01451
978 688 6466
www.antiquelight.com

Michigan

Ann Arbor Re-Use Center (reclamation yard: salvaged timber, furniture)

2420 South Industrial Highway
Ann Arbor
MI 48104
734 662 6288
www.recycleannarbor.org

Minneapolis

The ReUse Center (reclaimed building materials and salvaged furniture)

2801 21st Av S
Suite 190
Minneapolis
MN 55407
(enter on E. 29th Street off 21st Av S)
612 724 2608

New Hampshire

Nor'East Architectural Antiques (reclamation yard: huge range of reclaimed salvage for indoors and out)

16 Exeter Road
South Hampton
NH 03827
603 394 0006
www.noreast1.com

New York

Finger Lakes ReUse Inc (wide range of architectural salvage)

Triphammer Mall
2255 N. Triphammer Road
Ithaca, NY 14850
607 257 9699
www.fingerlakesreuse.org

Olde Good Things (reclamation yard: wide range of architectural salvage including gardenalia and household objects)

124 West 24th Street
New York
NY 10011
212 989 8401
www.ogtstore.com

Secondhand Rose (more than 1,000 original vintage wallpaper patterns, antique wallpaper in original rolls; quantities of Victorian antique papers, damask wallpaper, 1940s florals, Art Deco geometrics, novelties from the 1950s, 60s and 70s; also linoleum, furniture and lighting from around 1840)

230 5th Avenue
510
NY 10001
212 393 9002
www.secondhandrose.com

Pennsylvania

Olde Good Things (reclamation yard: wide range of architectural salvage including gardenalia and household objects)

400 Gilligan Street
Scranton
PA 18508
570 341 7668

Tennessee

Tailgate Antique Show (annual February antique and memorabilia fair)

Tennessee State Fairgrounds
625 Smith Ave
Nashville
TN 37203
317 598 0012

Vermont

Architectural Salvage Warehouse (reclamation yard: architectural salvage)

11 Maple Street
Five Corners
Essex Jct
Vermont 05452
802 879 4221

Washington

Earthwise Inc (reclamation yard: architectural salvage)

3447 4th Ave South
Suite E
Seattle
WA 98134
www.earthwise-salvage.com

Washington DC

The Brass Knob (architectural antiques)

2311 18th Street NW
Washington
DC 20009
202 332 3370

Also:

The Brass Knob Back Doors Warehouse (reclamation yard: all types of house parts, salvaged from local buildings)

57 N Street NW
Washington
DC 20009
202 332 3370

Internet Websites

- www.abundantearth.com – swings from recycled tyres and more recycled objects.
- www.antiqueweb.co.uk lists antique fairs by geographical areas giving date, venue and listing the sort of things that will be for sale. It includes England, Ireland (North and South), Scotland and Wales and a very few fairs and second-hand shops in Europe.
- www.architecturalreclamation.com – online catalogue of wide range of interior artefacts including flooring, sanitary ware, church interiors, fireplaces, doors, kitchenalia, gardenalia, lighting, pub stuff, radiators, reclaimed wood. Viewing by appointment only.
- www.arcsal.com – browser site of architectural salvage items available from dealers throughout Britain.
- www.beyondfrance.co.uk – vintage and new Hungarian domestic linens including fabric rolls, towels, tea towels, mattress covers; also grain sacks.
- www.eatsleeplive.co.uk – reclaimed parquet and other flooring; range of chunky furniture of wood from demolished buildings.
- www.ebay.co.uk – category: 'Antiques' and sub categories.
- www.gratcom.com – English and Asian-based company selling reclaimed Asian artefacts online including Chinese cabinets and other furniture, and other domestic items.

- **www.haes.co.uk** – reclaimed interior and exterior artefacts; architectural stone and terracotta, woodwork and panelling, flooring, windows and leaded glass, fireplaces, bathroom accessories, furniture and mirrors, kitchen units and accessories; interesting and unusual items, e.g. set of six Heals dining chairs. Can visit Lancashire yard by appointment only.
- **www.henandhammock.co.uk** – ecologically-minded items for home and garden including recycled hessian coffee sacks and planters made from old tyres.
- **www.kitschulike.com** – retro gifts and novelties including recycled rubber car tyre table and stool set.
- **www.norfolktextiles.co.uk** – among a lot of new oilcloths, furnishing fabrics and curtain linings are some interesting and desirable vintage textiles including lace, embroidery, table linen and bed linen.
- **www.oldegoodthings**.com – selling catalogue of over 2,000 salvaged artefacts and antiques; also an online calendar of upcoming shows, markets and fairs.
- **www.parna.co.uk** – vintage linen, hemp and embroidery from Central and Eastern Europe.
- **www.reclaimbuildingsupply.com** – national site for locating reclaimed building materials throughout the UK. Click onto 'Suppliers by County' or 'First Stop' if you want lists of materials with contact numbers (e.g. 'cast-iron bath'; 'London yellow stock bricks'; 'hand-operated sewing machine').
- **www.teaantiques.com** – selling catalogue of fine china and silver antique tea sets, teapots, sugar bowls and tea caddies, but they also collect lids so if you are looking for a replacement lid for a beloved teapot, this can be a good place to start (particular makes).
- **www.teessidearchitecturalsalvage.co.uk** – online selling catalogue of a wide range of reclaimed materials from demolished buildings in the North East and North Yorkshire, including building materials, brass taps, newel posts, leaded lights, architectural door furniture and window fittings, lighting, garden items and French glazed doors.
- **www.therecyclewarehouse.com** – online catalogue of domestic and office products made from recycled materials, including tables from recycled cable reels, cardboard furniture, tables, benches and beds from recycled timber.
- **www.vintage-home.co.uk** – online selling catalogue of vintage pretty things for the home including 1940s curtains, rosebud door plates, chromo prints and other miscellanea.
- **www.vintagefabricmarket.co.uk** – click onto 'Vintage Linen, Bedding' or 'Vintage fabric'; also sells Laura Ashley patchwork squares.

Picture Credits

All photographs by Barty Phillips except:

pp. 10t, 18b, 66b, 67t, 71t, 74, 103b, 107b, 114tl, 122t & b, 123t, 126t, 127, 134t, 139t, 150t, 167t, 194: Edward Haes

pp. 14b, 31, 102 all: Marcus Peel

pp. 19t & b, 46b, 75, 110tl & br, 174b: Retrouvius

p. 25: Ruby Kay

pp. 62, 135b, 163b: Antique Oak Flooring

pp. 66t, 178: Nor'East Architectural Salvage

pp. 103t, 106br, 115tl: Jenny Blanchard

p. 110bl: © Ryland Peters & Small/Loupe Images/Debi Treloar

p. 118t: Richard Westwood

pp. 134b, 143b: John Phillips